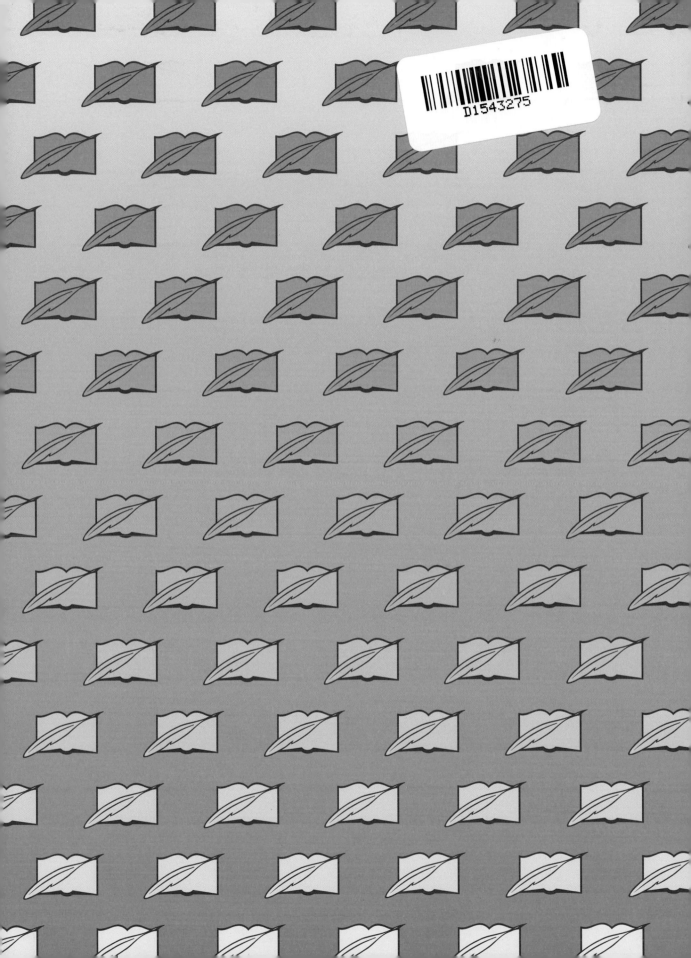

THE FICTION OF
L. RON HUBBARD

THE FICTION OF

L. RON HUBBARD

A COMPREHENSIVE BIBLIOGRAPHY & REFERENCE GUIDE TO PUBLISHED AND SELECTED UNPUBLISHED WORKS

BY WILLIAM J. WIDDER, M.A.

TABLE OF CONTENTS

FOREWORD

Without a doubt, L. Ron Hubbard is one of the most prolific and influential writers of the twentieth century. Until now, relatively few of his readers have been aware of the true scope of his creative genius. For the first time, this bibliography will allow Mr. Hubbard's international audience to fully appreciate the entire range of his productivity, including fiction, nonfiction, poetry, and music.

Hubbard's writings embody the essence of "The American Dream." In many forums, he stresses the need to maximize our potentials through education, practical experience, and old-fashioned hard work. Only this path allows each person to achieve what he or she is capable of. Mr. Hubbard further insists that life's challenges be met with courage, personal integrity, and mutual respect among all people. His fictional heroes often stand in stark contrast to the corrupt bureaucracies surrounding them, clearly suggesting the choices we must make.

This comprehensive, annotated bibliography brings together over fifty years of L. Ron Hubbard's published works. It also offers brief synopses of selected entries. The chronology of Mr. Hubbard's life allows the reader to place each piece in its appropriate historical context. This volume provides a long overdue tool for readers, critics, and scholars alike to explore the full extent and impact of a major writer's artistic contributions.

Stephen V. Whaley, Ph.D.
Professor of English and Foreign
Languages, California
Polytechnic University, Pomona

PREFACE

This bibliography marks the first time that all of L. Ron Hubbard's published works of fiction have been assembled in synoptic form, with full publishing histories and supplemental notes, in a single comprehensive reference work. Also in this volume will be found listings of his unpublished works of fiction which represent additional facets of his literary production and creative process.

Even a cursory examination will communicate a sense of the dimension of Hubbard's work: its immense range and diversity; his phenomenal productivity; and the creative scope of his perspectives and literary invention in a spectrum of major genres that includes western, mystery-detective, adventure, romance, science fiction and fantasy.

There are nearly four hundred individual works summarized and annotated in this bibliography. They encompass air and sea stories, tales of spies and pirates, of the rodeo and circus, of the Marine Corps and the Foreign Legion, and they traverse the South Pacific, the Caribbean, the China coast, the American frontier and even other speculative universes. With them goes the long and fabulous caravan of Hubbard characters from innumerable backgrounds and professions (he covered seventeen professions in his "Hell-Job" series alone, all reflecting his personal experiences and research [see Q2]). Some are from this world and other times; but there is also a rich and varied assortment of voyagers into, and visitors from, parallel worlds and strange galaxies.

Hubbard's professional career as a writer, spanning more than a half-century of prodigious work, reflected the colorful, Renaissance quality of his life. Like Melville and Twain, London and Hemingway, Hubbard's experiences and travels—as adventurer and master mariner; pilot and diver; prospector and photographer; artist and educator; composer and, always quintessentially, as writer—found their way into his fiction, and into American culture.

These are yarns and sagas transformed from Hubbard's endless exploration of lands, cultures and ideas into vivid, compelling and memorable literature. As author, editor and critic Frederik Pohl has said of Hubbard's stories:

> There are bits and pieces from [his] work that became part of the language in ways that very few other writers managed. I can still remember scenes from Hubbard's stories when I've forgotten most of the other things I was reading . . . He had a gift for inventing colorful pictures that still stay with me . . . Stories with these frequently memorable lines and quotable things. Pictures that stayed in your head.

This infusion of images into the consciousness of a culture is a hallmark of great literary craftsmen who have translated life experiences into literature with an unmistakable resonance of authenticity and intellectually and philosophically liberating perceptions and themes.

Although the authenticity and perceptions in Hubbard's stories are drawn from his extensive travels and broad cultural research, his literature is part of an intensely and genuinely American idiom of literary expression and thought that parallels the works of Hemingway, Steinbeck and Faulkner in the 1930s. Hubbard was a significant force in the popular fiction magazines that indelibly shaped American culture in the first half of this century with the post-modernist canon that also included Hammett and Chandler, Gardner, Burroughs and Heinlein. More trenchantly, Hubbard's influence has stayed with us and is now, perhaps even more forcefully, shaping the visage and direction of things to come.

Clearly, Hubbard's intensive research and penetrating direct observation were key to the incisive ideas and reality in his works, and may be seen as the springboard of his wide appeal and success. As J. S. Williams, an editor of one of the popular fiction magazines of the 1930s, once told his readers: ". . . [Hubbard's] been there, brothers. He's been and seen and done. And plenty of all three of them!" Both direct observation and immediate experience were fundamental and functional aspects of Hubbard's approach to life, as well as to his research and writing—as he commented later:

> To know life you've got to be part of life, you must get down there and <u>look</u>, you must get into the nooks and crannies of existence,

and you must rub elbows with all kinds and types of men before you can finally establish what man is. I lived with bandits in Mongolia and hunted with Pygmies in the Philippines—as a matter of fact I studied twenty-one different primitive races, including the white race—and my conclusions were that man, regardless of his state or culture, was essentially the same, that he was a spiritual being pulled down into the material, and I concluded finally that he needed a hand.

Hubbard's earliest published fiction—three short stories and a prize winning one-act play—appeared in the *University Hatchet Monthly Literary Review* at The George Washington University where he attended engineering classes, and took one of the earliest available courses in atomic and molecular phenomena. These academic disciplines would find detailed expression later in his adventure stories about engineers, and in his definitive science fiction tales of future history and Einsteinian space flight.

However, these initial yarns, set in pre–World War II China, readily reflect Hubbard's earlier journeys of more than a quarter of a million land and sea miles, before he was nineteen, to the remote western hills of China (in years when knowledge of these lands was fragmentary or apocryphal), and down the China coast to Java and the Sumatra Straits. His first short story published in the popular fiction magazines, "The Green God" (1934), again mirrored his Far Eastern experiences. And his first aviation story, "Hurtling Wings" (1934), reflected his background as a "stunt" pilot of gliders and powered aircraft, suffusing that story, and a score of subsequent aviation stories, with irresistible realism.

Hubbard's salient philosophy of artistic composition—formulated from his own life, his writer's discipline, his extensive reading, and his exacting research (his widely-read articles on writing and research are listed in section C of this bibliography)—catalyzed his immense literary production: more than eighteen million words of published fiction, as well as a diversity of related non-fiction articles about writing, flying and personal adventure.

For example, the germ of his short story "Mr. Tidwell, Gunner" (1936)—an impelling adventure with Nelson at the Battle of the Nile—began with Hubbard's discovery through his extensive research that there was a schoolmaster aboard the admiral's flagship to teach the midshipmen.

His landmark western, *Buckskin Brigades* (1937), came from his reading of Washington Irving's *Astoria,* and its description of the fur trade in the early years of the American republic. Hubbard married this aesthetically to relevant passages in the journals of the Lewis and Clark expedition, to memories of his own life in the rugged frontier country of turn-of-the-century Montana, and to his familiarity as a tribal blood brother with the Blackfeet Indians. The result was his first published book, a watershed novel in western fiction for its unconventionally sympathetic understanding and portrayal of Indian mores, sensibilities and culture, and its powerful historical detail.

The range of Hubbard's creative vision and originality, the span of his unique productive energies was, indeed, extraordinary. The whole spectrum of his fiction had a remarkably evocative power, a driving intensity of action and characterization, of time and place that could recreate for millions of readers the sense of the real—and the romantic—Old West, or the hard-edged tone of cities; the feel and perilous tempo of life at sea, or the sharp exhilaration and challenge of flight.

When he brought his compelling mastery of the storytelling art—honed in a variety of idioms—to the field of science fiction in July 1938 with his first science fiction story, "The Dangerous Dimension," he began to fundamentally and permanently change the face of the genre. Despite the fact that only about ten percent of his total body of fiction is written in this genre, he helped, with a few other major literary figures, to create what is still considered the great, classic "Golden Age of Science Fiction" (c. 1938–1950), and to definitively shape and dynamically enlarge the dimensions and imaginative vistas of living literature.

Fear, one of a triad of germinally influential works by Hubbard that were written and published in a single year (1940), had its genesis under the working title "Phantasmagoria." It was written at the request of his editor during a time when Hubbard was extensively researching classic literary fantasies. Now seen as the archetypical novel of psychological suspense and phantasmagoric horror in contemporary literature, *Fear* has been described as a vitally transforming work of psychological insight and moral complexity. It is a significant novel which continues, increasingly, to evoke extended comment from reviewers, critics and literary historians as a signally important work of modern American fiction. (See A15.)

Final Blackout remains Hubbard's austerely symbolic dystopia, his classic presage of a world of endless war, political disillusion and redeeming courage and leadership, written in the looming shadows of the most destructive war known to man. And *Typewriter in the Sky*, the last of this remarkable 1940 trio, is the seminally funny "journey into the mind" novel of the eternal and comedic literary struggle between author and characters that continues to exert derivative influence on various artistic forms, including theatre and motion picture.

There are three distinct motifs or recurring major themes that infuse virtually all of Hubbard's works: the imperishability of man, the indestructibility of the human spirit, and the unlimited potential of the human mind.

In his final, consummate novels—the massive, precedent-setting bestsellers *Battlefield Earth* (1982) and the ten-volume *Mission Earth* "dekalogy" (1985–87)—these motifs become allegory (good versus evil; creative intelligence versus blunt, brute force), parable (the tenacity of hope), and brilliant but savagely comic, Juvenalian satire (recalling, always, that satire is quintessentially protest and acrimony raised to the level of high art).

At this writing, more than 114 million copies of Hubbard's fiction and nonfiction works have been published in at least thirty languages and sold in more than one hundred countries. *Fear*, *Final Blackout*, *Buckskin Brigades*, *Battlefield Earth* and all ten volumes of *Mission Earth*, among other major titles, are regarded as both popular bestsellers and works of lasting literary merit and interest.

Unquestionably, the work of L. Ron Hubbard continues to significantly influence the writing of science fiction, fantasy and other literary genres, as well as the world of letters in general and the public at large.

William J. Widder
March 1994

EDITOR'S NOTE

Every bibliography, however extensive in its scope and scholarship, is provisional: on the day it is published, it ceases to reflect, with complete and immediate accuracy, the current status of the author's work. New editions of L. Ron Hubbard's published fiction and related non fiction, imprimis printings of previously unpublished fiction, and reviews, critical appreciations, and academic explications both of the whole extraordinary body of his fiction and of many of its most memorable individual works, continue to appear with growing frequency and import.

Consequently, supplements to this bibliography—periodically updating and clarifying its contents—are currently planned with a further view to publishing a revised, second edition. To that end, the editors invite and enthusiastically welcome all documented addenda and corrigenda, as well as relevant, published interpretive and expository commentary. These will receive prompt and full attention if sent to the Author's Affairs Director, Bridge Publications, Inc., 4751 Fountain Avenue, Los Angeles, California 90029.

INTRODUCTION

SCOPE OF THIS WORK

The major focus of this volume is the verification and description of the immense volume and range of L. Ron Hubbard's writings in one reference work, and a compilation of the growing list of literary appreciations and exegetical reviews of his most widely known works.

Thus, all published fiction works by L. Ron Hubbard (including those published under one of his many pen names) are listed here with synopses and international publishing histories. Relevant notes are also provided for those works which are currently considered to be literarily his most influential, prototypical and seminal.

The lists of unpublished plays, screenplays, stories and verse, and numerous sections with additional information about his life and achievements, are also included here to provide insight and research possibilities.

We offer this volume as an essential primary reference for both readers of Hubbard's fiction and scholars who wish to explore the depths and richness of these works, many of which are clearly powerful literary influences in their genres, as well as extraordinarily accurate expressions of a broad range of life, the mind, the human condition and man's ultimate potential.

ORGANIZATION OF THIS WORK

A description of the contents, methods of organization, cross-referencing and entry style for each section follows. A summary of these descriptions may also be found at the beginning of each section for easy reference. Abbreviations have been avoided to simplify the research and reference task.

CHRONOLOGIES

This section begins with a chronology of Hubbard's life that includes important fiction-related notes. It is segmented into nine major time periods and is cross-referenced to appropriate entries in other sections of this book, which are likewise cross-referenced to the life chronology.

Following this is a chronology listing the first date of publication for all of Hubbard's published fiction works. It is cross-referenced to the appropriate entries in Sections A (Books) and B (Magazine Fiction). There are separate chronologies for each of the major genres in which he wrote, also cross-referenced.

A. BOOKS

Organization of Sections A and B provides classification of a literary publishing phenomenon typical of the post-modernist canon of writers (see Preface), i.e., the author's works, even those of novel length, which most often first found expression in the popular fiction magazines of the time (1930–1950). Subsequently, these have been, or are being published in book form as a result of growing acclaim and interest.

Thus, all fiction works by Hubbard that have been published in *book* form are listed in Section A. Included are anthologies and collections such as *Ole Doc Methuselah* and *Lives You Wished to Lead but Never Dared*.

For those works which were published first as a book, the entries include an international publishing history, annotations and cross-references to secondary sources listed in Section L, where appropriate, and a synopsis.

Critical appreciations of the major works are quoted in Section I.

Where the story first appeared in magazine form, the entries in this section are cross-referenced to Section B, in which the synopses and annotations also appear.

Finally, Section AA provides a list of books to be published by Author Services, Inc., as part of the "L. Ron Hubbard Classic Fiction Series." These are also cross-referenced to Section B.

B. MAGAZINE FICTION

All fiction works by Hubbard (including those that appeared under one of his many pen names) first published in magazine form are listed in this section. This section is cross-referenced to Section A where the stories have been later published as a book, or to Section AA where they are scheduled to be published in book form. (See Section M1 for a list of pen names.)

All entries in Section B include full publishing histories and relevant annotations.

Section BB alphabetically lists and provides synopses for all known unpublished fiction stories.

C. MAGAZINE NONFICTION

This section lists published nonfiction writings which are relevant to the author's fiction writing career, such as articles on writers and writing, aviation and deep-sea diving.

The entry format follows the same style as previous sections.

D. VERSE

This section lists both published and unpublished verse, providing an insightful, albeit brief, glimpse of another facet of Hubbard's creative range.

In addition to some published poetry and the lyrics and verse related to his *Battlefield Earth* and *Mission Earth* novels, there does exist a large body of verse by Hubbard which is relevant to his fiction works, but which he never submitted for publication. All in this latter category, which appear to be complete, are listed alphabetically in sub-section DD. Most are undated works of free verse. However, where the work is of a different classification, this is noted. Additionally, where dates and bylines are on the original work, this is noted. Unnamed works are listed by the first line of the verse.

E. AUDIO TAPES AND RECORDINGS

Listed chronologically in this section are audio recordings related to Hubbard's fiction works, including recently released audio fiction recordings. Section EE lists the musical sound track recordings which the author wrote for *Battlefield Earth* and *Mission Earth*. These are cross-referenced to the book section.

F. PLAYS AND SCREENPLAYS

This section lists both published and unpublished fiction plays and screenplays to show his early success as well as his later creativity in this form. Also listed, in addition to the Hollywood movies on which Hubbard received screen credits for his stories, are those screenplays he worked on as a studio screenwriter in the 1930s but for which—consistent with conventional studio practice of the time—he received no screen credits.

G.   HONORS AND AWARDS FOR FICTION WORKS

Awards and recognitions that the author has received internationally for his fiction works are listed chronologically by category.

The categories are:

1. General author awards

2. Awards for specific titles

   a. *Battlefield Earth*

   b. *Mission Earth*

   c. *Writers of The Future*

H.   DOCTOR OF LITERATURE AWARD FROM MOSCOW UNIVERSITY

A description of the 1992 posthumous Doctor of Literature award and dedication of the L. Ron Hubbard Hall at Moscow University is provided in this section.

I.   CRITICAL APPRECIATION

This section provides a selection of critical appreciation for Hubbard and his major works from publications, reviewers and other authors. Included are statements ranging from the enthusiastic 1930s critiques by science fiction editor John W. Campbell, Jr. to Stephen King's more recent acclamation for the republication of *Fear*. The selections have been made on the basis of 1) relevance, 2) insight and 3) influence of the sources. The selected quotes are categorized alphabetically by book title as follows:

1. L. Ron Hubbard: the writer

2. *Buckskin Brigades*

3. *Battlefield Earth*

4. *Death's Deputy*

5. *Final Blackout*

6. *Fear*

7. *The Ghoul*

8. *The Indigestible Triton*

9. *Ole Doc Methuselah*

10. *Slaves of Sleep*

11. *To the Stars*

12. *Typewriter in the Sky*

13. *Mission Earth*

(An index to Section I—by author or periodical quoted—is in Section R.)

J.   ABOUT THE AUTHOR: LETTERS

This section includes excerpts from selected published and personal letters, and editorial comments regarding or from the period 1932–1948. See also "Life Chronology," part III and part IV.

These selections have been made to provide further insight into L. Ron Hubbard's life, particularly in reference to a) his popularity with readers, b) his influence in the genres in which he wrote and c) the view of peers, associates and friends during this time period.

K.   ABOUT THE AUTHOR: BIOGRAPHICAL ENTRIES & AWARDS

A list of the biographical reference books and awards listing L. Ron Hubbard and the entry awards.

L.   ABOUT THE AUTHOR: MONOGRAPHS, INTERVIEWS, REFERENCES & REVIEWS

This is a chronological list of reference works and materials which deal with the author or his works in depth or in passing.

M.   MISCELLANEA

This section includes the following lists:

1. Pen Names

2. Memberships

3. Colleges and Universities using L. Ron Hubbard's Fiction Works

4. Exhibitions and Displays

5. Aviation, Marine Navigation & Exploration Recognitions

6. Early Recognitions

N. INTRODUCTION TO *BATTLEFIELD EARTH*

Written by Hubbard as the introduction to his science fiction masterpiece, *Battlefield Earth*, this essay offers a retrospective look at his own rewarding career, a brief history of science fiction and a delineating statement on the genres of science fiction and fantasy.

O. L. RON HUBBARD PRESENTS *WRITERS OF THE FUTURE*

A description of this respected contest, its success and popularity, and Hubbard's lifetime efforts to assist other writers.

P. PHOTOGRAPHIC REFERENCE SECTION

A visual collection of Hubbard, his works, awards, exhibitions about him and the *Writers of the Future*. It is cross-referenced to other pertinent sections of the text of this bibliography.

Q. SERIES INDEX

This section lists Hubbard's works that comprise or form a series of stories. It provides a series synopsis and is cross-referenced to the individual entries in Sections A and B.

1. *The Conquest of Space*

2. *Hazardous Professions (Hell-Job Series)*

3. *Kilkenny Cats*

4. *Ole Doc Methuselah*

5. *The Secret of Treasure Island*

6. *Mission Earth*

R. AUTHOR INDEX TO QUOTES & CRITICAL APPRECIATIONS

An index to quotes about L. Ron Hubbard found in this bibliography.

S. TITLE INDEX

A general alphabetical index to L. Ron Hubbard's works and other authors and works mentioned in this bibliography.

CHRONOLOGIES OF L. RON HUBBARD'S LIFE AND FICTION WORKS

This section begins with a chronology of L. Ron Hubbard's life that includes important fiction-related notes. It is segmented into nine major time periods of his life and is cross-referenced to appropriate entries in other sections in this book which, in turn, are cross-referenced to the life chronology.

Following the life chronology is a chronology listing the first date of publication for all of Hubbard's published fiction works. It is cross-referenced to the appropriate entries in Sections A (Books) and B (Magazine Fiction). Additionally, there are separate chronologies for each of the major genres in which he wrote, and these are also cross-referenced.

1.   L. RON HUBBARD'S LIFE

I. EARLY YEARS   1911–1926

March 13, 1911:   Lafayette Ronald Hubbard is born in Tilden, Nebraska, to U.S. naval officer Harry Ross Hubbard and Ledora May Waterbury. In September they move to Durant, Oklahoma.

1912:   The Hubbard family lives briefly in the city of Kalispell, Montana. An early bond of friendship is formed in the fall as young Ron dances to the beat of Indian drums and impresses Blackfeet Indians at a tribal ceremony held on the outskirts of town.

L. Ron Hubbard spent his early years in the rugged environs of Helena, Montana.

From there, the Hubbards move to just outside of Helena, Montana, where the family ranch, affectionately referred to as the "Old Homestead," becomes their home. In the harsh frontier winter months they retreat to a three-story brick house on the corner of Fifth and Beatty in Helena. Here, in the rough and tough western "big-sky" country of pioneer Montana, young Ron Hubbard learns to read and write at an early age, rides horses and breaks broncos, pans for gold and is honored with the status of Blood Brother of the Blackfeet Indians by age six.

1918: Hubbard embarks with his grandfather on a springtime "automotive adventure" from Helena to Portland, Oregon, in a Model T Ford. He returns to Helena and from there adventures on his own by train to Tacoma, Washington. In 1919, he moves with his parents to San Diego and a year later to Oakland, California.

1923: The Hubbard family moves to Tacoma and Ron joins local Boy Scout Troop 31 in April.

In October, his father is ordered to report to Washington, D.C. The Hubbard family boards the USS *Ulysses S. Grant* on November 1 and they sail from San Francisco to New York, through the recently reopened Panama Canal. During this voyage, Hubbard meets U.S. Navy Commander Joseph "Snakc" Thompson who has recently returned from studies in Vienna with Sigmund Freud. In the course of the friendship that follows in Washington, D.C., Commander Thompson introduces him further to Freud's theories and encourages him to conduct his own investigations into the nature of the mind.

L. Ron Hubbard, age 13, became the youngest person to achieve the rank of Eagle Scout in 1924.

1924: Now an active member of Washington, D.C.'s Boy Scout Troop 10, he earns numerous merit badges, Life Scout and Star Scout medals, and on March 20, he represents his troop as he meets President Calvin Coolidge. Five days later on March 25, he becomes the nation's youngest Eagle Scout. The following day he returns to Montana by cross-country train.

II.   YOUTHFUL ADVENTURES   1927–1933

1927:   During early June, Hubbard travels to San Francisco and boards a steamer on a voyage to Guam via Hawaii, Japan, China, Hong Kong and the Philippines, where he boards another ship. In the first week of July he meets his father in Guam. During these travels, he carefully records his adventures and observations. Articles about his journeys appear in the Helena High School *Nugget* and the *Helena Independent*.

By September, he is back in Helena and becomes joke editor of the Helena High School *Nugget*. In October, he joins the Montana National Guard's 163rd Infantry.

Young Ron Hubbard on an early adventure to the Far East, 1928.

1928:   In early May, as the school year is drawing to a close, he organizes and enters a group of classmates in Helena's annual Vigilante Day Parade. They receive the "Most Original Cast" award for his entry of Spanish Main pirates.

He leaves Helena again in May, and in July travels aboard the USS *Henderson* from San Diego to Guam.

From there, during the next fourteen months, Hubbard journeys inland to the western hills of China, back to Japan, down to the Philippines, and south to Java. He befriends a British intelligence officer, Buddhist priests, the last in a line of magicians from the court of Khublai Khan, and meets people from many varied cultures and backgrounds. He gains greater nautical expertise aboard the twin-masted coastal schooner *Marianna Maru* as he plies the waters off the China coast as a helmsman and supercargo.

1929: Hubbard returns to the United States in September to complete his high school education. He attends Swavely Prep School in Manassas, Virginia. Here, he writes a number of school papers including "Should the Philippines be Liberated?" "Modernism," "Go Thou Fair Lad and Discover Thy Imagination," and a book report on *Revolt in the Desert* by T. E. Lawrence.

1930: In January, he enrolls at Woodward School for Boys in

L. Ron Hubbard in Washington, D.C. in the early '30s.

Washington, D.C. In March, he writes and delivers a prize-winning speech on "The Constitution—A Guarantee of Liberty to the Individual" in the regional oratory contest.

He enlists in the 20th Marine Corps Reserve, Company G, during May, is appointed first sergeant in June, and turns out a prize-winning drill team.

Hubbard graduates from Woodward and in September enrolls at The George Washington University (GWU). His studies include engineering courses and atomic and molecular phenomena, but here he also carries out his first investigation of the structure and function of the human mind. He performs ballads on local radio station WOL and writes dramas for another local station, WJSV.

1931: While Hubbard continues his studies at GWU, he takes up glider flying and becomes recognized as a daring pilot. He then becomes a powered flight pilot and barnstorms across the Midwest in September with a friend. He is also president of The George Washington University Flying Club, is secretary of the GWU chapter of the American Society of Civil Engineers and joins a team of surveyors who are sent to verify the U.S./Canadian border in Maine.

L. Ron Hubbard "barnstormed" with powered aircraft in 1931.

1932: In January, he sells his first magazine article, "Tailwind Willies," which appears in the aviation journal *Sportsman Pilot* (see C1), where he details the latest aviation developments and advises pilots on flight procedures in adverse conditions. (He receives his glider pilot license in September, see M5.)

As an editor and writer for *The University Hatchet* at GWU, his first published fiction story, "Tah," appears in February and a short adventure story, "Grounded," is published in April. He follows this in May by winning the Literary Award at GWU for the best one-act play with "The God Smiles." (See B1, B2, B3.)

In the spring, Hubbard organizes and leads the "Caribbean Motion Picture Expedition." He is joined on the two-and-a-half month, five-thousand-mile journey aboard the two hundred foot, four-masted schooner, *Doris Hamlin*, by more than fifty adventure-seeking college students. The voyage is complete by September. The crew brings numerous floral and reptile specimens back for the University of Michigan and photographs are sold to the *New York Times*.

A short time later, in October, he embarks upon a voyage to Puerto Rico. In this West Indies Mineralogical Expedition he not only completes the first mineralogical survey

L. Ron Hubbard in Puerto Rico during the West Indies Mineralogical Expedition in 1932.

of Puerto Rico as an American territory, but writes articles for *Sportsman Pilot* about flying through the Caribbean Islands. He also investigates and explores some of the area's diverse cultures and beliefs, including voodoo and Espiritismo.

In November, "Sans Power," appears in the *Sportsman Pilot* (C2). His first nautical-related story, "Submarine" (B4), appears in *The University Hatchet* during the same month.

1933:   The expedition to Puerto Rico is complete in April. In May, his article "Washington's Langley Day" (C3) appears in *Sportsman Pilot*.

During the summer, he writes a story a day for two months. By the end of the year, he is producing a hundred thousand words a month.

III. THE LEGEND BEGINS   1934–1936

1934:   "The Green God," Hubbard's first fiction story to be published in the popular fiction magazines, appears in *Thrilling Adventures* in February 1934. He continues to produce one hundred thousand words of fiction a month and by December 1934, hires an agent to represent his work. He uses a variety of pen names and publishes an average of more than one story every two weeks—a total of 138 novels, novelettes and short stories in a six-year period. The stories cover a wide spectrum of genres, including adventure, western, mystery and detective.

L. Ron Hubbard, center, as president of the New York chapter of the American Fiction Guild in 1936.

1935:   The New York chapter of the American Fiction Guild elects him president. He gives leadership to a group which includes Raymond Chandler, Dashiell Hammett and Edgar Rice Burroughs. He offers help to other writers through his articles for writer magazines and appears on radio shows with advice on how to improve the quality and saleability of stories. (See Section C for articles, and Section O for relevant material on *Writers of The Future.*)

1936:   Hubbard completes his first book, *Buckskin Brigades,* in November. It is published in August, 1937 by The Macaulay Company.

1937:   Columbia Pictures purchases film rights to his novel *Murder at Pirate Castle* and asks for his assistance with the screenplay adaptation, which is produced under the title "Secret of Treasure Island." He works on other big screen serials for Columbia: *The Mysterious Pilot* and *The Adventures of Wild Bill Hickock.* He also works on *The Spider Returns* with Norvell Page at Warner Bros. During his ten weeks in Hollywood, he writes a quarter of a million words of scripts and continues to produce for his New York editors. (See Section F.)

John W. Campbell, Jr. (right), editor of Astounding Science Fiction *magazine, with L. Ron Hubbard. (See Section N, Introduction to* Battlefield Earth.*)*

IV. CHANGING GENRES   **1938–1940**

1938:   Hubbard returns to New York where executives from Street & Smith, one of the world's largest publishers, enlist his help to fill the pages of their newly acquired magazine, *Astounding Science Fiction.* He is asked to boost sagging sales with stories about *real* people—not robots, planets and spaceships. He continues to write in other genres, but his decision to enter the field of science fiction is one which fundamentally and permanently changes the genre. "The Dangerous Dimension," his first story for *Astounding Science Fiction,* appears in the July issue. (See B115.)

1939:   In January, John W. Campbell, Jr., editor of *Astounding Science Fiction,* starts *Unknown* magazine to provide a venue for "fantasy" stories, particularly those which Hubbard writes. (See Section J.) His first story for *Unknown* magazine, "The Ultimate Adventure," appears in the April issue. (See B130.)

1940:   The Explorers Club elects him a member in February. "Death's Deputy" is published the same month. "Final Blackout" is published in three parts during April–June. In July , the same month that "Fear" is published in *Unknown,* he sets sail under Explorers Club flag number 105 from Seattle with the thirty-two foot ketch, *Magician,* on the Alaskan Radio Experimental Expedition. He charts previously inaccurate and unrecorded hazards and coastline for the U.S. Navy Hydrographic Office, conducts experiments on radio directional finding and examines local native cultures. He does a series of radio shows on KGBU in Ketchikan, Alaska. Then, in December, he announces a Christmas story writing contest for Alaska's amateur writers in the "Golden Pen Award" hour.

"The Kilkenny Cats" is published in September and "Typewriter in the Sky" is published in two parts in November–December.

The U.S. Bureau of Marine Inspection and Navigation awards him the "Master of Steam and Motor Vessels" license in December. After he is back home in the Seattle area on December 23, he resumes his writing and presents the U.S. Navy with hundreds of photographs and notes they have requested.

1941:   Hubbard receives the "Master of Sail Vessels" license for "Any Ocean" in late March. The United States Navy commissions him as lieutenant (jg) in the Navy Reserve in late June. With the outbreak of the war in early December, he receives orders to active duty. He reports to Australia where he coordinates naval intelligence activities and is Senior Officer Present Ashore. Fifteen stories, written earlier, are published between January 1941 and April 1943.

V. WAR YEARS 1942–1945

Hubbard returns to the United States from Australia and assumes command of a convoy escort YP 422 in Boston; attends submarine chaser school in Miami; commands the sub chaser PC 815 in the North Pacific, where he sinks at least one Japanese submarine in an engagement off the

Hubbard in 1943 when he captained the navy sub chaser PC 815.

coast of Oregon; instructs at the Small Craft Training Center in San Pedro, California; is a navigation officer aboard the USS *Algol;* and attends the U.S. Navy School of Military Government at Princeton University. As the war is coming to its final months, he is sent to Oak Knoll Naval Hospital in Oakland, California, to receive care for injuries sustained during the war.

At Oak Knoll, he conducts a series of experiments dealing with the endocrine system and discovers that contrary to long-standing beliefs, function monitors structure in the relationship between thought and the body. He begins to help friends "who had not survived the war too well."

VI. POST -WAR FICTION   1946–1949

The Navy releases him from active duty in February 1946, and he returns to writing as a means to support his intensified research. By July 1947, "The Chee-Chalker" is published. In the next three years (up to November 1950), he writes thirty-one science fiction, fantasy, western, mystery and detective stories. Among these are "Blood on His

L. Ron Hubbard in the late 1940s, while living in San Luis Obispo, California.

Spurs," "Ole Doc Methuselah," "Killer's Law," "To the Stars," "The Kingslayer," "Masters of Sleep," "Hoss Tamer," and "The Obsolete Weapon." During these years, he serves as a Special Officer with the Los Angeles Police Department; works with a public relations firm; and conducts *Dianetics*® research in cities across the United States—including Los Angeles, California; Savannah, Georgia; New York City, New York and Washington, D.C. He also writes the original thesis of Dianetics, which is circulated widely among doctors, engineers and scientists across the country, and publishes his first articles on the subject, such as "Terra Incognita" (*Explorers Club Journal,* Winter/Spring 1950), and "Dianetics: The Evolution of a Science" (*Astounding Science Fiction,* May 1950).

VII. Exploring Terra Incognita 1950–1979

In May 1950, Hermitage House publishes *Dianetics: The Modern Science of Mental Health,* which culminates his years of research on the subject of the mind. The public

L. Ron Hubbard in the late 1940s, during which he traveled the country extensively.

response is telling: a *New York Times* bestseller that remains on the list for twenty-six consecutive weeks; sweeping public interest and demand for more information and lectures. Hubbard leaves the field of fiction and Hollywood movie offers. By 1952, his researches lead him to develop *Scientology*® applied religious philosophy. And for the next three decades, he dedicates his life to writing and publishing millions of words of non-fiction concerning the nature of man and the betterment of the human condition.

During this time, he writes, lectures and researches extensively in fields ranging from drug rehabilitation and organizational management to art and communications, while he forwards his understanding of the human mind and spirit. Yet he still finds time for some notable achievements in exploration and writing.

1961:   Hubbard receives his second Explorers Club flag for the "Ocean Archeological Expedition to study underwater sites

L. Ron Hubbard doing a photoshoot in Jamaica, 1975.

of historical interest such as submerged cities," in the Aegean Sea.

1966:   He accepts his third Explorers Club flag for the Hubbard Geological Survey Expedition which examines and amplifies knowledge of Mediterranean history.

1976:   Writes a feature-length screenplay titled *Revolt in the Stars* (F12).

VIII. MONUMENTAL RETURN TO FICTION 1980–1981

During 1980–1981, Hubbard produces two million words of fiction. Among his writings are two unpublished feature-length screenplays, *Ai! Pedrito!* (F14), and *A Very Strange Trip* (F15), as well as his highly successful published works. These include the largest single-volume science fiction novel ever written, *Battlefield Earth: A Saga of the Year 3000* (A28), and his masterpiece of comic satire, *Mission Earth* (A29)—an unprecedented 1.2 million word science fiction novel in ten volumes, which he describes with the word *dekalogy*.

IX. ENVOI 1982–1985

From his California ranch, he researches and releases his new and final discoveries in Scientology. His own literary agency, Author Services, Inc., is established and he sees *Battlefield Earth* become an international bestseller after its 1982 release, as well as the release of the first volume of *Mission Earth* in 1985. He composes music and lyrics for both of these works—the first time a recorded "soundtrack" is created to directly accompany a best-selling novel. (See EE1, EE2.)

In 1983, he launches an international science fiction and fantasy short story and novelette competition for new and aspiring writers, which he calls the *Writers of The Future Contest*. (See Section O for complete information on the Writers Contest as well as the companion *Illustrators of The Future Contest*. The Illustrators' Contest was founded in 1988 by Author Services, Inc., to encourage the speculative fiction artist in much the same way the Writers' Contest has done for authors.)

January 24, 1986: L. Ron Hubbard departs this life. All ten volumes of his final novel, *Mission Earth*, become successive *New York Times* bestsellers and a twenty-year schedule to republish his masterpieces and unpublished works is started by Author Services, Inc., as the culmination of his literary legacy.

2. CHRONOLOGY OF FICTION WORKS—ALL GENRES

(By first publication date with cross references)
Total published fiction works: 226

[**Notes:** Screenplays, separately published poems and nonfiction are not included here. See sections D, E and F for these other listings.

The *Mission Earth* dekalogy is counted as one work although the 1.2 million word satire was published in ten volumes. See notes A28.]

1932	1932/Feb	Tah (B1)
	1932/Apr	Grounded (B2)
	1932/May	The God Smiles (B3, F1)
	1932/Nov	Submarine (B4)
1934	1934/Feb	The Green God (B5)
	1934/Apr	Calling Squad Cars! (B6)
	1934/May	Pearl Pirate (B7)
	1934/Jun	Sea Fangs (B8)
	1934/Jul	Dead Men Kill (B9)
	1934/Sept	Twenty Fathoms Down (B10)
	1934/Sept	Mouthpiece (B11)
	1934/Sept	Maybe Because—! (B12)
	1934/Oct	Yellow Loot (B13)
	1934/Nov	Hurtling Wings (B14)
	1934/Nov	The Carnival of Death (B15)
	1934/Nov	"Tooby" (B16)

1935	1935/Jan	The Phantom Patrol (B17)
	1935/Jan	The Trail of the Red Diamonds (B18)
	1935/Feb	The Red Dragon (B19)
	1935/Feb	Flame City (B20)
	1935/Mar	Destiny's Drum (B21)
	1935/Apr	Brass Keys to Murder (B22)
	1935/May	False Cargo (B23)
	1935/May	The Squad That Never Came Back (B24)

1935/May	The Drowned City (B25)
1935/May–Jun	The Cossack (B26)
1935/Jun	Man-Killers of the Air (B27)
1935/Jul	Hostage to Death (B28)
1935/Jul	Hell's Legionnaire (B29)
1935/Jul	Plans for the Boy (B30)
1935/Aug	The Contraband Crate (B31)
1935/Aug	Under the Black Ensign (B32)
1935/Aug	Yukon Madness (B33)
1935/Sept	The Bad One (B34)
1935/Sept	Buckley Plays a Hunch (B35)
1935/Sept	Medals for Mahoney (B36)
1935/Sept	The Sky Devil (B37)
1935/Oct	He Walked to War (B38)
1935/Oct	Murder Afloat (B39)
1935/Oct	Forbidden Gold (B40)
1935/Oct	Wind-Gone-Mad (B41)
1935/Nov	Five Mex for a Million (B42)
1935/Nov	The Adventure of "X" (B43)
1935/Nov	The Black Sultan (B44)
1935/Nov	Catapult Courage (B45)
1935/Dec	The Barbarians (B46)
1935/Dec	Machine Gun 21,000 (B47)

1936	1936/Jan	Trick Soldier (B48)
	1936/Jan	The Sky-Crasher (B49)
	1936/Jan	Starch and Stripes (B50)
	1936/Feb	Red Sand (B51)
	1936/Mar	The Price of a Hat (B52)
	1936/Mar	Raiders of the Beam (B53)
	1936/Mar	The Blow Torch Murder (B54)
	1936/Mar	Hurricane (B55)
	1936/Apr	Spy Killer (B56)
	1936/Apr	The Death Flyer (B57)
	1936/Apr	Marriage for Spite (B58)
	1936/May	Horse and Horse (B59)
	1936/May	They Killed Him Dead (B60)
	1936/May	Loot of the Shanung (B61)
	1936/Jun	Escape for Three (B62)

	1936/Jun	The Mad Dog Murder (B63)
	1936/Jul	The Grease Spot (B64)
	1936/Jul	Leaducation (B65)
	1936/Jul	Sleepy McGee (B66)
	1936/Jul	Don't Rush Me (B67)
	1936/Aug	The Neck Scarf (B68)
	1936/Aug	The Headhunters (B69)
	1936/Sept	Sky Birds Dare! (B70)
	1936/Sept	The Baron of Coyote River (B71)
	1936/Sept	The Slickers (B72)
	1936/Sept	Mr. Tidwell, Gunner (B73)
	1936/Sept	Golden Hell (B74)
	1936/Oct	Flaming Arrows (B75)
	1936/Oct	Tomb of the Ten Thousand Dead (B76)
	1936/Oct	Mr. Luck (B77)
	1936/Oct	Test Pilot (B78)
	1936/Oct	Deep-Sea Diver (B79)
	1936/Oct	The Big Cats (B80)
	1936/Oct	Black Towers to Danger (B81)
	1936/Nov	The No-Gun Gunhawk(B82)
	1936/Nov	Canteens (B83)
	1936/Nov	River Driver (B84)
	1936/Nov	The Ethnologist (B85)
	1936/Dec	Fifty-Fifty O'Brien (B86)
	1936/Dec	Mine Inspector (B87)
	1936/Dec	The Shooter (B88)
	1936/Dec	While Bugles Blow! (B89)
1937	1937/Jan	Steeplejack (B90)
	1937/Jan	Flying Trapeze (B91)
	1937/Feb	Mountaineer (B92)
	1937/Feb	The Bold Dare All (B93)
	1937/Mar	The Battling Pilot (B94)
	1937/Mar	Cattle King for a Day (B95)
	1937/Mar	A Lesson in Lightning (B96)
	1937/Jun	The Crate Killer (B97)
	1937/Jun	All Frontiers Are Jealous (B98)
	1937/Jul	The Dive Bomber (B99)
	1937/Aug.	Buckskin Brigades (A1)
	1937/Aug	Nine Lives (B100)

	1937/Sept	Reign of the Gila Monster (B101)
	1937/Oct	Red Death over China (B102)
	1937/Nov	The Devil—with Wings (B103)
	1937/Nov	Gunman's Tally (B104)
	1937/Nov	Cargo of Coffins (B105)
	1937/Dec	Tinhorn's Daughter (B106)
	1937/Dec	Orders Is Orders (B107)

1938	1938/Mar	Six-Gun Caballero (B108)
	1938/Mar	Under the Die-Hard Brand (B109)
	1938/Jun	The Toughest Ranger (B110)
	1938/Jun	Arctic Wings (B111)
	1938/Jun	Killer Ape (B112)
	1938/Jun–Jul	Hot Lead Payoff (B113)
	1938/Jul	King of the Gunmen (B114)
	1938/Jul	The Dangerous Dimension (B115)
	1938/Jul	Ride 'Em, Cowboy! (B116)
	1938/Aug	The Ghost Town Gun-Ghost (B117)
	1938/Aug	When Gilhooly Was in Flower (B118)
	1938/Sept	Boss of the Lazy B (B119)
	1938/Sept–Nov	The Tramp (B120)
	1938/Oct	Come and Get It (B121)
	1938/Oct	Branded Outlaw! (B122)
	1938/Oct	The Lieutenant Takes the Sky (a.k.a. The Lieutenant Takes the Air) (B123)
	1938/Oct	Death Waits at Sundown (B124)
	1938/Nov	Silent Pards (B125)
	1938/Dec	Ruin at Rio Piedras (B126)
	1938/Dec	Empty Saddles (B127)

1939	1939/Jan	Trouble on His Wings (B128)
	1939/Feb	Wings over Ethiopia (B129)
	1939/Apr	The Ultimate Adventure (B130)
	1939/Apr	The Falcon Killer (B131)
	1939/Apr	The Hurricane's Roar (B132)
	1939/May	Danger in the Dark (B133)
	1939/Jul	Slaves of Sleep (B134)

	1939/Aug	The Ghoul (B135)
	1939/Oct	The Ranch That No One Would Buy (B136)
1940	1940/Feb	The Professor Was a Thief (B137)
	1940/Feb	The Small Boss of Nunaloha (B138)
	1940/Feb	If I Were You (B139)
	1940/Feb	Death's Deputy (B140)
	1940/Apr	The Indigestible Triton (B141)
	1940/Apr–Jun	Final Blackout (B142)
	1940/May	On Blazing Wings (B143)
	1940/Jun	Shadows from Boothill (B144)
	1940/Jun	Inky Odds (B145)
	1940/Jul	The Iron Duke (B146)
	1940/Jul	Fear (B147)
	1940/Jul	The Idealist (B148)
	1940/Aug	Sabotage in the Sky (B149)
	1940/Sept	The Kilkenny Cats (B150)
	1940/Oct	The Devil's Rescue (B151)
	1940/Nov	One Was Stubborn (B152)
	1940/Nov–Dec	Typewriter in the Sky (B153)
1941	1941/Jan	The Traitor (B154)
	1941/Feb	The Crossroads (B155)
	1941/Apr	The Mutineers (B156)
	1941/Aug	The Case of the Friendly Corpse (B157)
	1941/Oct	Borrowed Glory (B158)
	1941/Nov	The Last Drop (B159)
1942	1942/Jan	The Invaders (a.k.a. Behind the Black Nebula) (B160)
	1942/Feb	He Didn't Like Cats (B161)
	1942/Mar	The Rebels (B162)
	1942/Apr	Strain (B163)
	1942/Apr	The Room (B164)
	1942/Jun	The Slaver (B165)
	1942/Jul	Space Can (B166)
	1942/Oct	The Beast (B167)

1943	1943/Apr	The Great Secret (B168)
1947	1947/Jul–Aug	The Chee-Chalker (B169)
	1947/Aug–Oct	The End Is Not Yet (B170)
	1947/Sept	Killer's Law (B171)
	1947/Oct	Ole Doc Methuselah (B172)
	1947/Nov	The Expensive Slaves (B173)

1948	1948/Mar	Her Majesty's Aberration (B174)
	1948/May	The Obsolete Weapon (B175)
	1948/Jun	The Magic Quirt (B176)
	1948/Jul	When Shadows Fall (B177)
	1948/Sept	The Great Air Monopoly (B178)
	1948/Dec	240,000 Miles Straight Up (B179)
	1948/Dec	Stacked Bullets (B180)

1949	1949/Jan	Forbidden Voyage (B181)
	1949/Feb	Gunman! (B182)
	1949/Mar	The Magnificent Failure (B183)
	1949/Apr	The Gunner from Gehenna (B184)
	1949/Apr	Plague! (B185)
	1949/Apr	Gun Boss of Tumbleweed (B186)
	1949/May	The Conroy Diary (B187)
	1949/May	The Incredible Destination (B188)
	1949/May	Battle of Wizards (B189)
	1949/Jun	A Sound Investment (B190)
	1949/Jul	The Unwilling Hero (B191)
	1949/Aug	Johnny, the Town Tamer (B192)
	1949/Aug	A Matter of Matter (B193)
	1949/Sept	Beyond the Black Nebula (B194)
	1949/Sept	Guns of Mark Jardine (B195)
	1949/Sept	Blood on His Spurs (B196)
	1949/Oct	The Automagic Horse (B197)
	1949/Oct	The Planet Makers (B198)
	1949/Nov	The Emperor of the Universe (B199)
	1949/Nov	Man for Breakfast (B200)
	1949/Dec	Stranger in Town (B201)
	1949/Dec	A Can of Vacuum (B202)

1950	1950/Jan	Ole Mother Methuselah (B203)
	1950/Jan	Hoss Tamer (B204)
	1950/Jan	Beyond All Weapons (B205)
	1950/Jan	The Last Admiral (B206)
	1950/Feb–Mar	To the Stars (a.k.a. Return to Tomorrow)(B207)
	1950/Feb	Devil's Manhunt (B208)
	1950/Winter	The Kingslayer (B209)
	1950/Apr	Greed (B210)
	1950/May	The No-Gun Man (B211)
	1950/Jun	Vengeance Is Mine! (B212)
	1950/Aug	Battling Bolto (B213)
	1950/Sept	Final Enemy (B214)
	1950/Oct	The Masters of Sleep (B215)
	1950/Nov	Tough Old Man (B216)
1981	1981/Oct	The Were-Human (B217)
1982	1982/May	Battlefield Earth (A27)
	1982/Sept	He Found God (B218)
1985	1985/Oct	Mission Earth Volume 1: The Invaders Plan (A28)
1986	1986/Mar	Mission Earth Volume 2: Black Genesis (A29)
	1986/Apr	Mission Earth Volume 3: The Enemy Within (A30)
	1986/Jul	Mission Earth Volume 4: An Alien Affair (A31)
	1986/Oct	Mission Earth Volume 5: Fortune of Fear (A32)
1987	1987/Jan	Mission Earth Volume 6: Death Quest (A33)
	1987/May	Mission Earth Volume 7: Voyage of Vengeance (A34)
	1987/Jul	Mission Earth Volume 8: Disaster (A35)
	1987/Sept	Mission Earth Volume 9: Villainy Victorious (A36)

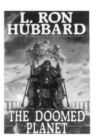

	1987/Nov	Mission Earth Volume 10: The Doomed Planet (A37)
1991	1991/Jun	Mariner's Mate (B219)
1992	1992/Jan	Model Gentleman (B220)
	1992/Jun	Hired Assassin (B221)
	1992/Jun	Gift from Heaven (B222)
1993	1993/Jun	The Secret of Skeleton Creek (B223)

3.   CHRONOLOGY OF FICTION WORKS—ADVENTURE

(By first publication date with cross references)
Total adventure fiction works: 91

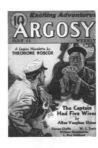

1932	1932/Feb	Tah (B1)
	1932/Apr	Grounded (B2)
	1932/May	The God Smiles (B3, F1)
1934	1934/Feb	The Green God (B5)
	1934/May	Pearl Pirate (B7)
	1934/Jun	Sea Fangs (B8)
	1934/Sept	Twenty Fathoms Down (B10)
	1934/Oct	Yellow Loot (B13)
	1934/Nov	Hurtling Wings (B14)

1935	1935/Jan	The Phantom Patrol (B17)
	1935/Jan	The Trail of the Red Diamonds (B18)
	1935/Feb	The Red Dragon (B19)
	1935/Mar	Destiny's Drum (B21)
	1935/May	False Cargo (B23)
	1935/May	The Squad That Never Came Back (B24)
	1935/May	The Drowned City (B25)
	1935/May–Jun	The Cossack (B26)

	1935/Jun	Man-Killers of the Air (B27)
	1935/Jul	Hostage to Death (B28)
	1935/Jul	Hell's Legionnaire (B29)
	1935/Aug	The Contraband Crate (B31)
	1935/Aug	Under the Black Ensign (B32)
	1935/Aug	Yukon Madness (B33)
	1935/Sept	Buckley Plays a Hunch (B35)
	1935/Sept	Medals for Mahoney (B36)
	1935/Sept	The Sky Devil (B37)
	1935/Oct	He Walked to War (B38)
	1935/Oct	Forbidden Gold (B40)
	1935/Oct	Wind-Gone-Mad (B41)
	1935/Nov	Five Mex for a Million (B42)

1935/Nov   The Adventure of "X" (B43)
1935/Nov   The Black Sultan (B44)
1935/Nov   Catapult Courage (B45)
1935/Dec   The Barbarians (B46)
1935/Dec   Machine Gun 21,000 (B47)

1936   1936/Jan   Trick Soldier (B48)
        1936/Jan   The Sky-Crasher (B49)
        1936/Jan   Starch and Stripes (B50)
        1936/Feb   Red Sand (B51)
        1936/Mar   The Price of a Hat (B52)
        1936/Mar   Raiders of the Beam (B53)
        1936/Mar   Hurricane (B55)
        1936/Apr   Spy Killer (B56)
        1936/May   Loot of the Shanung (B61)
        1936/Jun   Escape for Three (B62)

        1936/Jul   Sleepy McGee (B66)
        1936/Jul   Don't Rush Me (B67)
        1936/Aug   The Headhunters (B69)
        1936/Sept Sky Birds Dare! (B70)
        1936/Sept Mr. Tidwell, Gunner (B73)
        1936/Sept Golden Hell (B74)
        1936/Oct   Flaming Arrows (B75)
        1936/Oct   Tomb of the Ten Thousand
                   Dead (B76)

        1936/Oct   Mr. Luck (B77)
        1936/Oct   Test Pilot (B78)
        1936/Oct   Deep-Sea Diver (B79)
        1936/Oct   The Big Cats (B80)
        1936/Oct   Black Towers to Danger (B81)
        1936/Nov   River Driver (B84)
        1936/Nov   The Ethnologist (B85)
        1936/Dec   Fifty-Fifty O'Brien (B86)
        1936/Dec   Mine Inspector (B87)
        1936/Dec   The Shooter (B88)
        1936/Dec   While Bugles Blow! (B89)

1937   1937/Jan   Steeplejack (B90)
        1937/Jan   Flying Trapeze (B91)
        1937/Feb   Mountaineer (B92)
        1937/Feb   The Bold Dare All (B93)

	1937/Mar	The Battling Pilot (B94)
	1937/Mar	A Lesson in Lightning (B96)
	1937/June	The Crate Killer (B97)
	1937/June	All Frontiers Are Jealous (B98)
	1937/Jul	The Dive Bomber (B99)
	1937/Aug	Nine Lives (B100)
	1937/Oct	Red Death over China (B102)
	1937/Nov	The Devil—with Wings (B103)
	1937/Nov	Cargo of Coffins (B105)
	1937/Dec	Orders is Orders (B107)
1938	1938/Jun	Arctic Wings (B111)
	1938/Oct	The Lieutenant Takes the Sky (B123)
1939	1939/Jan	Trouble on His Wings (B128)
	1939/Feb	Wings over Ethiopia (B129)
	1939/Apr	The Falcon Killer (B131)
	1939/Apr	The Hurricane's Roar (B132)
1940	1940/Feb	The Small Boss of Nunaloha (B138)
	1940/Feb	If I Were You (B139)
	1940/May	On Blazing Wings (B143)
	1940/Jun	Inky Odds (B145)
	1940/Jul	The Iron Duke (B146)
	1940/Aug	Sabotage in the Sky (B149)
1991	1991/Jun	Mariner's Mate (B219)

4. CHRONOLOGY OF FICTION WORKS—WESTERN

(By first publication date with cross references)
Total western fiction works: 47

1934	1934/Sept	Maybe Because—! (B12)
	1934/Nov	"Tooby" (B16)
1935	1935/Jul	Plans for the Boy (B30)
	1935/Sept	The Bad One (B34)
1936	1936/Apr	Marriage for Spite (B58)
	1936/May	Horse and Horse (B59)
	1936/Jul	Leaducation (B65)
	1936/Aug	The Neck Scarf (B68)
	1936/Sept	The Baron of Coyote River (B71)
	1936/Nov	The No-Gun Gunhawk (B82)
	1936/Nov	Canteens (B83)
1937	1937/Mar	Cattle King for a Day (B95)
	1937/Aug	Buckskin Brigades (A1)
	1937/Sept	Reign of the Gila Monster (B101)
	1937/Nov	Gunman's Tally (B104)
	1937/Dec	Tinhorn's Daughter (B106)
1938	1938/Mar	Six-Gun Caballero (B108)
	1938/Mar	Under the Die-Hard Brand (B109)
	1938/Jun	The Toughest Ranger (B110)
	1938/Jun-Jul	Hot Lead Pay-Off (B113)
	1938/Jul	King of the Gunmen (B114)
	1938/Aug	The Ghost Town Gun-Ghost (B117)
	1938/Sept	Boss of the Lazy B (B119)
	1938/Oct	Come and Get It (B121)
	1938/Oct	Branded Outlaw! (B122)
	1938/Oct	Death Waits at Sundown (B124)
	1938/Nov	Silent Pards (B125)

	1938/Dec	Ruin at Rio Piedras (B126)
	1938/Dec	Empty Saddles (B127)
1939	1939/Oct	The Ranch that No One Would Buy (B136)
1940	1940/Jun	Shadows From Boothill (B144)
1948	1948/Jun	The Magic Quirt (B176)
	1948/Dec	Stacked Bullets (B180)
1949	1949/Feb	Gunman! (B182)
	1949/Apr	The Gunner from Gehenna (B184)
	1949/Apr	Gun Boss of Tumbleweed (B186)
	1949/Aug	Johnny, The Town Tamer (B192)
	1949/Sept	Guns of Mark Jardine (B195)
	1949/Sept	Blood on His Spurs (B196)
	1949/Nov	Man for Breakfast (B200)
	1949/Dec	Stranger in Town (B201)
1950	1950/Jan	Hoss Tamer (B204)
	1950/Feb	Devil's Manhunt (B208)
	1950/May	The No-Gun Man (B211)
	1950/Jun	Vengeance Is Mine! (B212)
1992	1992/Jun	Hired Assassin (B221)
1993	1993/Jun	The Secret of Skeleton Creek (B223)

5. CHRONOLOGY OF FICTION WORKS—MYSTERY/DETECTIVE

(By first publication date with cross references)

Total mystery/detective fiction works: 15

1934	1934/Apr	Calling Squad Cars! (B6)
	1934/Jul	Dead Men Kill (B9)
	1934/Sept	Mouthpiece (B11)
	1934/Nov	The Carnival of Death (B15)
1935	1935/Feb	Flame City (B20)
	1935/Apr	Brass Keys to Murder (B22)
	1935/Oct	Murder Afloat (B39)
1936	1936/Mar	The Blow Torch Murder (B54)
	1936/May	They Killed Him Dead (B60)
	1936/Jun	The Mad Dog Murder (B63)
	1936/Jul	The Grease Spot (B64)
	1936/Sept	The Slickers (B72)
1938	1938/Jun	Killer Ape (B112)
1947	1947/Jul–Aug	The Chee-Chalker (B169)
	1947/Sept	Killer's Law (B171)

6. CHRONOLOGY OF FICTION WORKS—FANTASY

(By first publication date with cross-references)
Total fantasy fiction works: 19

1936	1936/Apr	The Death Flyer (B57)
1939	1939/Apr	The Ultimate Adventure (B130)
	1939/May	Danger in the Dark (B133)
	1939/Jul	Slaves of Sleep (B134, A4)
	1939/Aug	The Ghoul (B135)
1940	1940/Feb	Death's Deputy (B140)
	1940/Apr	The Indigestible Triton (B141)
	1940/Jul	Fear (B147, A15)
	1940/Oct	The Devil's Rescue (B151)
	1940/Nov	One Was Stubborn (B152)
	1940/Nov-Dec	Typewriter in the Sky (B153)
1941	1941/Feb	The Crossroads (B155)
	1941/Aug	The Case of the Friendly Corpse (B157)
	1941/Oct	Borrowed Glory (B158)
1942	1942/Feb	He Didn't Like Cats (B161)
	1942/Apr	The Room (B164)
1949	1949/May	Battle of Wizards (B189)
1950	1950/Oct	The Masters of Sleep (B215)
1981	1981/Oct	The Were-Human (B217)

7. CHRONOLOGY OF FICTION WORKS—SCIENCE FICTION

(By first publication date with cross-references)
Total science fiction works: 49

1938	1938/Jul	The Dangerous Dimension (B115)
	1938/Sept-Nov	The Tramp (B120)

1940	1940/Feb	The Professor Was a Thief (B137)
	1940/Apr–Jun	Final Blackout (B142)
	1940/Jul	The Idealist (B148)
	1940/Sept	The Kilkenny Cats (B150)

1941	1941/Jan	The Traitor (B154)
	1941/Apr	The Mutineers (B156)
	1941/Nov	The Last Drop (B159)

1942	1942/Jan	The Invaders (also Behind the Black Nebula) (B160)
	1942/Mar	The Rebels (B162)
	1942/Apr	Strain (B163)
	1942/Jun	The Slaver (B165)
	1942/Jul	Space Can (B166)
	1942/Oct	The Beast (B167)

1943	1943/Apr	The Great Secret (B168)

1947	1947/Aug-Oct	The End Is Not Yet (B170)
	1947/Oct	Ole Doc Methuselah (B172)
	1947/Nov	The Expensive Slaves (B173)

1948	1948/Mar	Her Majesty's Aberration (B174)
	1948/May	The Obsolete Weapon (B175)
	1948/Sept	The Great Air Monopoly (B178)
	1948/Dec	240,000 Miles Straight Up (B179)

1949	1949/Jan	Forbidden Voyage (B181)
	1949/Mar	The Magnificent Failure (B183)
	1949/Apr	Plague! (B185)
	1949/May	The Conroy Diary (B187)

	1949/May	The Incredible Destination (B188)
	1949/Jun	A Sound Investment (B190)
	1949/Jul	The Unwilling Hero (B191)
	1949/Aug	A Matter of Matter (B193)
	1949/Sept	Beyond the Black Nebula (B194)
	1949/Oct	The Automagic Horse (B197)
	1949/Oct	The Planet Makers (B198)
	1949/Nov	The Emperor of the Universe (B199)
	1949/Dec	A Can of Vacuum (B202)
1950	1950/Jan	Ole Mother Methuselah (B203)
	1950/Jan	Beyond All Weapons (B205)
	1950/Jan	The Last Admiral (B206)
	1950/Feb–Mar	To the Stars (B207)
	1950/Winter	The Kingslayer (B209)
	1950/Apr	Greed (B210)
	1950/Aug	Battling Bolto (B213)
	1950/Sept	Final Enemy (B214)
	1950/Nov	Tough Old Man (B216)
1982	1982/May	Battlefield Earth (A27)
	1982/Sept	He Found God (B218)
1985	1985/Oct	Mission Earth Volume 1: The Invaders Plan (A28)
1986	1986/Mar	Mission Earth Volume 2: Black Genesis (A29)
	1986/Apr	Mission Earth Volume 3: The Enemy Within (A30)
	1986/Jul	Mission Earth Volume 4: An Alien Affair (A31)
	1986/Oct	Mission Earth Volume 5: Fortune of Fear (A32)
1987	1987/Jan	Mission Earth Volume 6: Death Quest (A33)
	1987/May	Mission Earth Volume 7: Voyage of Vengeance (A34)

	1987/Jul	Mission Earth Volume 8: Disaster (A35)
	1987/Sept	Mission Earth Volume 9: Villainy Victorious (A36)
	1987/Nov	Mission Earth Volume 10: The Doomed Planet (A37)
1992	1992/Jun	Gift from Heaven (B222)

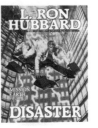

8. CHRONOLOGY OF FICTION WORKS—ROMANCE

(By first publication date with cross-references)
Total romance fiction works: 5

1932	1932/Nov	Submarine (B4)
1936	1936/Apr	Marriage for Spite (B58)
1938	1938/Jul	Ride 'Em Cowboy (B116)
	1938/Aug	When Gilhooly Was in Flower (B118)
1992	1992/Jan	Model Gentleman (B220)

A. Books

Organization of Sections A and B provides classification of a literary publishing phenomenon typical of the post-modernist canon of writers (see Preface), i.e., the author's works, even those of novel length, which most often first found expression in the popular fiction magazines of the time (1930–1950). Subsequently, these have been, or are now being published in book form as a result of growing acclaim and interest.

Thus, all fiction works by L. Ron Hubbard that have been published in *book* form are listed in Section A. Included are anthologies and collections such as *Ole Doc Methuselah* and *Lives You Wished to Lead But Never Dared*.

For those works which were published first as a book, the entries include an international publishing history, annotations and cross-references to secondary sources listed in Section L, where appropriate, and a synopsis.

Critical appreciations of the major works are quoted in Section I.

Where the story first appeared in magazine form, the entries in this section are also cross-referenced to Section B, in which the synopses and annotations appear.

Finally, Section AA provides a list of books to be published by Author Services, Inc., as part of the *L. Ron Hubbard Classic Fiction Series*. These are also cross-referenced to Section B.

A.   BOOKS

All of L. Ron Hubbard's fiction works published in *book* form are listed here chronologically by first publication date of the book. Subsequent book publishings of the same title are listed chronologically under the entry for each original publishing.

Publishing histories of the works which have also been individually published in magazine form are provided in Section B. The publishing histories in Section B reflect the complete publishing history of both magazine and book publishings of the individual work.

For those works which were published *first* in book form, the synopses and notes are also provided here in Section A. For all others, see Section B cross-reference.

Section AA lists the scheduled release dates of works in the *Classic Fiction Series* being produced by Author Services, Inc. These are also cross-referenced to Section B for synopses and, where applicable, annotation.

A1.   **Buckskin Brigades.**   New York: Macaulay, 1937, cloth, 316p. First hardcover edition.

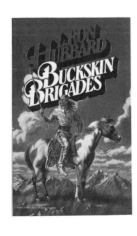

[**Note:** The entry for *Buckskin Brigades* appears in this section only. Therefore included below are all magazine printings, in addition to all publications in book form.]

b.   *Complete Northwest Novel Magazine*, Vol. 5, No. 6, Oct., 1938: 6-69. Condensed version.

c.   London: Wright & Brown, c. 1938, cloth, 265p.

d.   *Triple Western Magazine*, Vol. 5, No. 3, Oct., 1949: 112+. Condensed version.

e.   Clearwater, Florida: Theta Publishing, 1977, cloth, 316p.

f.   Los Angeles: Bridge Publications, Inc., 1987, paper, 312p. Includes extensive additional material.

g.   Thorndike Press, 1988, cloth and paper, 386p. Large print edition.

h.   Los Angeles: Author Services, Inc., 1993, leather. Limited edition.

On May 14, 1804, the Corps of Discovery—more familiarly known as the Lewis and Clark Expedition—left St. Louis, Missouri, to explore the newly acquired Louisiana territory: 900,000 square miles of the North American continent purchased by the Jefferson administration from France for 15 million dollars. The famous journal of that expedition records that just after the expedition split briefly into two parts, Lewis first encountered the Blackfeet Indians. Hubbard writes in the Foreword that in a briefly violent encounter on the banks of the Marias River a chief of the Blackfeet is killed. In the same journal, just a few pages earlier, is a reference to an unnamed white man who has been raised by, or is living with, the Blackfeet.

With this historical background as an introduction, Hubbard begins *Buckskin Brigades* with the death of the chief, and chronicles the daring journey of the blonde white man the Blackfeet call "Yellow Hair"—identified by Hubbard as scout and warrior Michael Kirk—through the rugged, unmapped country that is now Montana, across the Canadian wilderness to the shore of the great Hudson Bay, and back.

The central elements of the plot and conflict include: the Nor'Westers—avaricious fur traders who build their own fortified trading posts and trap indiscriminately and ruthlessly on Indian land; the Hudson's Bay Company, whose territorial dominion is menaced by the traders and whose "brigades" (of the title) build forts to fend off intruders; and the Blackfeet, whose very survival depends—in the face of foreign encroachment, predatory traders, and their own tribal enmities—on the success of Yellow Hair's perilous journey. Told, uniquely, from the Indian point of view, the story is a significant departure from the "another redskin bit the dust" stereotypes of traditional western fiction.

Notes: Hubbard's first published book, and most celebrated western, it pervasively reflects his own experiences growing up in turn-of-the-century frontier Montana, esp., his ceremonial induction as a tribal blood brother into the Blackfeet tribe at age six. (See Chronologies: Part 1. Also, cf. other Western titles: See Chronologies: Part 4.) This watershed novel has been recognized for its unconventionally sympathetic understanding and portrayal of Indian life, mores, and culture; its vigorously authentic historical detail; and its strong, pioneering environmentalism.

Addressing the stereotypes of the Western novel, the following excerpt from Hubbard's comments in the (original) 1937 preface is worth noting:

> ". . . It required a peculiar kind of courage to condemn one's own race, a worse kind of cowardice to malign men dead these hundred years."

> ". . . But, my interest has been, primarily, with the Blackfeet."

> ". . . I cannot forget everything I have found to their credit, and in this book I have tried to present them, not as they are, but as they were at the height of their power—the mightiest body of fighters on the plains; the truest of gentlemen."

A2.   **Final Blackout.**   Providence: Hadley Publishing Co., 1948, cloth, 154p. (1940; see B142.)

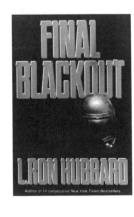

b.   as "L'ultimo vessillo." Piacenza: La Tribuna Editrice, 1965, paper, 164p. [Italian]

c.   Hollywood: Leisure Books, 1970, paper, 191p.

d.   New York: Garland Publishing, 1975, cloth, 191p.

e.   as *Il tenente*. Translated by Maria Benedetta de Castiglione. *Urania No. 701*, Milano: Mondadori, 1976, paper. [Italian]

f.   as "L'ultimo vessillo." Bologna: Libra Editrice, 1982, paper, 191p. [Italian]

g.   Los Angeles: Bridge Publications, Inc., 1989, cloth, 184p. Introduction by Algis Budrys.

h.   Los Angeles: Bridge Publications, Inc., 1991, paper,

h.   Los Angeles: Bridge Publications, Inc., 1991, paper, 218p. Introduction by Algis Budrys.

i.   Garden City, NY: Doubleday, Science Fiction Bookclub, 1992, cloth. Illustrated by Sergey V. Poyarkov. Introduction by Algis Budrys.

j.   Paris: Presses de la Cité, New Era Publications, 1992, paper. [French]

k.   Norwalk, CT: The Easton Press, 1994, leather, 218p. Introduction by Algis Budrys. Illustrated by Sergey V. Poyarkov.

A3.   **Death's Deputy.**   Los Angeles: Fantasy Publishing Co., 1948, paper, 167p. (1940; see B140.) Illustrated by Lou Goldstone.

b.   in *From Death to the Stars*. Los Angeles: Fantasy Publishing, 1950, cloth, 11-167. Collection. See A9.

c.   as *Le Bras Droit de la Mort*. Translated by Igor B. Maslowski. Collection Enigme - Romans Extraordinaires. Paris: Librairie Hachette, 1951, paper. [French]

d.   Hollywood: Leisure Books, 1970, paper, 158p.

e.   in *L'uomo che non poteva morire*. Translated by Manuela Fugenzi & Roberta Rambelli. Bologna: Libra Editrice, 1982. Contains "Death's Deputy" and "The Ultimate Adventure." (See also A12.) [Italian]

f.   as *Shi No Dailinin*. Tokyo: New Era Publications Japan, 1992, cloth, 241p. [Japanese]

g.   Tokyo: New Era Publications Japan, 1994, paper, 271p. [Japanese]

A4.   **Slaves of Sleep.**   Chicago: Shasta, 1948, cloth, 206p. (1939; see B134).

b.   New York: Lancer Books, 1967, paper, 176p.

c.   *Schiavi del sonno & Signori del sonno*. Milano: Armenia Editore, 1978, cloth. Translation of the two novels "Slaves of Sleep" and "The Masters of Sleep." See A20. [Italian]

    d.   *Versklavte Seelen.* Germany: ein Ullstein Buch, 1978, paper, 128p. [German]

    e.   New York: Dell Publishing Co., 1979, paper, 190 p.

    f.   with "Masters of Sleep." Los Angeles: Bridge Publications, Inc., 1993, cloth, 392p.

A5.   **Triton.** Los Angeles: Fantasy Publishing, 1949, cloth and paper. This collection includes: "The Indigestible Triton" (1940; see B141) and "Battle of Wizards" (1949; see B189).

    b.   In *Quintette.* Los Angeles: Fantasy Publishing, 1950, 9-53. Science fiction and fantasy anthology.

    c.   *Il segno del tritone.* Milano: Collana Siro #1, Edizioni Onda Tivu Srl, 1980, paper. [Italian]

    d.   *The Indigestible Triton.* Los Angeles: Author Services, Inc., 1993, leather, 225p.

A6.   **The Kingslayer.** Los Angeles: Fantasy Publishing, 1949, cloth, 208p. This collection includes: "The Kingslayer" (1949; see B209); "The Beast" (1942; see B167) and "The Invaders" (1942; see B160).

    b.   Los Angeles: Author Services, Inc., 1991, leather, 179p. (1949; see B209). See also A6, A14 and A18. [novel]

A7.   **Guns of Mark Jardine.** Malian Press Pty. Ltd., c. 1950, cloth (1949; see B195). Australia.

    b.   Los Angeles: Author Services, Inc., 1991, leather, 225p.

A8.   **Typewriter in the Sky.** New York: Gnome Press, 1951, cloth, 256p. This collection includes "Typewriter in the Sky" (1940; see B153) and "Fear" (1940; see B147).

    b.   London: Fantasy Books, Kemsley Newspapers, Cherry Tree Book #409, 1951, paper, 190p.

    c.   *Fear and Typewriter in the Sky.* New York: Popular Library, 1977, paper, 286p. See A15.

    d.   Los Angeles: Author Services, Inc., 1994, leather (1940; see B153.) (See also A8 and A14.)

A9.   **From Death to the Stars.** Los Angeles: Fantasy Publishing Co., 1950, cloth, 208p. This collection includes: "Death's

Deputy" (1940; see B140); "The Kingslayer" (1949; see B209); "The Beast" (1942; see B167) and "The Invaders" (1942; see B160).

A10.   **Roda Vingar.**   [Red Wings] Göteborg: Romanförlaget, 1954, paper ("On Blazing Wings," 1940; see B143). [Swedish]

A11.   **Return to Tomorrow.**   New York: Ace Books, 1954, paper, 157p. (originally "To the Stars," 1950; see B207).

    b.   *Utyu Koro* (The Way of a Spaceship). Tokyo: Gen Gen Sha, cloth, 1956, 239p. Translated by Yuich Ohama. [Japanese]

    c.   as *A Retour à Demain.* Paris: Editions Fleuve Noir, 1957, paper, 187p. [French]

    d.   as *Återkomst Till Morgondagen.* Stockholm: Wennerberg Förlaget AB, paper, 1957, 144p. [Swedish]

    e.   London: Panther Book—Hamilton & Co., 1957, paper, 144p.

    f.   as *Fremitiden Tur-Retur.* Copenhagen: Winthers Forlag, paper, 1958, 144p. [Danish]

    g.   as *Ritorno al domani.* Milano: Oscar Mondadori, paper, 1974, 185p. [Italian]

    h.   as *Återkomst Till Morgondagen.* Delta Förlaget AB, 1974. [Swedish]

    i.   New York: Garland Publishing, 1975, cloth, 157p.

    j.   *Ritorno al domani.* Bologna: Libra Editrice, paper, 1981, 185p. [Italian]

A12.   **L'uomo che non poteva morire.**   Translated by Patrizio Dalloro. *Urania No. 5*, Milano: Mondadori, 1954, paper. Italy. This collection includes: "L'uomo che non poteva morire" [Death's Deputy] (1940; see B140) and "L'avventura delle mille e una notte" [The Ultimate Adventure] (1939; see B130). [Italian]

    b.   Translated by Manuela Fugenzi and Roberta Rambelli. Bologna: Libra Editrice, 1982, cloth. [Italian]

A13.   **Le quattro ore di satana.**   [The Four Hours of Satan] Bologna: Mondadori, Urania No. 89, 1955, paper. This collection includes: "La paura" [Fear] (1940; see B147); "Il cadavere affezionato" [The Case of the Friendly Corpse] (1941; see B157); "Il ghoul" [The Ghoul] (1939; see B135) and "Il tritone indigesto" [The Indigestible Triton] (1940; see B141). [Italian]

A14.   **La trama tra le nubi.**   Mondadori, Urania No. 105, 1955, paper. This collection includes: "La trama tra le nubi" [Typewriter in the Sky] (1940; see B153) and "Il regicida" [The Kingslayer] (1950; see B209). [Italian]

  b.   Bologna: Libra Editrice, 1980, cloth. [Italian]

A15.   **Fear.**   Galaxy Science Fiction Novel No. 29. New York: Galaxy Publishing Corp., 1957, paper, 125p. (1940; see B147).

  b.   *Fear/Typewriter in the Sky.* New York: Gnome Press, 1951, cloth, 135-256.

  c.   *Fear/Typewriter in the Sky.* Fantasy Books, Kemsley Newspapers, 1951, paper, 100-190.

  d.   in *Le quattro ore di satana.* Bologna: Mondadori, Urania No. 89, 1955, paper. [Italian]

  e.   *Fear & The Ultimate Adventure.* Berkley Medallion, Mar., 1970, paper, 9-131. See A17.

  f.   as *Dodens Timer* [The Hour of Death]. Translated by Frits Remar. Iskolde Gys #6, Copenhagen: Winther Forlag, 1973, paper. [Danish]

  g.   as *Omansklig Fasa.* Kalla Karar #17, B. Wahlstroms Bokforlag, 1973, paper. [Swedish]

  h.   *Fear & Typewriter in the Sky.* New York: Popular Library, 1977, paper, 157-286.

  i.   in *Le quattro ore di satana.* Bologna: Mondadori, 1978, paper. [Italian]

  j.   as *Omansklig Fasa.* B. Wahlstroms Bokforlag, 1980, paper. [Swedish]

  k.   in *Le quattro ore di satana.* Bologna: Libra Editrice, 1981, cloth. [Italian]

l.   Los Angeles: Bridge Publications, Inc., 1991, cloth, 188p. Illustrated by Derek Hegsted.

m.   Redhill, Surrey, England: New Era Publications United Kingdom, Ltd., 1991, cloth. United Kingdom.

n.   as *Au Bout du Cauchmar*. Paris: Presses de la Cité, 1991, paper. [French]

o.   as *Miedo*. Madrid: Nueva Era Dinámica, S.A., 1991, paper. [Spanish]

p.   as *Retteges*. Budapest: Phoenix, 1992, cloth, 201p. [Hungarian]

q.   as *CTPAX*. Moscow: Image, 1992, cloth, 183p. [Russian]

r.   as *KYOUFU*. Tokyo: New Era Publications Japan, 1992, cloth, 210p. [Japanese]

s.   with "Borrowed Glory." Los Angeles: Bridge Publications, Inc., 1992, paper, 1-205. See B158.

t.   as *CTPAX*. Sofia: Vuzev, 1993, cloth, 161p. [Bulgarian]

u.   as *Des*. Czechoslovakia: Svoboda, 1993, paper, 102p. [Czechoslovakian]

A16.   **Ole Doc Methuselah.**   Austin: Theta Press, 1970, cloth, 175p. First hardcover edition. This collection includes: "Ole Doc Methuselah" (1947; see B172); "Her Majesty's Aberration" (1948; see B174); "The Expensive Slaves" (1947; see B173); "The Great Air Monopoly" (1948; see B178); "Plague" (1949; see B185); "A Sound Investment" (1949; see B190) and "Ole Mother Methuselah" (1950; see B203).

b.   New York: Daw Books, 1970, paper, 190p. Cover art by Josh Kirby.

c.   Los Angeles: Bridge Publications, 1992, cloth, 270p. Introduction by Robert Silverberg.

d.   as *Doc Mathusalem*. Paris: Presses de la Cité and New Era Publications France, 1993, paper, 305p. [French]

e.   East Grinstead: New Era Publications, Ltd., United Kingdom, 1993, cloth, 270p.

      f.   London: Book Club Associates, 1993, cloth, 270p.

A17.   **Fear & The Ultimate Adventure.**   New York: Berkley Publishing Corp., Berkley Medallion, 1970, paper, 221p. This collection includes: "Fear" (1940; see B147) and "The Ultimate Adventure" (1939; see B130).

A18.   **Seven Steps to the Arbiter.**   Chatsworth, CA: Major Books, 1975, paper, 192p. This collection includes: "The Kingslayer" (1949; see B209); "The Beast" (1942; see B167) and "The Invaders" (1942; B160).

A19.   **Lives You Wished To Lead But Never Dared.**   St. Louis: Theta Books Inc., 1978, cloth, 385p. This collection includes: "Sleepy McGee" (1936; see B66); "Don't Rush Me" (1936; see B67); "Mr. Luck" (1936; see B77); "Test Pilot" (1936; see B78); "Deep Sea Diver" (1936; see B79); "The Big Cats" (1936; see B80); "River Driver" (1936; see B84); "The Ethnologist" (1936; see B85); "Mine Inspector" (1936; see B87); "The Shooter" (1936; see B88); "Steeplejack" (1937; see B90); "Flying Trapeze" (1937; see B91); "Mountaineer" (1937; see B92); "A Lesson in Lightning" (1937; see B96); "Nine Lives" (1937; see B100); "Cargo of Coffins" (1937; see B105) and "Orders Is Orders" (1937; see B107).

A20.   **Schiavi del sonno & Signori del sonno.**   Milano: Armenia Editore, 1978, cloth. Italy. This collection includes "Slaves of Sleep" (1939; see B134) and "The Masters of Sleep" (1950; see B215). [Italian]

A21.   **L'ultima avventura del soldato della luce.**   [The Last Adventure of the Soldier of Light]. Nova SF No. 39. Bologna: Libra Editrice, 1978, paper. ("Ole Mother Methuselah," 1950; see B203). [Italian]

A22.   **L'epidemia.**   Nova SF No. 40. Bologna: Libra Editrice, July, 1979, and Feb., 1980, paper. ("Plague," 1949; see B185.) [Italian]

A23.   **La macchina infernale.**   Nova SF No. 41. Bologna: Libra Editrice, 1980, paper. ("A Sound Investment," 1949; see B190.) [Italian]

A24.   **I ribelli dell'universo.**   [The Rebels of the Universe]. Bologna: Libra Editrice, 1980, paper. This collection includes:

"L'idealista" ["The Idealist"] (1940; see B148); "I lupi di Sirio" ["Kilkenny Cats"] (1940; see B150); "La febbre verde" ["The Traitor"] (1941; see B154); "Gli ammutinati del cielo" ["The Mutineers"] (1941; see B156) and "Attacco al planeta" ["The Rebels"] (1942; see B162). [Italian]

A25.   **L'impero dei mille soli.**   [The Empire of the Thousand Suns]. Bologna: Libra Editrice, 1981, cloth. First hardcover edition of the "Conquest of Space" stories. This collection includes: "Altraterra, 1953: La conquista della luna" ["Forbidden Voyage"] (1949; see B181); "Altraterra, 1981: La conquista di Marte" ["The Magnificent Failure"] (1949; see B183); "Altraterra, 2001: Oltre i confini del Sistema Solare" ["The Incredible Destination"] (1949; see B188); "Altraterra, 2099: Al di la del centauro" ["The Unwilling Hero"] (1949; see B191); "Altraterra, 2175: La conquista dei grandi spazi" ["The Last Admiral"] (1950; see B206); "Altraterra, 2204: La nascita dell'Impero" ["Beyond the Black Nebula"] (1949, see B194); "Altraterra, 2284: L'Imperatore dell'Universo" ["The Emperor of the Universe"] (1949; see B199); "Altraterra, 2352: Nel fulgore dell'Impero" ["Tough Old Man"] (1950; see B216) and "Altraterra, 2499: Il crepuscolo dell'Impero" ["When Shadows Fall"] (1948; see B177). See also, Q1 for series notes. [Italian]

A26.   **I guerrieri del tempo.**   ["The End Is Not Yet"]. Bologna: Libra Editrice, 1982, cloth (1947; see B170). [Italian]

A27.   **Battlefield Earth: A Saga of the Year 3000.**   New York: St. Martin's Press, 1982, cloth, 819p.

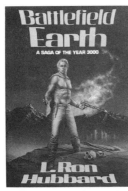

b.   Notting Hill Gate London: Quadrant, 1984, 819p., cloth. United Kingdom.

c.   as *Terra campo de batalha*. Lisbon: Europa-America, 1984, in two volumes, paper. [Portuguese]

d.   Los Angeles: Bridge Publications, Inc., 1985, paper, 1056p.

e.   Redhill, Surrey, England: New Era Publications United Kingdom, Ltd., 1985, paper, 1064p.

f.   Paddington, N.S.W.: New Era Publications Australia Pty. Ltd., 1985, cloth. Australia and New Zealand.

g. as *Terre Champ de Bataille*. Paris: Presses de la Cité and New Era Publications France, 1985, in two volumes, paper. [French]

h. as *Terre Champ de Bataille, Édition Intégrale*. Paris: Presses de la Cité, 1985, cloth, 494p. [French]

i. as *Terre Champ de Bataille, les Derniers Hommes*. Translated by Michel Demuth. Montreal: Albert Soussan editions, 1985, cloth, 399p. [French-Canadian]

j. as *Kampf um die Erde*. Neu Wulmstorf: New Era Publications Deutschland GmbH, 1985, in three volumes, cloth. [German]

k. as *Campo de Batalla: La Tierra, El Enemigo* and *La Victoria*. Barcelona: Editorial Planeta, 1985, paper. In two volumes. [Spanish]

l. as *Batolufiiludo Aas*. Tokyo: Sanryo, 1985, in six volumes, paper. [Japanese]

m. as *Terre Champ de Bataille*. Paris: France Loisirs (Bookclub), 1986, in two volumes, cloth. [French]

n. as *Terre Champ de Bataille*. Montreal: Albert Soussan editions, 1986, in two volumes, paper. [French-Canadian]

o. as *Campo de Batalla: La Tierra, El Enemigo/ La Victoria*. Barcelona: Editorial Planeta, 1986, paper, 826p. Both stories published in one volume for Mexico edition. [Spanish]

p. as *Battaglia per la terra*. Milano: Rizzoli Editore, 1986, cloth, 518p. [Italian]

q. as *Battaglia per la terra*. Milano: Euroclub (Bookclub), 1986, in two volumes, cloth. [Italian]

r. as *Campo de Batalha Terra*. Rio de Janeiro: Editora Record, 1986, paper, 885p. [Brazilian-Portuguese]

s. as *Bojno Polje Zemlja*. Zagreb: Mladost, 1986, in two volumes, paper. [Serbo-Croatian]

t. as *Terre Champ de Bataille.* Quebec: Quebec Loisirs (Bookclub), 1987, in two volumes, cloth. [French-Canadian]

u. as *Bumi Medan Pertempuran.* Jakarta: Pt Pradnya Paramita, 1987, in five volumes, paper. [Bahasa Indonesian]

v. as *Terre Champ de Bataille.* Paris: Presses Pocket, 1988, in three volumes, paper. [French]

w. as *Battaglia per la terra.* Milano: New Era Publications Italia Srl., 1988, in three volumes, paper. [Italian]

x. as *Kampf um die Erde.* Gütersloh: Science Fiction & Fantasy Club (Bookclub Edition), 1988, cloth, 442p. [German]

y. as *Batofuliiludo Aas.* Tokyo: New Era Publications Japan, 1990, in four volumes, cloth. [Japanese]

z. Tel Aviv: Zmora-Bitan, 1990, in two volumes, cloth. [Hebrew]

aa. as *Kampf um die Erde.* Neu Wulmstorf: New Era Publications GmbH, 1993, in 3 volumes, paper. [German]

bb. as *Campo de Batalla La Tierra, El Enemigo.* Madrid: Nueva Era Dinámica, S.A., 1993, 285p. [Spanish]

cc. as *Pole Bitewne Ziemia.* Poland: Amber, 1993, paper. In two volumes so far; another is expected. [Polish]

dd. as [Bulgarian characters]. Sofia: Vuzev, 1993, paper, in three volumes, paper. [Bulgarian]

It is the year 3000 A.D. and Man, in the judgement of his cruelest tormentor, is an "endangered species." The Earth has been ruthlessly ruled for a thousand years by a space-plundering race of nine-foot high, gas-breathing conquerors from the planet Psychlo. One of these creatures, the security guard Terl, plans to enslave a man-creature, force him to mine Earth gold, teleport the gold to Psychlo and then return in stolen comfort back to the planet himself.

That slave emerges in the person of Jonnie Goodboy Tyler, a member of a community of human survivors— there are no more than 35,000 left on Earth—hiding in the mountains near Denver. Terl captures Jonnie, cages him, teaches him to use the highly advanced Psychlo machinery, but does not share with Jonnie the secret of teleportation (a recurrent theme in Hubbard's fiction; cf. "The Dangerous Dimension" [B115] and "The Tramp" [B120]). Jonnie, under Terl's direction, recruits a band of Scots to mine the gold, but secretly enlists their help to overthrow Terl and the Psychlo tyranny. Jonnie discovers that deposits of uranium in the Rocky Mountains have been enfeebling his people, and that uranium is unstable and explosive in the presence of the gas the Psychlos breathe. When Terl finally prepares to teleport his gold in coffins to Psychlo, Jonnie and his collaborators replace the gold with uranium. Psychlo is destroyed, the multi-galactic empire of the Psychlos is irretrievably broken, and Terl is subdued and imprisoned.

Then, in an audacious financial transaction, Terl "sells" Earth to Jonnie's bitter competitor, and—unaware that Psychlo no longer exists—blasts off haplessly into oblivion, leaving his teleportation apparatus behind. An interplanetary banker appears, claiming Earth as collateral on a multi-trillion dollar Psychlo loan, now in obvious default. Psychlo's former subject planets are accepted as an alternate settlement of the loan. A vast congress of planetary emissaries—summoned by Jonnie—agrees to universal peace.

Notes: Thematically and structurally, *Battlefield Earth* is Hubbard's most powerfully visualized and most elaborately characterized story, and the biggest *single* volume novel in science fiction literature—1000 pages, and 450,000 words with more than 150 characters (cf. *Mission Earth* [A28 and Q6]). An enormous international bestseller, widely honored and in academic use today, it is seen as his culminating and creatively defining work of fiction, embodying elements of allegory, parable and comic irony, and propounding fascinating theses of economics, government and business.

The much-quoted introduction to the novel is both a retrospectively personal and apostrophic memoir on the Golden Age of Science Fiction, and a delineating essay on science fiction (as "the herald of possibility") and fantasy (as postulating "no limits at all"). See Section N for the complete text of the introduction, and Section D and EE respectively for the accompanying lyrics and musical "soundtrack" to *Battlefield Earth*. The soundtrack, with words and music by the author, marked the first musical score ever composed to directly accompany a novel. Also, see, *The New Encyclopedia of Science Fiction*, passim (L46). (For Awards, see Section G.)

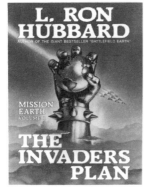

A28. **Mission Earth Vol. 1, The Invaders Plan.** Los Angeles: Bridge Publications, 1985, cloth, 559p.

b. Garden City, New York: Doubleday, 1985, cloth, 559p. Science Fiction Bookclub edition.

c. Taiwan: Imperial Book Sound & Gift Co., 1985, cloth, 559p.

d. Tonbridge, Kent: New Era Publications United Kingdom, Ltd., 1986, cloth, 559p.

e. London: Book Club Associates, 1986, cloth, 559p.

f. as *Le Plan des Envahisseurs*. Paris: Presses de la Cité and New Era Publications France, 1988, paper, 412p. [French]

g. as *Rencana Penyerbuan (Bagian 1)*. Jakarta: Pt. Pradnya Paramita, 1988, paper, 363p. [Bahasa Indonesian]

h. as *Missão Terra, O Plano Invasor*. Lisbon: Europa-America, 1988, paper, 457p. [Portuguese]

i. Tonbridge, Kent: New Era Publications United Kingdom, Ltd., 1988, paper, 615p.

j. as *Gli invasori tramano*. Milano: New Era Publications Italia Srl., 1988, cloth, 693p. [Italian]

k. as *Gli invasori tramano*. Milano: Euroclub (Bookclub), 1988, cloth, 507p. [Italian]

l.   Benrose: New Era South Africa,1988, paper, 615p.

m.   Los Angeles: Bridge Publications, 1988, paper, 615p.

n.   as *Mission Terre, Le Plan des Envahisseurs*. Paris: France Loisir (Bookclub), 1988, cloth, 631p. [French]

o.   as *O Plano dos Invasores*. Rio de Janeiro: Editora Record, 1989, paper, 480p. [Brazilian-Portuguese]

p.   as *Mission Erde, Die Verschwörer planen*. Neu Wulmstorf: New Era Publications Deutschland GmbH, 1989, cloth, 631p. [German]

q.   as *Le Plan des Envahisseurs*. Paris: Presses Pocket, 1991, paper, 586p. [French]

r.   New Delhi: Lancer Publishers Pvt. Ltd., 1992, paper, 615p.

Prefaced by an anxiously "official" disclaimer (by one Lord Invay) that such a place as Blito-P3 (Earth) actually exists, or has ever existed, *Mission Earth* begins with the brilliantly complex, self-expiatory, rowdily satirical first-person "confession" of the jailed Soltan Gris (pronounced "grease"). Gris is a former executive of the forbidding Coordinated Information Apparatus (CIA), of the planet Voltar.

Gris claims that Earth has long been targeted for invasion by the planet Voltar as a supply base on its space route to further galactic conquest. When prodigously gifted Fleet Combat Engineer Jettero Heller discovers on a scouting mission that Earth is polluting itself so rapidly it may become uninhabitable—hence, unusable—long before the invasion date, Heller is sent on a subsequent mission to covertly slow the process. This jeopardizes the plans of dreaded Apparatus chief, Lombar Hisst (as reptilian as his name) to subvert and overthrow the 110-planet Voltarian Confederacy with drugs he has cached on Earth. He enlists Gris's help to sabotage Heller. At Spiteos, the Apparatus's notorious mountain prison, Heller meets and falls in love with the beautiful wild animal trainer Countess Krak.

Unknown to Heller, secretly implanted devices in Heller's head allow Gris to "see" and "hear" through Heller himself. Piloting the spacecraft "Tug" and its "will-be-was" time-drive, Heller departs for Earth with Gris as a passenger. The people of Earth are, of course, unaware of the invasion that clandestinely has already begun.

Notes on the *Mission Earth* **dekalogy:** Hubbard's unprecedented 1.2 million word masterpiece of comic satire in ten volumes—the longest science fiction novel in the history of the genre, and generally considered to be Hubbard's "magnum opus" for its imaginative scope and bold complexities of character, plot and situation, its technically innovative use of narrative viewpoint, and as a tour de force of broad satire and antic farce. Cf. *Battlefield Earth* (A28), the biggest *single-volume* novel in the literature of science fiction. Not sequels, both novels are considered milestone works of mainstream fiction, and both have enjoyed extraordinary popular and critical success. All ten volumes of the *Mission Earth* dekalogy—a word introduced by the author to describe the novel's unique ten-volume structure—became international bestsellers as they were released. See *The New Encyclopedia of Science Fiction*, op. cit., passim (L46).

Hubbard's introduction to *Mission Earth*, in Vol. 1, is a widely-admired and informed causerie on the nature and history of satire as a literary form and its germinal role in the evolution of science fiction. See Section O for the complete text of the *Mission Earth* introduction. See also Sections D and E, respectively, for the accompanying lyrics, verse and musical soundtrack, also written by Hubbard.

A29.   **Mission Earth Vol. 2, Black Genesis.**   Los Angeles: Bridge Publications, 1986, cloth, 431p.

b.   Garden City, New York: Doubleday, 1986, cloth, 431p. Science Fiction Bookclub edition.

c.   Tonbridge, Kent: New Era Publications United Kingdom Ltd., 1986, 431p., cloth.

d.   London: Book Club Associates, 1986, cloth, 431p.

e.   Taiwan: Imperial Book Sound & Gift Co., 1987, cloth, 431p.

f.   Los Angeles: Bridge Publications, 1988, paper, 477p.

g.   Tonbridge, Kent: New Era Publications United Kingdom, Ltd., 1988, 477p., paper.

h.   as *La forteresse du mal.* Paris: Presses de la Cité and New Era Publications France, 1988, paper, 346p. [French]

i.   as *Genesi nera.* Milano: New Era Publications Italia Srl., 1988, cloth, 507p. [Italian]

j.   as *Rencana Penyerbuan (Bagian 2).* Jakarta: Pt. Pradnya Paramita, 1988, paper. [Bahasa Indonesian]

k.   as *Genesi nera.* Milano: Euroclub (Bookclub), 1989, cloth, 507p. [Italian]

l.   Benrose: New Era South Africa, 1989, paper. South Africa.

m.   as *Der Anfang vom Untergang.* Neu Wulmstorf: New Era Publications Deutschland GmbH, 1989, cloth, 483p. [German]

n.   as *Génese Negra.* Rio de Janeiro: Editora Record, 1989, cloth, 349p. [Brazilian-Portuguese]

o.   as *Missão Terra, Génese Negra.* Lisbon: Europa-America, 1990, paper, 349p. [Portuguese]

p.   as *La forteresse du mal.* Paris: Presses Pocket, 1991, paper, 438p. [French]

q.   New Delhi: Lancer Publishers Pvt. Ltd., 1992, paper, 477p.

Equipped with papers falsely identifying him as the son of John Rockecenter, the richest man in the world, Heller reaches Washington, D.C., meets Rockecenter's lawyer, and escapes an attempted assassination. Heller then moves into gaudy splendor near the United Nations building, acquires a Mafia bodyguard, and encounters a man who wants to build a corporate empire around him.

A30.   **Mission Earth Vol. 3, The Enemy Within.**   Los Angeles: Bridge Publications, 1986, cloth, 393p.

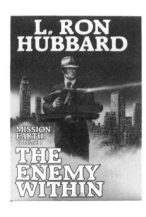

b.   Garden City, New York: Doubleday, 1986, cloth, 393p. Science Fiction Bookclub edition.

c.   Tonbridge, Kent: New Era Publications United Kingdom Ltd., 1987, cloth, 393p.

d.   London: Book Club Associates, 1987, cloth, 393p.

e.   Taiwan: Imperial Book Sound & Gift Co., 1987, cloth, 393p.

f.   Los Angeles: Bridge Publications, 1988, paper, 429p.

g.   as *L'ennemi intérieur.* Paris: Presses de la Cité and New Era Publications France, 1988, paper, 318p. [French]

h.   Tonbridge, Kent: New Era Publications United Kingdom Ltd., 1989, paper, 424p.

i.   Benrose: New Era South Africa, ApS, 1989, paper. South Africa.

j.   as *Il nemico é fra noi.* Milano: New Era Publications Italia Srl., 1989, cloth, 491p. [Italian]

k.   as *Der Feind im Innern.* Neu Wulmstorf: New Era Publications Deutschland GmbH, 1989, cloth. [German]

l.   as *Il nemico é fra noi.* Milano: Euroclub (BookClub), 1990, cloth, 491p. [Italian]

m.   as *L'ennemi interieur.* Paris: Presses Pocket, 1991, paper. [French]

n.   as *O Inimigo Está Entre Nós.* Rio de Janeiro: Editora Record, 1991, paper, 412p. [Brazilian-Portuguese]

o.   New Delhi: Lancer Publishers Pvt. Ltd., 1992, paper, 424p.

Dismayed by Heller's progress, Gris sends for the Countess Krak and the infamous Dr. Crobe (a "cellologist" of sorts who specializes in creating biological freaks), hoping that one of them will disrupt Heller's mission. Then, when Jettero begins work on a device that will power an automobile without gasoline, and thus drastically reduce pollution, Gris informs Rockecenter about this threat to his control of world oil supplies. A plan to discredit Heller with publicity—or eliminate him at a challenge car race—takes sinister shape.

A31.   **Mission Earth Vol. 4, An Alien Affair.**   Los Angeles: Bridge Publications, 1986, cloth, 329p.

b.   Garden City, New York: Doubleday, 1986, cloth, 431p. Science Fiction Bookclub edition.

c.   Tonbridge, Kent: New Era Publications United Kingdom Ltd., 1987, paper, 329p.

d.   London: Book Club Associates, 1987, cloth, 353p.

e.   Taiwan: Imperial Book Sound & Gift Co., 1987, cloth, 329p.

f.   Los Angeles: Bridge Publications, 1989, paper, 353p.

g.   as *Une affaire très étrange.* Paris: Presses de la Cité, 1989, paper, 277p. [French]

h.   Tonbridge, Kent: New Era Publications United Kingdom Ltd., 1989, paper, 353p.

i.   Benrose: A New Era South Africa, ApS, 1990, paper. South Africa.

j.   as *Passione aliena.* Milano: New Era Publications Italia Srl, 1991, cloth, 376p. [Italian]

k.   as *Passione aliena.* Milano: Euroclub (BookClub), 1991, cloth. [Italian]

l.   as *Uma Aventura Alienígena.* Rio de Janeiro: Editora Record, 1991, paper. [Brazilian-Portuguese]

m.   as *Une affaire très étrange.* Paris: Presses Pocket, 1992, paper, 276p. [French]

n.   New Delhi: Lancer Publishers Pvt. Ltd., 1992, paper, 347p.

Heller—but not his car—survives the car race. Gris, in desperation, flees to his Turkish base to escape hounding creditors. He undergoes a Voltarian regeneration process that among other things heightens his libido. When Countess Krak and Dr. Crobe finally arrive on Earth, Gris imprisons the Doctor, and implants the same "audio" and "viseo" monitors in Krak's head as he has implanted in Heller's. Ready to send her to the United States to find Heller, Gris falls asleep.

A32.

Mission Earth Vol. 5, Fortune of Fear.   Los Angeles: Bridge Publications, 1986, cloth, 365p.

b.   Garden City, New York: Doubleday, 1986, cloth, 365p. Science Fiction Bookclub edition.

c.   Tonbridge, Kent: New Era Publications United Kingdom Ltd., 1987, cloth, 365p.

d.   London: Book Club Associates, 1987, cloth, 365p.

e.   Taiwan: Imperial Book Sound & Gift Co., 1987, cloth, 365p.

f.   Los Angeles: Bridge Publications, 1989, paper, 395p.

g.   as *L'Empire de la peur.* Paris: Presses de la Cité and New Era Publications International ApS, 1989, paper, 307p. [French]

h.   Tonbridge, Kent: New Era Publications United Kingdom, Ltd., 1990, paper, 390p.

i.   Benrose: New Era South Africa, ApS, 1991, paper. South Africa.

j.   as *L'Empire de la peur.* Paris: Presses Pocket, 1992, paper, 307p. [French]

k.   as *As Ondas do Medo.* Rio de Janeiro: Editora Record, 1993, paper, 379p. [Brazilian-Portuguese]

l.   New Delhi: Lancer Publishers Pvt. Ltd., 1993, paper, 395p.

Gris wakes up to find that Krak has escaped and gone off to find Heller. The arrival of a shipment of gold makes Gris rich enough to not only destroy Heller and Krak, but to satisfy his creditors. Meanwhile, an impecunious Jettero Heller, now reunited with Krak, uses a space-flight device that enables him to see into the future to break the bank at an Atlantic City casino. Heller then makes a killing in the commodities market, while Gris, chased by women who have discovered the wonder of his Voltarian "rejuvenation," flees to New York. Discouraged by his persistent failure to destroy Heller, he decides the Countess is the real problem and retains professional help to dispose of her.

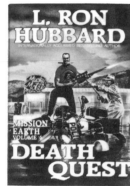

A33.   **Mission Earth Vol. 6, Death Quest.**   Los Angeles: Bridge Publications, 1987, cloth, 351p.

b.   Garden City, NY: Doubleday, 1987, cloth, 351p. Science Fiction Bookclub edition.

c.   Tonbridge, Kent: New Era Publications United Kingdom, Ltd., 1987, cloth, 351p.

d.   London: Book Club Associates, 1987, cloth, 365p.

e.   Taiwan: Imperial Book Sound & Gift Co., 1987, cloth, 351p.

f.   Los Angeles: Bridge Publications, 1989, paper, 391p.

g.   as *Objectif mort.* Paris: Presses de la Cité and New Era Publications France, 1989, paper. [French]

h.   as *Objectif mort.* Paris: Presses Pocket, 1992, paper. [French]

i.   Benrose: New Era South Africa, 1992, paper. South Africa.

j.   New Delhi: Lancer Publishers Pvt. Ltd., 1993, paper, 385p.

k.   as *Plano Mortal.* Rio de Janeiro: Editora Record, 1993, paper, 381p. [Brazilian-Portuguese]

Gris hires a Mafia hit man to assassinate Krak, but the attempt hilariously misfires. Heller, now pursuing an air decontamination project, continues to be the target of a defamatory public relations campaign run by the notorious potentate of PR, J. Walter Madison. Sued by women, once again penniless, Heller makes his peace with the Countess Krak, who goes off to prove the lawsuits are false—using a "hypno-helmet" to elicit the truth.

A34. **Mission Earth Vol. 7, Voyage of Vengeance.** Los Angeles: Bridge Publications, 1987, cloth, 381p.

    b.   Garden City, NY: Doubleday, 1987, cloth, 381p. Science Fiction Bookclub edition.

    c.   Taiwan: Imperial Book Sound & Gift Co., 1987, cloth, 381p.

    d.   Redhill, Surrey, England: New Era United Kingdom Publications, Ltd., 1988, cloth, 381p.

    e.   London: Book Club Associates, 1988, cloth, 381p.

    f.   Los Angeles: Bridge Publications, 1990, paper, 425p.

    g.   as *Destination vengeance.* Paris: Presses de la Cité and New Era Publications France, 1990, paper, 328p. [French]

    h.   as *A Viagem da Vingança.* Rio de Janeiro: Editora Record, 1991, paper, 415p. [Brazilian-Portuguese]

    i.   Redhill, Surrey, England: New Era Publications United Kingdom, Ltd., 1992, paper, 419p.

    j.   as *Destination Vengeance.* Paris: Presses Pocket, 1993, paper, 328p. [French]

    k.   New Delhi: Lancer Publishers Pvt. Ltd., 1993, paper, 419p.

Jettero Heller returns to cleaning up the air on Earth; Gris takes off with Madison on a globe-girdling yacht, and Heller's imposter "double" is kidnapped on national television by a specially trained calico cat. Gris finally believes he has disposed of Heller and the Countess permanently. He is soon to find out how wrong he is.

A35. **Mission Earth Vol. 8, Disaster.** Los Angeles: Bridge Publications, 1987, cloth, 337p.

    b.   Garden City, NY: Doubleday, 1987, cloth, 337p. Science Fiction Bookclub edition.

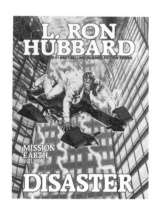

c.   Taiwan: Imperial Book Sound & Gift Co., 1987, cloth, 337p.

d.   Redhill, Surrey, England: New Era Publications United Kingdom, Ltd., 1988, cloth, 337p.

e.   London: Book Club Associates, 1988, cloth, 337p.

f.   Los Angeles: Bridge Publications, 1990, paper, 363p.

g.   as *Catastrophe*. Paris: Presses de la Cité and New Era Publications France, 1990, paper, 286p. [French]

h.   Redhill, Surrey, England: New Era Publications United Kingdom, Ltd., 1993, paper, 363p.

i.   Paris: Presses Pocket, 1993, paper, 286p. [French]

From the spacecraft *Tug One*, Heller disables the world's refineries, takes control of the world's oil industries when the bottom drops out of the stock market, captures Gris, and with Countess Krak returns to Voltar. Gris escapes on Voltar, and voluntarily goes to prison. Here, the narrative confession by Gris ends. It is now one hundred years later; the Gris manuscript has been found by Monte Pennwell who seeks out the rest of the story: Heller and Gris have clashed; Heller kidnaps the drug-addicted Emperor of Voltar and, with Countess Krak, returns to Earth.

A36.   **Mission Earth Vol. 9, Villainy Victorious.**   Los Angeles: Bridge Publications, 1987, cloth, 419p.

b.   Garden City, NY: Doubleday, 1987, cloth, 419p. Science Fiction Bookclub edition.

c.   Redhill, Surrey, England: New Era Publications United Kingdom, Ltd., 1988, cloth, 419p.

d.   London: Book Club Associates, 1988, cloth, 419p.

e.   Taiwan: Imperial Book Sound & Gift Co., 1988, cloth, 419p.

f.   Los Angeles: Bridge Publications, 1990, paper, 465p.

g.   as *Noire victoire*. Paris: Presses de la Cité and New Era Publications France, 1990, paper. [French]

h. Paris: Presses Pocket, 1993, paper, 362p. [French]

i. Redhill, Surrey, England: New Era Publications United Kingdom, Ltd., 1993, paper, 465p.

Rockecenter dies in a car crash. Madison, now on Voltar courtesy of Gris, meets Lombar Hisst, is given carte blanche and money to run his anti-Heller public relations campaign on Voltar and persuades Hisst to declare himself Emperor. Heller—convinced now, by the Countess, of the menace posed by Hisst, Madison and the Apparatus—comes to Voltar, saves his sister Hightee, and is declared an outlaw when Gris goes on trial and blames everything on him.

A37. **Mission Earth Vol. 10, The Doomed Planet.** Los Angeles: Bridge Publications, 1987, cloth, 331p.

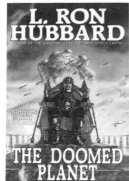

b. Garden City, New York: Doubleday, 1987, cloth, 331p. Science Fiction Bookclub edition.

c. Redhill, Surrey, England: New Era Publications United Kingdom, Ltd., 1988, cloth, 333p.

d. London: Book Club Associates, 1988, cloth, 333p.

e. Taiwan: Imperial Book Sound & Gift Co., 1988, cloth, 333p.

f. Los Angeles: Bridge Publications, 1990, paper, 359p.

g. as *Requiem pour une planète*. Paris: Presses de la Cité and New Era Publications France, 1991, paper, 282p. [French]

h. Paris: Presses Pocket, 1994, paper, 281p. [French]

In a swirling climax to the foregoing events, Gris exposes the machinations of the Apparatus during his trial. Riots break out and Voltar begins to disintegrate. Heller chases now Emperor Hisst from Spiteos to Palace City, then destroys a small, time-warping black hole that has kept the city invincibly fifteen minutes in the future, returning it to the present time so that the city can be—and is—attacked. Hisst is captured and put on trial; Madison is exposed and exiled; and, having been found guilty, both Hisst and Gris are sent to a distant prison camp. In a sardonic epilogue, Monte Pennwell urges an invasion of Earth to capture its resources, then exchanges letters with his publisher questioning the wisdom of releasing *Mission Earth*. (For Awards, see G; for series see Q6.)

A38.   **Spy Killer.**   Los Angeles: Author Services, Inc., 1990, leather, 119p. (1936; see B56.)

A39.   **Arctic Wings.**   Los Angeles: Author Services, Inc., 1991, leather, 129p. (1938; see B111.)

A40.   **Empty Saddles.**   Los Angeles: Author Services, Inc., 1991, leather, 161p. (1938; see B127.)

A41.   **The Case of the Friendly Corpse.**   Los Angeles: Author Services, Inc., 1991, leather, 199p. (1941; see B157.)

A42.   **Black Towers to Danger.**   Los Angeles: Author Services, Inc., 1991, leather, 137p. (1936; see B81).

A43.   **The Carnival of Death.**   Los Angeles: Author Services, Inc., 1991, leather, 113p. (1934; see B15).

A44.   **The Red Dragon.**   Los Angeles: Author Services, Inc., 1991, leather, 145p. (1935; see B19).

A45.   **Six-Gun Caballero.**   Los Angeles: Author Services, Inc., 1991, leather, 137p. (1938; see B108).

A46.   **The Ghoul.**   Los Angeles: Author Services, Inc., 1991, leather, 273p. (1939; see B135).

A47.   **Inky Odds.**   Los Angeles: Author Services, Inc., 1992, leather, 129p. (1940; see B145).

A48.   **The Kilkenny Cats Series.**   Los Angeles: Author Services, Inc., 1992, leather, 265p. (See Q3.)

A49.   **Hot Lead Pay-Off.**   Los Angeles: Author Services, Inc., 1992, leather, 225p. (1938; see B113).

A50.   **The Ultimate Adventure.**   Los Angeles: Author Services, Inc., 1992, leather, 177p. (1939; see B130).

A51.   **Forbidden Gold.**   Los Angeles: Author Services, Inc., 1992, leather, 145p. (1935; see B40).

A52. **The Chee-Chalker.** Los Angeles: Author Services, Inc., 1992, leather, 129p. (1947; see B169).

A53. **Wind-Gone-Mad & The Hurricane's Roar.** Los Angeles: Author Services, Inc., 1992, leather, 161p. This collection includes: "Wind-Gone-Mad" (1935; see B41), and "The Hurricane's Roar" (1939; see B132).

A54. **Adventure Short Stories, Vol. 1.** Los Angeles: Author Services, Inc., 1992, leather, 145p. This collection includes: "Five Mex for a Million" (1935; see B42); "The Price of a Hat" (1936; see B52), and "The Cossack" (1935; see B26).

A55. **The Tramp.** Los Angeles: Author Services, Inc., 1992, leather, 169p. (1938; see B120).

A56. **Western Short Stories, Vol. 1.** Los Angeles: Author Services, Inc., 1992, leather, 129p. This collection includes: "Hoss Tamer" (1950; see B204), "Stranger in Town" (1949; see B201) and "The Ghost Town Gun-Ghost" (1938; see B117).

A57. **Sea Fangs.** Los Angeles: Author Services, Inc., 1992, leather, 113p. (1934; see B8.)

A58. **Adventure Short Stories, Vol. 2.** Los Angeles: Author Services, Inc., 1992, leather, 193p. This collection includes: "The Black Sultan" (1935; see B44), "Red Sand" (1936; see B51) and "The Barbarians" (1935; see B46).

A59. **The Battling Pilot.** Los Angeles: Author Services, Inc., 1993, leather, 121p. (1937; see B94.)

A60. **Western Short Stories, Vol. 2.** Los Angeles: Author Services, Inc., 1993, leather, 168p. This collection includes: "The Toughest Ranger" (1938; see B110); "The Bad One" (1935; see B34); "Marriage for Spite" (1936; see B58) and "Horse and Horse" (1936; see B59).

A61. **Brass Keys to Murder.** Los Angeles: Author Services, Inc., 1993, leather, 144p. (1935; see B22.)

A62. **Fantasy Short Stories, Vol. 1.** Los Angeles: Author Services, Inc., 1993, leather, 144p. This collection includes: "240,000 Miles Straight Up" (1948; see B179); "He Found God" (1982; see B218) and "The Were-Human" (1981; see B217).

A63. **Adventure Short Stories, Vol. 3.**   Los Angeles: Author Services, Inc., 1993, leather, 193 p. This collection includes: "The Trail of the Red Diamonds" (1935; see B18); "Tomb of the Ten Thousand Dead" (1936; see B76) and "Golden Hell" (1936; see B74).

A64. **The Sky-Crasher.**   Los Angeles: Author Services, Inc., 1993, leather, 98p. (1936; see B49.)

A65. **Science Fiction Short Stories, Vol. 1.**   Los Angeles: Author Services, Inc., 1993, leather, 128p. This collection includes: "The Invaders" (1942; see B160) and "The Beast" (1942; see B167).

A66. **Western Short Stories, Vol. 3.**   Los Angeles: Author Services, Inc., 1993, leather, 129p. This collection includes: "Tinhorn's Daughter" (1937; see B106); "Vengeance Is Mine!" (1950; see B212) and "Johnny, the Town Tamer" (1949; see B192).

A67. **Hurtling Wings.**   Los Angeles: Author Services, Inc., 1993, leather, 130p. (1934; see B14.)

A68. **Fantasy Short Stories, Vol. 2.**   Los Angeles: Author Services, Inc., 1993, leather, 129p. This collection includes: "The Room" (1942; see B164), 89-120; "The Crossroads" (1941; see B155), 89-120; and "The Devil's Rescue" (1940; see B151).

A69. **Western Short Stories, Vol. 4.**   Los Angeles: Author Services, Inc., 1993, leather, 161p. This collection includes: "Blood on His Spurs" (1949; see B196), 111-112; "Man for Breakfast" (1949; see B200), 85-110; and "The Baron of Coyote River" (1936; see B71).

A70. **Adventure Short Stories, Vol. 4.**   Los Angeles: Author Services, Inc., 1994, leather, 129p. This collection includes: "Starch and Stripes" (1936; see B50), 1-35; "Trick Soldier" (1935; see B48), 39-76; and "Mr. Tidwell, Gunner" (1936; see B73).

A71. **Hostage to Death & Killer Ape.**   Los Angeles: Author Services, Inc., 1994, leather. This collection includes: "Hostage to Death" (1935; see B28), 1-112; and "Killer Ape" (1938; see B112).

A72. **Trouble on His Wings.** Los Angeles: Author Services, Inc., 1994, leather, 115p. (1939; see B128.)

A73. **The Automagic Horse.** Los Angeles: Bridge Publications, 1994, cloth. (1949; see B197.)

AA. FUTURE RELEASES

Scheduled continuation of the *L. Ron Hubbard Classic Fiction Series* in chronological order.

AA1. **Branded Outlaw.** Los Angeles: Author Services, Inc., 1994, leather (1938; see B122).

AA2. **Sabotage in the Sky.** Los Angeles: Author Services, Inc., 1994, leather (1940; see B149).

AA3. **Mystery/Suspense Short Stories, Vol. 1.** Los Angeles: Author Services, Inc., 1994, leather. This collection includes: "Calling Squad Cars!" (1934; see B6); "The Grease Spot" (1936; see B64); "The Blow Torch Murder" (1936; see B54) and "Killer's Law" (1947; see B171).

AA4. **Science Fiction Short Stories, Vol. 2.** Los Angeles: Author Services, Inc., 1994, leather. This collection includes: "Beyond All Weapons" (1950; see B205); "The Obsolete Weapon" (1948; see B175) and "The Planet Makers" (1949; see B198).

AA5. **Adventure Short Stories, Vol. 5.** Los Angeles: Author Services, Inc., 1994, leather. This collection includes: "Red Death over China" (1937; see B102); "Grounded" (1932; see B2); "Yellow Loot" (1934; see B13); "Tah" (1932; see B1) and "Submarine" (1932; see B4).

AA6. **Western Short Stories, Vol. 5.** Los Angeles: Author Services, Inc., 1994, leather. This collection includes: "The No-Gun Gunhawk" (1936; see B82); "The Neck Scarf" (1936; see B68) and "Devil's Manhunt" (1950; see B208).

AA7. **The Falcon Killer.** Los Angeles: Author Services, Inc., 1994, leather (1939; see B131).

AA8. **The Iron Duke.** Los Angeles: Author Services, Inc., 1994, leather (1940; see B146).

AA9. **To the Stars** (a.k.a. "Return to Tomorrow"). Los Angeles: Author Services, Inc., 1995, leather (1950; see B207).

AA10. **Western Short Stories, Vol. 6.** Los Angeles: Author Services, Inc., 1995, leather. This collection includes: "Maybe Because—!" (1934; see B12); "Tooby" (1934; see B16); "Plans for the Boy" (1935; see B30) and "Under the Die-Hard Brand" (1938; see B109).

AA11. **Adventure Short Stories, Vol. 6.** Los Angeles: Author Services, Inc., 1995, leather. This collection includes: "The Squad That Never Came Back" (1935; see B24); "The Adventure of 'X'" (1935; see B43) and "Escape for Three" (1936; see B62).

AA12. **Fantasy Short Stories, Vol. 3.** Los Angeles: Author Services, Inc., 1995, leather. This collection includes: "Danger in the Dark" (1939; see B133); "Battle of Wizards" (1949; see B189) and "Tough Old Man" (1950; see B216).

AA13. **Western Short Stories, Vol. 7.** Los Angeles: Author Services, Inc., 1995, leather. This collection includes: "Ride 'Em, Cowboy!" (1938; see B116); "When Gilhooly Was in Flower" (1938; see B118); "Canteens" (1936; see B83) and "The Ranch That No One Would Buy" (1939; see B136).

AA14. **Adventure Short Stories, Vol. 7.** Los Angeles: Author Services, Inc., 1995, leather. This collection includes: "The Crate Killer" (1937; see B97); "He Walked to War" (1935; see B38) and "The Sky Devil" (1935; see B37).

AA15. **Man-Killers of the Air.** Los Angeles: Author Services, Inc., 1995, leather (1935; see B27).

AA16. **Fear.** Los Angeles: Author Services, Inc., 1995, leather (1940; see B147). See also A15 and A17.

AA17. **Science Fiction Short Stories, Vol. 3.** Los Angeles: Author Services, Inc., 1995, leather. This collection includes: "One Was Stubborn" (1940; see B152); "A Matter of Matter" (1949; see B193) and "The Dangerous Dimension" (1938; see B115).

AA18. **Adventure Short Stories, Vol. 8.** Los Angeles: Author Services, Inc., 1995, leather. This collection includes: "Yukon Madness" (1935; see B33); "Flaming Arrows" (1936; see B75) and "Medals for Mahoney" (1935; see B36).

AA19. **Western Short Stories, Vol. 8.** Los Angeles: Author Services, Inc., 1995, leather. This collection includes: "The Magic Quirt" (1948; see B176); "Stacked Bullets" (1948; see B180) and "The No-Gun Man" (1950; see B211).

AA20. **Adventure Short Stories, Vol. 9.** Los Angeles: Author Services, Inc., 1995, leather. This collection includes: "Boomerang Bomber (The Contraband Crate)" (1935; see B31); "Catapult Courage" (1935; see B45); "Raiders of the Beam" (1936; see B53) and "Wings Over Ethiopia" (1939; see B129).

AA21. **Mystery/Suspense Short Stories, Vol. 2.** Los Angeles: Author Services, Inc., 1996, leather. This collection includes: "Dead Men Kill" (1934; see B9); "The Mad Dog Murder" (1936; see B63) and "Mouthpiece" (1934; see B11).

AA22. **The Devil—With Wings.** Los Angeles: Author Services, Inc., 1996, leather (1937; see B103).

AA23. **Death's Deputy.** Los Angeles: Author Services, Inc., 1996, leather (1940; see B140). (See also A3 and A9.)

AA24. **The Hell Job Series, 1.** Los Angeles: Author Services, Inc., 1996, leather. This collection includes: "Sleepy McGee" (1936; see B66); "Don't Rush Me" (1936; see B67) and "Mr. Luck" (1936; see B77). Also see A19. Also, Q2 for series description.

AA25 **The Hell Job Series, 2.** Los Angeles: Author Services, Inc., 1996, leather. This collection includes: "Test Pilot" (1936; see B78); "Deep-Sea Diver" (1936; see B79) and "The Big Cats" (1936; see B80). Also see A19. Also, Q2 for series description.

AA26. **The Hell Job Series, 3.** Los Angeles: Author Services, Inc., 1996, leather. This collection includes: "River Driver" (1936; see B84); "The Ethnologist" (1936; see B85) and "Mine Inspector" (1936; see B87). Also see A19. Also, Q2 for series description.

AA27. **The Hell Job Series, 4.** Los Angeles: Author Services, Inc., 1996, leather. This collection includes: "The Shooter" (1936; see B88); "Steeplejack" (1937; see B90) and "Flying Trapeze" (1937; see B91). Also see A19. Also, Q2 for series description.

AA28.   **The Hell Job Series, 5.**   Los Angeles: Author Services, Inc., 1996, leather. This collection includes: "A Lesson in Lightning" (1937; see B96); "Mountaineer" (1937; see B92) and "Nine Lives" (1937; see B100). Also see A19. Also, Q2 for series description.

AA29.   **The Hell Job Series, 6, Cargo of Coffins.** Los Angeles: Author Services, Inc., 1996, leather (1937; see B105). Also see A19. Also, Q2 for series description.

AA30.   **The Hell Job Series, 7, Orders Is Orders.** Los Angeles: Author Services, Inc., 1996, leather (1937; see B107). Also see A19. Also, Q2 for series description.

AA31.   **Western Short Stories, Vol. 9.**   Los Angeles: Author Services, Inc., 1996, leather. This collection includes: "Come and Get It" (1938; see B121); "Death Waits at Sundown" (1938; see B124) and "Cattle King for a Day" (1937; see B95).

AA32.   **On Blazing Wings.**   Los Angeles: Author Services, Inc., 1996, leather (1940; see B143). Also see A10.

AA33.   **Science Fiction/Fantasy Short Stories, Vol. 4.**   Los Angeles: Author Services, Inc., 1997, leather. This collection includes: "Strain" (1942; see B163); "The Slaver" (1942; see B165) and "Space Can" (1942; see B166).

AA34.   **Murder Afloat & Flame City.**   Los Angeles: Author Services, Inc., 1997, leather. "Murder Afloat" (1935; see B39) and "Flame City" (1935; see B20).

AA35.   **Adventure Short Stories, Vol. 10.**   Los Angeles: Author Services, Inc., 1997, leather. This collection includes: "If I Were You" (1940; see B139); "Fifty-Fifty O'Brien" (1936; see B86) and "Machine Gun 21,000" (1935; see B47).

AA36.   **Western Short Stories, Vol. 10.**   Los Angeles: Author Services, Inc., 1997, leather. This collection includes: "Leaducation" (1936; see B65); "Reign of the Gila Monster" (1937; see B101) and "Gun Boss of Tumbleweed" (1949; see B186).

AA37.   **Final Blackout.**   Los Angeles: Author Services, Inc., 1997, leather (1940; see B142). See also A2.

AA38. **The Phantom Patrol.** Los Angeles: Author Services, Inc., 1997, leather (1935; see B17).

AA39. **Ole Doc Methuselah Series.** Los Angeles: Author Services, Inc., 1997, leather. This collection includes: "Ole Doc Methuselah" (1947; see B172); "Her Majesty's Aberration" (1948; see B174); "The Expensive Slaves" (1947; see B173); "The Great Air Monopoly" (1948; see B178); "Plague" (1949; see B185); "A Sound Investment" (1949; see B190) and "Ole Mother Methuselah" (1950; see B203). See also A16, A21, A22 and A23; also Q4 for series description.

AA40. **Sky Birds Dare!** Los Angeles: Author Services, Inc., 1997, leather (1936; see B70).

AA41. **He Didn't Like Cats & The Professor Was a Thief.** Los Angeles: Author Services, Inc., 1997, leather. "He Didn't Like Cats" (1942; see B161) and "The Professor Was a Thief" (1940; see B137).

AA42. **Buckskin Brigades.** Los Angeles: Author Services, Inc., 1997, leather (1937). See A1.

AA43. **The Dive Bomber.** Los Angeles: Author Services, Inc., 1997, leather (1937; see B99).

AA44. **Science Fiction Short Stories, Vol. 5.** Los Angeles: Author Services, Inc., 1997, leather. This collection includes: "The Great Secret" (1943; see B168); "Battling Bolto" (1950; see B213) and "The Automagic Horse" (1949; see B197).

AA45. **Ruin at Rio Piedras & Gunman's Tally.** Los Angeles: Author Services, Inc., 1998, leather. This collection includes: "Ruin at Rio Piedras" (1938; see B126) and "Gunman's Tally" (1937; see B104).

AA46. **Destiny's Drum.** Los Angeles: Author Services, Inc., 1998, leather (1935; see B21).

AA47. **Slaves of Sleep.** Los Angeles: Author Services, Inc., 1998, leather (1939; see B134). See also A4 and A20.

AA48. **Western Short Stories, Vol. 11.** Los Angeles: Author Services, Inc., 1998, leather. This collection includes: "Gunman!" (1949; see B182); "Shadows from Boothill" (1940; see B144); "Silent Pards" (1938; see B125) and "King of the Gunmen" (1938; see B114).

AA49.   **False Cargo.**   Los Angeles: Author Services, Inc., 1998, leather (1935; see B23).

AA50.   **Mystery/Suspense Short Stories, Vol. 3.**   Los Angeles: Author Services, Inc., 1998, leather. This collection includes: "The Green God" (1934; see B5); "The Death Flyer" (1936; see B57); "The Slickers" (1936; see B72) and "They Killed Him Dead" (1936; see B60).

AA51.   **Twenty Fathoms Down.**   Los Angeles: Author Services, Inc., 1998, leather (1934; see B10).

AA52.   **The Masters of Sleep.**   Los Angeles: Author Services, Inc., 1998, leather (1950; see B215). See also A20.

AA53.   **The Gunner from Gehenna & Boss of the Lazy B.**   Los Angeles: Author Services, Inc., 1998, leather. This collection includes: "The Gunner from Gehenna" (1949; see B184) and "Boss of the Lazy B" (1938; see B119).

AA54.   **Under the Black Ensign.**   Los Angeles: Author Services, Inc., 1998, leather (1935; see B32).

AA55.   **Fantasy Short Stories, Vol. 4.**   Los Angeles: Author Services, Inc., 1998, leather. This collection includes: "The Last Drop," with L. Sprague de Camp, (1941; see B159); "A Can of Vacuum" (1949; see B202) and "Borrowed Glory" (1941; see B158).

AA56.   **While Bugles Blow.**   Los Angeles: Author Services, Inc., 1998, leather (1936; see B89).

AA57.   **Science Fiction Short Stories, Vol. 6.**   Los Angeles: Author Services, Inc., 1999, leather. This collection includes: "Greed" (1950; see B210); "Final Enemy" (1950; see B214).

AA58.   **Loot of the Shanung.**   Los Angeles: Author Services, Inc., 1999, leather (1936; see B61).

AA59.   **Hurricane.**   Los Angeles: Author Services, Inc., 1999, leather (1936; see B55).

AA60.   **The Lieutenant Takes the Sky.**   Los Angeles: Author Services, Inc., 1999, leather (1938; see B123).

AA61.   **The Headhunters.**   Los Angeles: Author Services, Inc., 1999, leather (1936; see B69).

AA62.   **The End Is Not Yet.**   Los Angeles: Author Services, Inc., 1999, leather (1947; see B170 and A26).

AA63.   **The Conquest of Space Series, Vol. 1.**   Los Angeles: Author Services, Inc., 1999, leather. This collection includes: "When Shadows Fall" (1948; see B177); "Forbidden Voyage" (1949; see B181) and "The Magnificent Failure" (1949; see B183 and A25; also see Q1).

AA64.   **The Conquest of Space Series, Vol. 2.**   Los Angeles: Author Services, Inc., 1999, leather. This collection includes: "The Unwilling Hero" (1949; see B191); "Beyond the Black Nebula" (1949; see B194); "The Emperor of the Universe" (1949; see B199) and "The Last Admiral" (1950; see B206 and A25; also see Q1).

AA65.   **The Bold Dare All.**   Los Angeles: Author Services, Inc., 1999, leather (1937; see B93).

AA66.   **Adventure Short Stories, Vol. 11.**   Los Angeles: Author Services, Inc., 1999, leather. This collection includes: "Pearl Pirate" (1934; see B7); "The Small Boss of Nunaloha" (1940; see B138) and "The Drowned City" (1935; see B25).

B. Magazine Fiction

All fiction works by Hubbard (including those that appeared under one of his many pen names) first published in magazine form are listed in this section. This section is cross-referenced to Section A where the stories have been later published as a book, or to Section AA where they are scheduled to be published in book form. (See Section M1 for a list of pen names.)

All entries in Section B include full publishing histories and relevant annotations.

Section BB alphabetically lists and provides synopses for all known unpublished fiction stories.

B.   MAGAZINE FICTION

B1.   **"Tah."**   *The University Hatchet Monthly Literary Review* (George Washington University), Vol. 28, No. 18, Feb. 9 1932: 1-4.

b.   Scheduled for publication in book form by Author Services, Inc., in Summer 1994. (See AA5.)

Twelve-year-old Tah dies in battle after an all-night forced march.

Notes: L. Ron Hubbard's earliest known published work of fiction. A story of pre-World War II China, reflecting the author's extensive travels through the Orient.

B2.   **"Grounded."**   *The University Hatchet Monthly Literary Review* (George Washington University), Vol. 28, No. 25, Apr. 5 1932: 1-4.

b.   Scheduled for publication in book form by Author Services, Inc., in Summer 1994. (See AA5.)

With his reputation tainted by the inadvertent death of a friend in an air incident, a Royal Air Force lieutenant redeems himself at the cost of his own life. The setting is pre-World War II China.

B3.   **"The God Smiles."**   *The University Hatchet Monthly Literary Review* (George Washington University), Vol. 28, No. 33, May 24, 1932.

The setting is the Wai Cafe in the Chinese city of Tsingtau. Dimi, a hostess, and the man she loves, Alex Konrad, resourcefully contrive to incapacitate the local warlord and escape to Manila.

Notes: The prize-winning one-act play in a contest conducted by the George Washington *University Hatchet Monthly Literary Review* reflects Hubbard's first-hand familiarity with pre-war China.

B4. **"Submarine."** *The University Hatchet Monthly Literary Review* (George Washington University), Vol. 29, No. 7, Nov. 1, 1932.

  b. Scheduled for publication in book form by Author Services, Inc., in Summer 1994. (See AA5.)

On a 72-hour liberty from his submarine, a young sailor and his girlfriend experience romance, unexpected danger, and ominous separation when he is abruptly recalled to his ship.

Notes: Hubbard's first published story with a naval background, reflecting his working knowledge of the sea as a young helmsman and supercargo, and his widely traveled background as the son of a U.S. naval officer. (See Chronologies, Part 1.)

B5. **"The Green God."** *Thrilling Adventures*, Vol. 8, No. 3, Feb. 1934: 56-66.

  b. Scheduled for publication in book form by Author Services, Inc., in Spring 1998. (See AA50.)

A U.S. Navy intelligence officer endures burial alive and ingenious tortures while searching for a missing Green Idol in pre-World War II Tientsin.

Notes: Hubbard's first commercially published story, and the first of 91 stories of adventure and action, published between 1934 and 1991.

B6. **"Calling Squad Cars!"** *Phantom Detective*, Vol. 5, No. 2, Apr. 1934: 92-102.

  b. Scheduled for publication in book form by Author Services, Inc., in Summer 1994. (See AA3.)

A police dispatcher suspected of helping a gang of bank robbers, vindicates himself after being dismissed.

Notes: The first of 15 stories of mystery and detection, published between 1934 and 1947.

B7. **"Pearl Pirate."** *Thrilling Adventures*, Vol. 9, No. 3, May 1934: 132-46.

b.   Scheduled for publication in book form by Author Services, Inc., in Fall 1999. (See AA66.)

A nautical tale of deceit and treachery, set in the pre-World War II Coral Sea, leaves a schooner skipper in possession of two vessels and a box of black pearls.

B8.   **"Sea Fangs."**   *Five Novels Monthly*, Vol. 26, No. 3, June 1934: 129-60.

b.   Los Angeles: Author Services, Inc., 1992, 113p., leather. (See A57.)

Bob Sherman, stripped of his Venezuelan oil fields, twice imprisoned by pirates when he takes to the sea in an effort to regain his fields, is helped by a beautiful companion.

B9.   **"Dead Men Kill."**   *Thrilling Detective*, Vol. 11, No. 2, July 1934: 12-52.

b.   Scheduled for publication in book form by Author Services, Inc., in Winter 1996. (See AA21.)

Detective Terry Lane, on the trail of a series of murders, fights corpses that carry the scent of moist earth and undertaker perfumes.

Notes: A sinister story of zombies, reflecting a close knowledge of Haitian culture augmented during Hubbard's West Indies mineralogical expedition.

B10.   **"Twenty Fathoms Down."**   *Five Novels Monthly*, Vol. 27, No. 3, Sept. 1934: 9-37.

b.   *World Stories*, (United Kingdom) No. 79, Oct. 1934: 49+.

c.   Scheduled for publication in book form by Author Services, Inc., in Spring 1998. (See AA51.)

Recovering gold and emeralds proves almost fatally dangerous for diver Hawk Ridley as he contends with a ruthless salvage crew and a girl stowaway.

B11.   **"Mouthpiece."**   *Thrilling Detective*, Vol. 12, No. 1, Sept. 1934: 65-73.

b.   Scheduled for publication in book form by Author Services, Inc., in Winter 1996. (See AA21.)

Mat Lawrence returns from building a power dam in the desert to track down the murderer of his gangster father.

B12.   **"Maybe Because—!"** (Ken Martin) *Cowboy Stories*, Vol. 26, No. 3, Sept. 1934: 30-38.

b.   Scheduled for publication in book form by Author Services, Inc., in Winter 1995. (See AA10.)

Two old-time gunfighters, released from prison, steal $10,000, save a woman, and come face-to-face with the truth about themselves.

Notes: Hubbard's first published western story, reflecting his experience growing up in frontier Montana, and the first of 47 western tales he published between 1934 and 1993.

B13.   **"Yellow Loot."**   *Thrilling Adventures*, Vol. 11, No. 2, Oct. 1934: 137-45.

b.   Scheduled for publication in book form by Author Services, Inc., in Summer 1994. (See AA5.)

A search for precious amber ends in a tumultuous race for freedom on the Great Wall of China.

Notes: Hubbard's pre-World War II visits to the remote reaches of China lend the story a cogent authenticity at a time when knowledge of the Chinese interior was fragmentary or apocryphal.

B14.   **"Hurtling Wings."**   *Five Novels Monthly*, Vol. 28, No. 2, Nov. 1934: 8-40.

b.   *World Stories*, (United Kingdom) No. 81, Dec. 1934: 36+.

c.   Los Angeles: Author Services, Inc., 1993, 130p., leather. (See A67.)

With valuable air mail contracts at stake, a daredevil racing pilot contends with an unscrupulous competitor to win the National Air Meet.

Notes: The first of Hubbard's aviation stories, drawing on his experiences as a barnstormer and glider pilot in the early years of commercial flight.

B15. **"The Carnival of Death."** *Popular Detective*, Vol. 1, No. 1, Nov. 1934: 118-44.

b. Los Angeles: Author Services, Inc., 1991, 113p., leather. (See A43.)

A U.S. treasury agent, in the incognito of a carnival detective, solves a series of bizarre murders and exposes a drug ring.

B16. **"Tooby."** (Ken Martin) *Cowboy Stories*, Vol. 26, No. 5, Nov. 1934: 78-85.

b. Scheduled for publication in book form by Author Services, Inc., in Winter 1995. (See AA10.)

A story of competing musical bands, veined with humor, and written in the western parlance Hubbard knew from childhood. The "Tooby" is a tuba.

B17. **"The Phantom Patrol."** *Five Novels Monthly*, Vol. 29, No. 1, Jan. 1935: 42-73.

b. *World Stories*, (United Kingdom) No. 83, Feb. 1935: 12+.

c. Scheduled for publication in book form by Author Services, Inc., in Spring 1997. (See AA38.)

In a tale that combines air and sea themes, a drug runner and murderer almost succeeds in a scheme to disgrace a Coast Guard officer.

B18. **"The Trail of the Red Diamonds."** (Lt. Jonathan Daly) *Thrilling Adventures*, Vol. 12, No. 2, Jan. 1935: 74-91.

b. *Adventure Short Stories, Vol. 3.* Los Angeles: Author Services, Inc., 1993, 1-58, leather. (See A63.)

A fateful expedition into the depths of China to unearth a fabulous fortune in red diamonds involves a naval lieutenant in a dark maze of espionage, treachery and death.

B19. **"The Red Dragon."** *Five Novels Monthly*, Vol. 29, No. 2, Feb. 1935: 10-43.

  b. Los Angeles: Author Services, Inc., 1991, 145p., leather. (See A44.)

A failed scheme to kidnap "the last emperor" of China, and a set of priceless idols in a mysterious black chest, pose problems and dangers for a red-haired soldier of fortune in occupied China.

B20. **"Flame City."** *Thrilling Detective*, Vol. 13, No. 3, Feb. 1935: 81-94.

  b. Scheduled for publication in book form by Author Services, Inc., in Winter 1997. (See AA34.)

Fire Chief Blaze Delaney, his job in jeopardy, gets help from his son to stop an epidemic of fires and bring the arsonists to justice.

B21. **"Destiny's Drum."** *Five Novels Monthly*, Vol. 29, No. 3, Mar. 1935: 124-60.

  b. Scheduled for publication in book form by Author Services, Inc., in Winter 1998. (See AA46.)

Adventurer Phil Sheridan cleverly enlists native head-hunters to help him oust the predatory local regime.

B22. **"Brass Keys to Murder."** (Michael Keith) *Five Novels Monthly*, Vol. 30, No. 1, Apr. 1935: 98-127.

  b. Los Angeles: Author Services, Inc., 1993, 144p., leather. (See A61.)

A navy lieutenant, accused of murder, risks his life to find the real killer and discovers the motive: the brass keys.

B23. **"False Cargo."** *Five Novels Monthly*, Vol. 30, No. 2, May 1935: 44-71.

  b. Scheduled for publication in book form by Author Services, Inc., in Spring 1998. (See AA49.)

An insurance company investigator combats insurance fraud, organized ship scuttlings, and the apparent death of his best friend to bring criminals to justice.

B24. **"The Squad That Never Came Back."** (Legionnaire 148) *Thrilling Adventures*, Vol. 13, No. 3, May 1935: 70-89.

b. Scheduled for publication in book form by Author Services, Inc., in Winter 1995. (See AA11.)

Threatened with death, a corporal leads a group of fellow legionnaires to a lost treasure in the Moroccan desert.

B25. **"The Drowned City."** *Top-Notch*, Vol. 96, No. 5, May 1935: 98-117.

b. Scheduled for publication in book form by Author Services, Inc., in Fall 1999. (See AA66.)

Two divers fight off a dangerous adversary and find lost treasure in a hidden, undersea tunnel.

B26. **"The Cossack."** *New Mystery Adventures*, Vol. 1, No. 3, May-June 1935: 36-46.

b. *Adventure Short Stories, Vol. 1*, Los Angeles: Author Services, Inc., 1992, leather, 93-125. (See A54.)

A final confrontation between Colonel Komroff and the woman he had spurned in pre-revolutionary Russia ends in death for both.

B27. **"Man-Killers of the Air."** *Five Novels Monthly*, Vol. 30, No. 3, June 1935: 8-39.

b. Scheduled for publication in book form by Author Services, Inc., in Summer 1995. (See AA15.)

A daredevil pilot wins an international air race, foiling a scheme to sabotage his plane.

B28. **"Hostage to Death."** *Five Novels Monthly*, Vol. 31, No. 1, July 1935: 38-67.

b. "Den Avhuggna Handen." *Detektivmagasinet*, Vol. 22, No. 37, Göteborg: *Romanforlaget* 1955. [Swedish]

c. Scheduled for publication in book form by Author Services, Inc., in Winter 1994. (See A71.)

The Foreign Legion exacts full pay for an officer's mistake by sending him into "Suicide Section"—the Intelligence Service. And so Bill Reilly goes into enemy country as a renegade, a derelict of the Legion.

B29. **"Hell's Legionnaire."** (Capt. L. Ron Hubbard) *New Mystery Adventures*, Vol. 1, No. 4, July 1935: 46-54.

An American deserter from the French Foreign Legion, fleeing undeserved punishment, rescues a young woman from torture.

B30. **"Plans for the Boy."** (Ken Martin) *Cowboy Stories*, Vol. 28, No. 1, July 1935: 23-31.

b.   Scheduled for publication in book form by Author Services, Inc., in Winter 1995. (See AA10.)

The son of a rancher saves his father's spread from a mesa fire set by enemies, and dramatically changes his own future.

B31. **"The Contraband Crate."** *Sky Birds Magazine*, Vol. 19, No. 1, Aug. 1935: 41-49.

b.   as "Boomerang Bomber," *Sky Aces Magazine*, Vol. 1, No. 1, June 1938: 53-60.

c.   Scheduled for publication in book form by Author Services, Inc., in Fall 1995. (See AA20.)

In the guise of an army pilot, a U.S. naval intelligence officer contrives to have himself seized by the Japanese, photographs a military installation, and escapes.

B32. **"Under the Black Ensign."** *Five Novels Monthly*, Vol. 31, No. 2, Aug. 1935: 74-103.

b.   Scheduled for publication in book form by Author Services, Inc., in Fall 1998. (See AA54.)

A rousing swashbuckler romance—set in the Caribbean of the 17th century—that blends piracy, British men-of-war, a girl of aristocratic birth disguised as a boy, and an officer unjustly stripped of rank.

Notes: One of Hubbard's three published historical adventure/romances. See A1, *Buckskin Brigades*, and B73, "Mr. Tidwell, Gunner."

B33.   **"Yukon Madness."**   (Capt. L. Ron Hubbard) *New Mystery Adventures*, Vol. 1, No. 5, Aug. 1935: 46-54.

b.   Scheduled for publication in book form by Author Services, Inc., in Fall 1995. (See AA18.)

Though wounded, Mounty Tom McKenna uses a ruse to vanquish the rampaging Itauk the Madman, and then leaves him to the wolves.

B34.   **"The Bad One."**   (Ken Martin) *Cowboy Stories*, Vol. 28, No. 3, Sept. 1935: 37-45.

b.   *Western Short Stories, Vol. 2.* Los Angeles: Author Services, Inc., 69-90, leather. (See A60.)

Thousands of pounds of angry bull—called "Old Renegade" with careful affection—comes to the assistance of a beleaguered ranch hand with his back to the wall.

B35.   **"Buckley Plays a Hunch."**   (Bernard Hubbel) *Top-Notch*, Vol. 97, No. 3, Sept 1935: 126-138.

Jim Buckley, looking for members of a lost expedition, finds three madmen on an island in the Pacific.

B36.   **"Medals for Mahoney."**   (Ken Martin) *Top-Notch*, Vol. 97, No. 3, Sept. 1935: 36-45.

b.   Scheduled for publication in book form by Author Services, Inc., in Fall 1995. (See AA18.)

Mahoney and a native medicine man collaborate to thwart a murderous plot to defraud the trading company.

B37.   **"The Sky Devil."**   *Top-Notch*, Vol. 97, No. 3, Sept. 1935: 54-77.

b.   Scheduled for publication in book form by Author Services, Inc., in Spring 1995. (See AA14.)

Exhausted, wounded and almost out of gas, an adventuring pilot lands his plane at a Sahara oasis, where he uses his cunning—and gasoline—to outwit a dangerous opponent and marry the local king's daughter.

B38.   **"He Walked to War."**   *Adventure*, Vol. 93, No. 5, Oct. 1, 1935: 105-15.

b.   Scheduled for publication in book form by Author Services, Inc., in Spring 1995. (See AA14.)

Tired of walking, E.Z. Go transfers from Marine signalman to airplane gunner, only to find himself walking, once again, through the Nicaraguan underbrush.

B39.   "Murder Afloat."   *Star Detective Magazine*, Vol. 1, No. 3, Oct. 1935: 42-55.

b.   Scheduled for publication in book form by Author Services, Inc., in Winter 1997. (See AA34.)

With killers and thieves free to commit murder and rapine on the S.S. Cubana, an ace government operative sets out with singlehanded boldness to end their reign of terror.

B40.   "Forbidden Gold."   *Five Novels Monthly*, Vol. 32, No. 1, Oct. 1935: 94-126.

b.   as "Förbjudet Guld." *Svenska Novellmagasinet No. 15*, Göteborg Romanforlaget, 1955. [Swedish]

c.   Los Angeles: Author Services, Inc., 1992, leather, 145p. (See A51.)

A dead man's hatred challenging him to accomplish the apparently impossible, an adventurer-aviator braves the perils of the Yucatan jungle to find a missing gold nugget and inherit a fortune.

B41.   "Wind-Gone-Mad."   *Top-Notch*, Vol. 97, No. 4, Oct. 1935: 20-43.

b.   with "Hurricane's Roar." Los Angeles: Author Services, Inc., 1992, leather, 1-69. (See A53.)

Strongly defined tale of a madman's plan to wipe out an entire province in pre-war China and how it is thwarted by the man they call "Feng-Feng"—the Chinese word for hurricane or "Wind-Gone-Mad."

Notes: The first of two stories featuring this character and locale. (See B132, "The Hurricane's Roar.")

B42. **"Five Mex for a Million."** *Top-Notch*, Vol. 97, No. 5, Nov. 1935: 10-33.

 b. *Adventure Short Stories, Vol. 1,* Los Angeles: Author Services, Inc., 1992, leather, 1-67. (See A54.)

An outcast in pre-war Peiping (Peking), with a price on his head for murder, Captain Royal Sterling buys a mysterious black chest whose contents surprise and dazzle him.

B43. **"The Adventure of 'X'."** (Ken Martin) *Top-Notch*, Vol. 97, No. 5, Nov. 1935: 96-115.

 b. Scheduled for publication in book form by Author Services, Inc., in Winter 1995. (See AA11.)

An ex-U.S. Army lieutenant, now a French Legionnaire, nearly succumbs to a Tuareg ruse, then leads his fellow legionnaires against them.

B44. **"The Black Sultan."** *Thrilling Adventures*, Vol. 15, No. 3, Nov. 1935: 12-42.

 b. *Adventure Short Stories, Vol. 2.* Los Angeles: Author Services, Inc., 1992, 1-100. (See A58.)

American Eddie Moran saves the life of the true "Sultan of the Black City," then helps him depose the man—the "Black Sultan"—who has usurped the throne.

B45. **"Catapult Courage."** (Ken Martin) *Bill Barnes Air Trails*, Vol. 5, No. 2, Nov. 1935: 24+.

 b. Scheduled for publication in book form by Author Services, Inc., in Fall 1995. (See AA20.)

Despite repeated attempts to kill him, an airmail pilot flies a secret code to New York, thwarting a plot to blow up the Panama Canal.

B46. **"The Barbarians."** *Dime Adventure Magazine*, Vol. 1, No. 5, Dec. 1935: 38-48.

 b. *Adventure Short Stories, Vol. 2.* Los Angeles: Author Services, Inc., 1992, leather, 135-166. (See A58.)

Captain Jack Harvey of the Legion beheads the Berber tribal chief, avenging his comrade's equally violent death, then comes to a new, philosophically clearer view of the nature of war.

B47. **"Machine Gun 21,000."** *Dynamic Adventure*, Vol. 1, No. 3, Dec. 1935: 90-100.

    b. Scheduled for publication in book form by Author Services, Inc., in Winter 1997. (See AA35.)

Blake loses machine gun number 21,000, then, facing court martial, finds the man who stole it and quells a mutiny.

B48. **"Trick Soldier."** *Top-Notch*, Vol. 98, No. 1, Jan. 1936: 26-38.

The officer they called the "trick soldier"—long on drill and routine and short on courage—and the recruit who has physically bullied him, meet under fire 10 years later, and reverse their roles. (See A70.)

B49. **"The Sky-Crasher."** *Five Novels Monthly*, Vol. 33, No. 1, Jan. 1936: 68-89.

Despite his well-earned nickname, Caution Jones finally risks the hazards of a breathtaking around-the-world flight while a rival airline desperately tries to sabotage his every move. (See A64.)

B50. **"Starch and Stripes."** *Dime Adventure Magazine*, Vol. 1, No. 6, Jan. 1936: 36-47.

A marine captain ensnares a dangerous rebel leader, and saves his camp and his men from congressional disapproval. (See A70.)

B51. **"Red Sand."** (Kurt von Rachen) *Top-Notch*, Vol. 98, No. 2, Feb. 1936: 107-16.

    b. *Adventure Short Stories, Vol. 2*, Los Angeles: Author Services, Inc., 1992, leather, 105-131. (See A58.)

Hubbard deftly blends genres—adventure and mystery/detective—in this tale of the Foreign Legion, a desert ambush, a phantom gunner and an ex-Chicago detective who solves the mystery.

B52.   **"The Price of a Hat."**   *Thrilling Adventures*, Vol. 17, No. 1, Mar. 1936: 63-69.

  b.   *Adventure Short Stories, Vol. 1*, Los Angeles: Author Services, Inc., 1992, leather, 71-89. (See A54.)

A fur hat with a secret message stitched into its hatband costs the lives of six men in a belated effort to save the lives of Nicholas II, the last Russian Tsar, and his family.

Notes: How an ordinary wastebasket inspired this story and was transformed into a salient work of fiction is described by Hubbard in "Magic Out of a Hat," *Writer's Digest*, Vol. 16, No. 2, Jan. 1936. (See C15.)

B53.   **"Raiders of the Beam."**   (Ken Martin) *Bill Barnes Air Trails*, Vol. 5, No. 6, Mar. 1936: 22+.

  b.   Scheduled for publication in book form by Author Services, Inc., in Fall 1995. (See AA20.)

An attempt to hijack a commercial airliner "riding the beam" through zero visibility is resourcefully thwarted by the co-pilot.

B54.   **"The Blow Torch Murder."**   *Detective Fiction Weekly*, Vol. 100, No. 5, Mar. 14, 1936: 117-126.

  b.   Scheduled for publication in book form by Author Services, Inc., in Summer 1994. (See AA3.)

A cleverly devised murder—that appears to have been committed with a blow torch—is solved by a homicide detective.

B55.   **"Hurricane."**   *Five Novels Monthly*, Vol. 33, No. 3, Mar. 1936: 8-39.

  b.   as "Mannen från Helvetet" (Man from Hell). Göteborg: *Romanforlaget*, 1955, paperback. [Swedish]

  c.   Scheduled for publication in book form by Author Services, Inc., in Winter 1999. (See AA59.)

Captain Spar, determined to find the man who contrived his imprisonment on Devil's Island, escapes from the infamous penal colony, encounters a hurricane at sea and a forbidden Caribbean castle, and discovers the identity of his betrayer.

B56. **"Spy Killer."** *Five Novels Monthly*, Vol. 34, No. 1, Apr. 1936: 8-37.

    b.   as "Spion i Kina." [A Spy in China] *Detektivmagasinet*, Vol. 22, No. 24, Göteborg: *Romanforlaget*, 1955. [Swedish]

    c.   Los Angeles: Author Services, Inc., 1990, leather, 119p. (See A38.)

Innocent of the murder and grand larceny that he is charged with, Kurt Boyd alights in Shanghai, where he reluctantly accepts a mission from a traitorous bandit to eliminate a spy. A series of surprising identity changes are pivotal in this tale of Japanese-occupied China.

B57. **"The Death Flyer."** *Mystery Novels Magazine*, Vol. 3, No. 5, Apr. 1936: 115-21.

    b.   Scheduled for publication in book form by Author Services, Inc., in Spring 1998. (See AA50.)

The Death Flyer tears through the blackness, a ghost train with Jim Bellamy aboard, trying to save the life of a girl who died in its wreckage ten years before.

Notes: Hubbard's earliest known blending of mystery and the supernatural.

B58. **"Marriage for Spite."** (Ken Martin) *Romantic Range Magazine*, Vol. 1, No. 6, Apr. 1936: 107-16.

    b.   *Western Short Stories, Vol. 2*. Los Angeles: Author Services, Inc., 1993, leather, 95-117. (See A60.)

A rancher, a beautiful neighbor who wants his land, and a preacher incognito, in one of Hubbard's purely romantic stories.

B59. **"Horse and Horse."** (Ken Martin) *Cowboy Stories*, Vol. 29, No. 5, May 1936: 30-39.

    b.   *Western Short Stories, Vol. 2*. Los Angeles: Author Services, Inc., 1993, leather, 121-45. (See A60.)

Two cowpokes break broncs, avenge a monetary wrong, and earn the money they need to buy the ranch they want.

B60.   "They Killed Him Dead." *Detective Fiction Weekly*, Vol. 101, No. 6, May 2, 1936: 116-26.

b.   Scheduled for publication in book form by Author Services, Inc., in Spring 1998. (See AA50.)

Notorious for his case cracker thoroughness, "Careful" Cassidy changes his tactics, arresting five men for committing the same murder before finding the real cause of death.

B61.   "Loot of the Shanung." *Smashing Novels Magazine*, Vol. 1, No. 1, May 1936: 42-70.

b.   Scheduled for publication in book form by Author Services, Inc., in Winter 1999. (See AA58.)

An American reporter in China, and the heiress daughter of a missing American oil magnate, combine forces to find her father.

B62.   "Escape for Three." *Thrilling Adventures*, Vol. 18, No. 1, June 1936: 95-99.

b.   Scheduled for publication in book form by Author Services, Inc., in Winter 1995. (See AA11.)

With Berber tribesmen on a rampaging killing spree, a hard-boiled trio of French Legionnaires raid the Berber camp and rescue a captive.

B63.   "The Mad Dog Murder." *Detective Fiction Weekly*, Vol. 102, No. 5, June 6, 1936: 128-37.

b.   Scheduled for publication in book form by Author Services, Inc., in Winter 1996. (See AA21.)

An ingenious and cold-blooded plan turns a harmless Pekinese dog into an insidious agent of murder.

B64.   "The Grease Spot." *Thrilling Detective*, Vol. 19, No. 2, July 1936: 67-76.

b.   Scheduled for publication in book form by Author Services, Inc., in Summer 1994. (See AA3.)

The dangerously enterprising owner of a wrecking company finds himself a captive, at gunpoint, and needing help from the men in blue.

B65. **"Leaducation."** (Ken Martin) *Cowboy Stories*, Vol. 30, No. 1, July 1936: 100-10.

b. Scheduled for publication in book form by Author Services, Inc., in Spring 1997. (See AA36.)

Two feuding ranchers test their rivalry in a spelling bee and a declamation contest, then join forces against a "wild bunch" of thieves.

B66. **"Sleepy McGee."** *Argosy*, Vol. 265, No. 5, July 11, 1936: 84-95.

b. *Lives You Wished To Lead But Never Dared.* Clearwater, FL: Theta Books, Inc., 1978, cloth, 1-16. Collection. (See A19.)

c. Scheduled for publication in book form by Author Services, Inc., in Spring 1996. (See AA24.)

Only the laziest civil engineer in the world can build a road through ten miles of rain-soaked jungle!

Notes: Hubbard's initial story, at the age of 25, in *Argosy*—the first, most respected, and ultimately longest-lived of the adventure/action, all-story magazines. "Sleepy McGee" was also the first of an unexampled series of 17 "Hell Job" stories dealing with hazardous professions that Hubbard published in *Argosy*, under his own byline, over the next 17 months. Others in the series include: "Don't Rush Me" (B67), "Mr. Luck" (B77), "Test Pilot" (B78), "Deep-Sea Diver" (B79), "The Big Cats" (B80), "River Driver" (B84), "The Ethnologist" (B85), "Mine Inspector" (B87), "The Shooter" (B88), "Steeplejack" (B90), "Flying Trapeze" (B91), "Mountaineer" (B92), "A Lesson in Lightning" (B96), "Nine Lives" (B100), "Cargo of Coffins" (B105), and "Orders Is Orders" (B107). (See also Q2 for series information.)

In a 1935 radio interview on WFAS (Nov. 28, 1935) Hubbard described his involvement in this story—where the hero fights the rain 24 hours a day—as so intense that after he completed writing it he put on his raincoat to go outside, only to discover that it was a sunny day.

B67.   **"Don't Rush Me."**   *Argosy*, Vol. 265, No. 6, July 18, 1936: 82-95.

    b.   *Lives You Wished To Lead But Never Dared.* Clearwater, FL: Theta Books, Inc., 1978, cloth, 17-34. Collection. (See A19.)

    c.   Scheduled for publication in book form by Author Services, Inc., in Spring 1996. (See AA24.)

The trench he's ordered to dig is never dug—yet Sergeant "Don't Rush Me" Marshall has to defend it from the enemy.

Notes: The second in the "Hell-Job" series.

B68.   **"The Neck Scarf."**   (Ken Martin) *Cowboy Stories*, Vol. 30, No. 2, Aug. 1936: 114-21.

    b.   Scheduled for publication in book form by Author Services, Inc., in Fall 1994. (See AA6.)

The story of a red neckerchief, its infinite utility on the range, and how a cowboy uses it to keep alkali dust out of his mouth, fight off bulls, and find his way out of a maze of thornbushes.

B69.   **"The Headhunters."**   *Five Novels Monthly*, Vol. 35, No. 2, Aug. 1936: 8-37.

    b.   as "Huvudjagarna." *Detektivmagasinet*, Vol. 22, No. 30, Göteborg: *Romanforlaget*, 1955. [Swedish]

    c.   Scheduled for publication in book form by Author Services, Inc., in Spring 1999. (See AA61.)

In the jungles of the Solomon Islands, an explorer-prospector, and a man who had mistakenly trusted a tough and treacherous renegade in the jungle, encounter head-hunters and the ploys of a desperate enemy.

B70.   **"Sky Birds Dare!"**   *Five Novels Monthly*, Vol. 35, No. 3, Sept. 1936: 44-71.

b. as "Sensation i luften." *Svenska Novellmagasinet,* Vol. 18, No. 5, Göteborg: *Romanforlaget,* 1952. [Swedish]

c. Scheduled for publication in book form by Author Services, Inc., in Summer 1997. (See AA40.)

A glider pilot, trying to demonstrate the value of gliders and gliding techniques in war, survives both a competitor's ruthless attempts to destroy him and engine failure in a powered aircraft.

B71. **"The Baron of Coyote River."** *All Western Magazine,* Vol. 18, Whole No. 53, Sept. 1936: 58-79.

A cowpuncher with a price on his head for murder joins forces with a mystery man of the range to bring rustlers to a harsh accounting. (See A69.)

B72. **"The Slickers."** *Detective Fiction Weekly,* Vol. 105, No. 1, Sept. 12, 1936: 36-48.

b. Scheduled for publication in book form by Author Services, Inc., in Spring 1998. (See AA50.)

The sheriff of Cactus County learns a little about city slickers—and teaches the New York City Police a few elementary things about dealing summarily with criminals.

B73. **"Mr. Tidwell, Gunner."** *Adventure,* Vol. 95, No. 5, Sept. 1936: 97-109.

b. *Adventure Short Stories, Vol. 4.* Los Angeles: Author Services, Inc., 1994, 77-121, leather. (See A70.)

With Nelson challenging Napoleon's fleet for dominance of the Mediterranean Sea, ex-schoolmaster Tidwell calculates a grenade's trajectory, sinks a French flagship, and meets the admiral, himself.

Notes: See the Preface discussion of the research Hubbard did for this story.

B74. **"Golden Hell."** (Captain Humbert Reynolds) *Thrilling Adventures,* Vol. 19, No. 1, Sept. 1936: 40-54.

b. *Adventure Short Stories, Vol. 3.* Los Angeles: Author Services, Inc., 1993, 59-126, leather. (See A63.)

Told in the first person by the man who, tortured and shackled, is condemned to work deep within the bowels of a Mongolian mine, then leads a daring escape.

B75.   **"Flaming Arrows."**   *Mystery Adventure Magazine*, Vol. 4, No. 2, Oct. 1936: 108-23.

b.   Melrose Highlands, MA: Odyssey Publications, 1976: 98+

c.   Scheduled for publication in book form by Author Services, Inc., in Fall 1995. (See AA18.)

An accused embezzler, while trying to rescue his friend and employer, fights valiantly though he knows that escape can only mean prison.

B76.   **"Tomb of the Ten Thousand Dead."**   (Capt. Charles Gordon) *Thrilling Adventures*, Vol. 19, No. 2, Oct. 1936: 66-80.

b.   *Adventure Short Stories, Vol. 3.* Los Angeles: Author Services, Inc., 1993, 127-170 leather. (See A63.)

A search for the lost treasures of Baluchistan leads to an ancient tomb, murder, and the obliteration of an entire expedition. Told in the first person by the pilot of the expedition, the only man to escape alive.

B77.   **"Mr. Luck."**   *Argosy*, Vol. 267, No. 5, Oct. 3, 1936: 58-73.

b.   *Lives You Wished To Lead But Never Dared.* Clearwater, FL: Theta Books, Inc., 1978, cloth, 35-55. Collection. (See A19.)

c.   Scheduled for publication in book form by Author Services, Inc., in Spring 1996. (See AA24.)

To build a railroad in South America, "Shoot-the-Works" Kelly needs all the luck he can get. He finds it in a small boy whose singular ability to come up with money to pay the bills remains a mystery until the very end.

Notes: Third in the "Hell-Job" series. (See Q2.)

B78.   **"Test Pilot."**   *Argosy*, Vol. 268, No. 1, Oct. 17, 1936: 86-98.

b.   *Lives You Wished To Lead But Never Dared.* Clearwater, FL: Theta Books, Inc., 1978, cloth, 57-72. Collection. (See A19.)

c.   Scheduled for publication in book form by Author Services, Inc., in Spring 1996. (See AA25.)

A feckless test pilot, confronted with the ultimate trial of courage, sacrifices his own life to save his younger brother.

Notes: Fourth in the "Hell-Job" series. (See Q2.)

B79. **"Deep-Sea Diver."**   *Argosy*, Oct. 24, 1936: 72-82.

b.   *Lives You Wished To Lead But Never Dared*. Clearwater, FL: Theta Books, Inc., 1978, cloth, 73-86. Collection. (See A19.)

c.   Scheduled for publication in book form by Author Services, Inc., in Spring 1996. (See AA25.)

An unfaithful wife, a treacherous friend and unmerited jealousy bring two salvage divers close to death beneath the sea.

Notes: Fifth in the "Hell-Job" series. (See Q2.)

B80. **"The Big Cats."**   *Argosy*, Vol. 268, No. 3, Oct. 31, 1936: 33-45.

b.   *Lives You Wished To Lead But Never Dared*. Clearwater, FL: Theta Books, Inc., 1978, cloth, 87-101. Collection. (See A19.)

c.   Scheduled for publication in book form by Author Services, Inc., in Spring 1996. (See AA25.)

Two wild animal trainers, vying for top billing in the circus, each comes close to death under the slashing claws of the big cats.

Notes: Sixth in the "Hell-Job" series. (See Q2.)

B81. **"Black Towers to Danger."**   *Five Novels Monthly*, Vol. 36, No. 1, Oct. 1936: 8-38.

b.   Los Angeles: Author Services, Inc., 1991, leather, 137p. (See A42.)

Drilling for oil in Venezuela, Murphy encounters murder, a vengeful woman, and the destruction of his rig before he uncovers the truth.

B82.   **"The No-Gun Gunhawk."**   *Western Aces Magazine*, Vol. 7, No. 1, Nov. 1936: 103-27.

   b.   Scheduled for publication in book form by Author Services, Inc., in Fall 1994. (See AA6.)

Forced to change clothes with a masked rider, the son of a dead gunslinger takes up the gun he disavowed, to expose a plot.

B83.   **"Canteens."**   (Ken Martin) *Cowboy Stories*, Vol. 30, No. 5, Nov. 1936: 119-27.

   b.   Scheduled for publication in book form by Author Services, Inc., in Spring 1995. (See AA13.)

A Texas Ranger trails three renegade cowhands pursuing a gold prospector and his daughter into the desert. The true protagonist, Hubbard makes clear, is the desert and water.

B84.   **"River Driver."**   *Argosy*, Vol. 268, No. 4, Nov. 7, 1936: 62-73.

   b.   *Max Brand's Western Magazine*, Vol. 3, No. 4, Feb. 1951: 44-56.

   c.   *Lives You Wished To Lead But Never Dared.* Clearwater, FL: Theta Books, Inc., 1978, cloth, 103-118. Collection. (See A19.)

   d.   Scheduled for publication in book form by Author Services, Inc., in Spring 1996. (See AA26.)

The soft-fingered, banjo-playing son of rough and tough Christopher Plunkett gets a million dollars if he has the nerve to go into one of his father's logging camps and kill John Newcome.

   Notes: Seventh in the "Hell-Jobs" series.

B85.   **"The Ethnologist."**   *Argosy*, Vol. 269, No. 1, Nov. 28, 1936: 112-22.

   b.   *Lives You Wished To Lead But Never Dared.* Clearwater, FL: Theta Books, Inc., 1978, cloth, 119-135. Collection. (See A19.)

c.   Scheduled for publication in book form by Author Services, Inc., in Spring 1996. (See AA26.)

Reading a musty book, or out-witching witch doctors in the midst of a fear-crazed jungle tribe is all in a day's work for a good ethnologist.

Notes: Eighth in the "Hell-Job" series. (See Q2.)

B86.   **"Fifty-Fifty O'Brien."**   *Top-Notch*, Vol. 99, No. 6, Dec. 1936: 42-54.

b.   Scheduled for publication in book form by Author Services, Inc., in Winter 1997. (See AA35.)

An ex-carnival barker becomes a marine sharpshooter during a guerrilla war in Nicaragua, saves another marine's life, then has the favor returned.

B87.   **"Mine Inspector."**   *Argosy*, Vol. 269, No. 2, Dec. 5, 1936: 52-63.

b.   *Lives You Wished To Lead But Never Dared.* Clearwater, FL: Theta Books, Inc., 1978, cloth, 137-151. Collection. (See A19.)

c.   Scheduled for publication in book form by Author Services, Inc., in Spring 1996. (See AA26.)

Delaney is only a "blueprint" miner, who stays above ground, hated for his good clothes, his office, and his education. When he goes into the mine and finds dangerous gas, an encounter with his physically intimidating nemesis ends in a dramatic reversal of roles.

Notes: Ninth in the "Hell-Job" series. (See Q2.)

B88.   **"The Shooter."**   *Argosy*, Vol. 269, No. 3, Dec. 12, 1936: 92-104.

b.   *Lives You Wished To Lead But Never Dared.* Clearwater, FL: Theta Books, Inc., 1978, cloth, 153-170. Collection. (See A19.)

c.   (*Ron, The Writer* Magazine, Issue I, *Hollywood: Dynasty, Master Designers*, 1989, 22-39.

d.   Scheduled for publication in book form by Author Services, Inc., in Summer 1996. (See AA27.)

Mike McGraw uses unconventional methods—"drilling" an oil well with high explosives and the unexpected help of his dog, George, to bring in a gusher.

Notes: Tenth story in the "Hell-Job" series. (See Q2.)

B89.   **"While Bugles Blow!"**   *Five Novels Monthly*, Vol. 36, No. 3, Dec. 1936: 116-60.

b.   as "Slavinna till salu." *Svenska Novellmagasinet Vol. 21*, No. 23, 1955. [Swedish]

c.   Scheduled for publication in book form by Author Services, Inc., in Fall 1998. (See AA56.)

Against a horde of fierce men of the desert, and cut off from all help, an American commandant and sixty loyal Legionnaires put up a valiant defense of their post.

B90.   **"Steeplejack."**   *Argosy*, Vol. 270, No. 1, Jan. 9, 1937: 75-87.

b.   *Lives You Wished To Lead But Never Dared.* Clearwater, FL: Theta Books, Inc., 1978, cloth, 171-187. Collection. (See A19.)

c.   Scheduled for publication in book form by Author Services, Inc., in Summer 1996. (See AA27.)

The Lanning line of nerveless steeplejacks appears to have ended with young Terry, but the physically unprepossessing youngster proves worthy of his lineage when he tackles a church steeple in a raging storm.

Notes: Eleventh in the "Hell-Job" series. (See Q2.)

B91.   **"Flying Trapeze."**   *Argosy*, Vol. 270, No. 3, Jan. 23, 1937: 104-15.

b.   *Lives You Wished To Lead But Never Dared.* Clearwater, FL: Theta Books, Inc., 1978, cloth, 189-206. Collection. (See A19.)

c.   Scheduled for publication in book form by Author Services, Inc., in Summer 1996. (See AA27.)

A master of the trapeze, forced to masquerade as a prince, gives the performance of his life and quiets his critics.

Notes: Twelfth in the "Hell-Job" series. (See Q2.)

B92. **"Mountaineer."** *Argosy*, Vol. 270, No. 5, Feb. 6, 1937: 56-66.

    b. *Lives You Wished To Lead But Never Dared.* Clearwater, FL: Theta Books, Inc., 1978, cloth, 207-222. Collection. (See A19.)

    c. Scheduled for publication in book form by Author Services, Inc., in Summer 1996. (See AA28.)

Three mountain climbers assail the highest unscaled peak in the world, but only one achieves the goal; and he makes it to the top only with the help of the others, though it means his own death.

Notes: Thirteenth in the "Hell-Job" series. (See Q2.)

B93. **"The Bold Dare All."** *Five Novels Monthly*, Vol. 37, No. 2, Feb. 1937: 34-61.

    b. as "Man i Jarn." (Men in Iron) *Detektivmagasinet*, Vol. 22, No. 40, Göteborg: *Romanforlaget*, 1955. [Swedish]

    c. Scheduled for publication in book form by Author Services, Inc., in Fall 1999. (See AA65.)

A sadistic taskmaster is subdued by an incognito U.S. Army lieutenant who then seeks—and finds—his father's killer.

B94. **"The Battling Pilot."** *Five Novels Monthly*, Vol. 37, No. 3, Mar. 1937: 90-117.

    b. Los Angeles: Author Services, Inc., 1993, leather, 121p. (See A59.)

An airline pilot finds his flight routine disrupted by a princess with a cause when she takes to the air with him. An aerial dogfight with a desperate antagonist, and the discovery that the "princess" is not who she pretends to be, climax the story.

B95. **"Cattle King for a Day."** *All Western Magazine,* Vol. 20, No. 59, Mar. 1937: 8-31.

b. Scheduled for publication in book form by Author Services, Inc., in Fall 1996. (See AA31.)

The real identity of the man who arranged to kill Chinook Shannon's grandfather and is trying to steal his ranch provides an ending with a jolting twist.

B96. **"A Lesson in Lightning."** *Argosy,* Vol. 271, No. 5, Mar. 20, 1937: 30-49.

b. *Lives You Wished To Lead But Never Dared.* Clearwater, FL: Theta Books, Inc., 1978, cloth, 223-247. Collection. (See A19.)

c. Scheduled for publication in book form by Author Services, Inc., in Summer 1996. (See AA28.)

Blustering, brave George Potts always wanted a rugged son—but got small, pale, half-blind, stoop-shouldered physicist Horace Purdy Potts instead. Horace proves he is his father's son in the flaming hold of a Caribbean tramp steamer.

Notes: Fourteenth in the "Hell-Job" series. (See Q2.)

B97. **"The Crate Killer."** *War Birds Magazine,* Vol. 33, No. 2, June 1937: 48-55.

b. Scheduled for publication in book form by Author Services, Inc., in Spring 1995. (See AA14.)

After parachuting nine times from airplanes coming apart around him, "Jumper" Bailey faces his tenth—and most challenging—test flight.

B98. **"All Frontiers Are Jealous."** *Five Novels Monthly,* Vol. 38, No. 3, June 1937: 122-60.

b. as "Knock out i Djungeln." *Detektivmagasinet,* Vol. 23, No. 37, Göteborg: *Romanforlaget,* 1955. [Swedish]

An American engineer surveying the route of a railway in Africa, saves a girl from the fierce Dinkas, then takes on the tribal chief in a face-to-face encounter.

B99. **"The Dive Bomber."** *Five Novels Monthly,* Vol. 39, No. 1, July 1937: 8-38.

b. Scheduled for publication in book form by Author Services, Inc., in Fall 1997. (See AA43.)

A famous test pilot clashes with the man who wants to sell planes to a foreign government and will stop at nothing, from sabotage to savage attacks in the air, to destroy his competitor.

Notes: Warner Bros. Pictures, Inc. used Hubbard's title for a movie of the same name in 1941. The movie starred Errol Flynn and Fred McMurray.

B100. **"Nine Lives."** *Argosy,* Vol. 275, No. 3, Aug. 21, 1937: 50-68.

b. *Lives You Wished To Lead But Never Dared.* Clearwater, FL: Theta Books, Inc., 1978, cloth, 249-73. Collection. (See A19.)

c. Scheduled for publication in book form by Author Services, Inc., in Summer 1996. (See AA28.)

It's a well known fact that a cat in the cockpit is worse than a bee in your britches. So what do you do if your sweetheart gives you a black cat as a mascot?

Notes: Fifteenth in the "Hell-Job" series. (See Q2.)

B101. **"Reign of the Gila Monster."** *Western Aces Magazine,* Vol. 9, No. 3, Sept. 1937.

b. Scheduled for publication in book form by Author Services, Inc., in Spring 1997. (See AA36.)

When Howdy Johnson relieves the town of its murderous sheriff—called "Gila Monster" because of his formidable size—he loses his life in the exchange of gunfire. Or does he?

B102. **"Red Death Over China."** *War Birds Magazine,* Vol. 34, No. 1, Oct. 1937: 75-81.

    b.   Scheduled for publication in book form by Author Services, Inc., in Summer 1994. (See AA5.)

A fighter pilot who espouses no cause worth dying for finds one over war-torn China.

B103.   **"The Devil—with Wings."**   *Five Novels Monthly*, Vol. 40, No. 2, Nov. 1937: 10-41.

    b.   as "Flygande Fantomen." *Flygets Hjältar #15*, Göteborg: Flygets Hjaltars Forlag, 1954. [Swedish]

    c.   Scheduled for publication in book form by Author Services, Inc., in Winter 1996. (See AA22.)

A British pilot in black garb and flying an ominous black plane challenges the Japanese in their attempted conquest of China.

B104.   **"Gunman's Tally."**   *All Western Magazine*, Vol. 23, No. 67, Nov. 1937: 10-32.

    b.   as "Massmordaren." *Svenska Novellmagasinet*, Vol. 22, No. 17, Göteborg; Romanforlaget, 1956. [Swedish]

    c.   Scheduled for publication in book form by Author Services, Inc., in Winter 1998. (See AA45.)

Easy Bill and his undeserved reputation as a gunman survive a scheme to kill him and seize his ranch.

B105.   **"Cargo of Coffins."**   *Argosy*, Vol. 277, No. 3, Nov. 13, 1937: 32-66.

    b.   *Lives You Wished To Lead But Never Dared.* Clearwater, FL: Theta Books, Inc., 1978, cloth, 275-320. Collection. (See A19.)

    c.   Scheduled for publication in book form by Author Services, Inc., in Summer 1996. (See AA29.)

The man who considers murder a pastime—Paco Covino, now a chief steward—and the man he doomed to a penal colony—Lars Martin, now captain of an ocean-going yacht—confront each other at sea.

Notes: Sixteenth in the "Hell-Jobs" series. (See Q2.)

B106. **"Tinhorn's Daughter."** *Western Romances Magazine,* Vol. 27, No. 79, Dec. 1937: 10-30.

    b. *Western Short Stories, Vol. 3.* Los Angeles: Author Services, Inc., 1993, leather, 1-67. (See A66.)

A western romance about a girl from the east and her outlawed sweetheart—gallant, red-haired Sunset Maloney—who has sworn to shoot it out with her tinhorn fraud of a father.

B107. **"Orders Is Orders."** *Argosy,* Vol. 278, No. 2, Dec. 18, 1937: 48-85.

    b. *Lives You Wished To Lead But Never Dared.* Clearwater, FL: Theta Books, Inc., 1978, cloth, 321-81. Collection. (See A19.)

    c. Scheduled for publication in book form by Author Services, Inc., in Fall 1996. (See AA30.)

Two marines and a girl dodge bullets on a 200-mile trek through embattled China to bring serum and food to the American consulate, an isolated island of safety in a sea of dead and dying.

    Notes: Seventeenth and last in the "Hell-Job" series. (See Q2.)

B108. **"Six-Gun Caballero."** *Western Story Magazine,* Vol. 163, No. 4, Mar. 12, 1938: 6-40.

    b. Los Angeles: Author Services, Inc., 1991, leather, 137p. (See A45.)

Michael Patrick Obañon, who may have an Irish name, but has the soul of a Spanish gentleman, loses his hundred-thousand-acre spread and has to fight his renegade foes with cunning and firepower.

B109. **"Under the Die-Hard Brand."** *Western Aces Magazine,* Vol. 11, No. 1, Mar. 1938: 10-27.

    b. Scheduled for publication in book form by Author Services, Inc., in Winter 1995. (See AA10.)

The son of the sheriff, disguised in his father's clothes, eliminates the town menace in a gunfight and restores the old sheriff's reputation.

B110. **"The Toughest Ranger."** *Western Story Magazine*, Vol. 165, No. 5, June 11, 1938: 40-61.

b. *Western Short Stories, Vol. 2.* Los Angeles: Author Services, Inc., 1993, leather, 1-65. (See A60.)

Scared, exhausted, half-starved young Petey McGuire, a saddle tramp on the run from one beating to another, crying sensitively when a lame horse has to be shot, finally gets angry and becomes the toughest Ranger.

B111. **"Arctic Wings."** *Five Novels Monthly*, Vol. 42, No. 3, June 1938: 68-96.

b. Los Angeles: Author Services, Inc., 1991, leather, 129p. (See A39.)

Without compassion, convinced that all suspects are evil, a Canadian Mounty brings harsh justice to the Arctic until he is framed by a false witness, and must clear his name.

B112. **"Killer Ape."** *Detective Yarns*, Vol. 1, No. 1, June 1938: 35-44.

b. With "Hostage To Death." Los Angeles: Author Services, Inc.,   1994, leather. (See A71.)

When Joe the orangutan escapes from his owner and is accused of killing a man, Bill flees in terror through the forest, pursued by his erstwhile animal friend. But, friendship triumphs and Bill proves Joe's innocence and his owner's complicity.

B113. **"Hot Lead Payoff."** *Western Story Magazine*, Part 1, Vol. 166, No. 1, June 25, 1938: 6-26; Part 2, Vol. 166, No. 2, July 2, 1938: 40-57; Part 3, Vol. 166, No. 3, July 9, 1938: 82-100; Part 4, Vol. 166, No. 4, July 16, 1938: 94-107.

b. Los Angeles: Author Services, Inc., 1992, leather, 225p. (See A49.)

Tom Noland risks everything he's got—including his neck—to save Rio Camarca from the harsh domination of one man.

B114. **"King of the Gunmen."** *Western Yarns*, Vol. 1, No. 3, July 1938: 6-29.

b. Scheduled for publication in book form by Author Services, Inc., in Spring 1998. (See AA48.)

Kit Gordon escapes into the desert, only to become embroiled in the conflict between the cattlemen and the sheepherders.

B115. **"The Dangerous Dimension."** *Astounding Science Fiction*, Vol. 21, No. 5, July 1938: 100-12.

b. *Futures to Infinity*. New York: Pyramid Books, 1970: 121-42. Anthology, edited by Sam Moskowitz.

c. as "La Dimension Perilleuse." *Futures to Infinity*, L'Age d'Or de la Science Fiction, *Quatrieme Serie #230.* Paris: Editions Opta, Fiction Special No. 21, 1973, paper. Anthology. [French]

d. as "Die Negative Dimension." *Die Gesichter der Zukunft.* (Futures to Infinity anthology) Rastatt: Pabelhaus Erich Pabel, Verlag KG, Sept. 1973. [German]

e. in *Ron the Writer.* Hollywood: Dynasty, Master Designers, 1982.

f. Scheduled for publication in book form by Author Services, Inc., in Summer 1995. (See AA17.)

Meek, diffident Dr. Henry Mudge undergoes a striking personality change when he discovers a mathematical equation that defines a negative dimension, enabling him to go anywhere he thinks of—even when he doesn't want to.

Notes: Hubbard's first appearance in *Astounding Science Fiction*, the most prominent and vitally influential magazine in the history of the genre, and conventionally considered Hubbard's first published science fiction story (but see below). Considered a conceptually seminal work in the literature of the "Golden Age of Science Fiction" (c. 1938-1950), "The Dangerous Dimension" marks the earliest use of teleportation (the ability to move oneself by the power of the mind alone) as the central theme of a story (distinct from the "spirit-journeys" in earlier works of speculative fiction). See "The Tramp" (B120), and *Battlefield Earth* (A27), where teleportation of objects over vast distances is effected technologically. See also: *The New Encyclopedia of Science Fiction*, edited by James Gunn, passim (L46).

Hubbard subsequently characterized "Dangerous Dimension" as "actually fantasy because it was based on a spiritualistic idea." See: *Dream Makers Vol. II: The Uncommon Men and Women Who Write Science Fiction*, pages 182-183 (L 35), and the Introduction to *Battlefield Earth*, section N, for Hubbard's delineating comments on science fiction and fantasy.

B116.   **"Ride 'Em, Cowboy!"**   *Western Story Magazine*, Vol. 166, No. 6, July 30, 1938: 114-28.

    b.   Scheduled for publication in book form by Author Services, Inc., in Spring 1995. (See AA13.)

When a champion bronco-buster and the girl he wants to marry—but constantly quarrels with—compete for the same prize at a rodeo, the results are unexpectedly romantic.

B117.   **"The Ghost Town Gun-Ghost."**   *Western Action Magazine*, Vol. 4, No. 5, Aug. 1938: 100-14.

    b.   *Western Short Stories, Vol. 1.* Los Angeles: Author Services, Inc., 1992, leather, 63-107. (See A56.)

An old cowpoke and a young one—a step ahead of his pursuer—confront outlaws looking for money in a ghost town.

B118.   **"When Gilhooly Was in Flower."**   (Barry Randolph) *Romantic Range*, Vol. 6, No. 4, Aug. 1938: 116+.

    b.   Scheduled for publication in book form by Author Services, Inc., in Spring 1995. (See AA13.)

The trouble with Jigsaw, according to Mary Ann, is there is no romance in his soul. But a reading of *Ivanhoe*, a knightly joust with a bull, and conquest of two local desperadoes prove her wrong.

B119. **"Boss of the Lazy B."** *Western Story Magazine*, Vol. 167, No. 6, Sept. 10, 1938: 66-84.

b. Scheduled for publication in book form by Author Services, Inc., in Summer 1998. (See AA53.)

There's only one kind of justice for a kidnapper and a thief—and the taciturn boss of the Lazy B dispenses it with authority.

B120. **"The Tramp."** *Astounding Science Fiction*, Part 1, Vol. 22, No. 1, Sept. 1938: 70-86; Part 2, Vol. 22, No. 2, Oct. 1938: 90-105; Part 3, Vol. 22, No. 3, Nov. 1938: 46-65.

b. Los Angeles: Author Services, Inc., 1992, leather, 169p. (See A55.)

A hobo, endowed with phenomenal mental powers after a brain operation to save his life, attempts to seize control of the government of the United States.

Notes: Another "Golden Age" landmark for its synergistic use of themes of telekinesis (ability to move objects by sheer force of mind), telepathy (generally the ability to read another person's thoughts and/or communicate nonverbally), and, implicitly, of teleportation. Hubbard considered "The Tramp" his first science fiction story. See: "The Dangerous Dimension" (B115); *Dream Makers Vol. II*, op. cit. pg. 183 (L35) and *The New Encyclopedia of Science Fiction*, op. cit., passim (L46).

B121. **"Come and Get It."** *Western Story Magazine*, Vol. 168, No. 5, Oct. 15, 1938: 31-43.

b. Scheduled for publication in book form by Author Services, Inc., in Fall 1996. (See AA31.)

An Eastern tenderfoot inherits a huge Wyoming ranch and the mystery of his father's death. He becomes a cook, learns to shoot, and uncovers the real culprit and his own identity.

B122.   **"Branded Outlaw!"**   (Barry Randolph) *Five Novels Monthly*, Vol. 44, No. 1, Oct. 1938: 127-62.

b.   Scheduled for publication in book form by Author Services, Inc., in Spring 1994. (See AA1.)

Blamed for the rustling of 2,000 head of cattle, almost lynched, and with every man's hand against him, Lee Weston relentlessly searches for his father's killer.

B123.   **"The Lieutenant Takes the Sky."**   *Five Novels Monthly*, Vol. 44, No. 1, Oct. 1938: 8-35.

b.   as "Tvärs Genom Galler." [Through Iron Bars] *Detektivmagasinet*, Vol. 21, No. 29, Göteborg: Romanförlaget, 1954. [Swedish]

c.   Scheduled for publication in book form by Author Services, Inc., in Spring 1999. (See AA60.)

Sentenced unjustly to five years in a penal colony, Malloy disrupts a planned revolt.

Notes: *Five Novels Monthly* titled the story on the magazine cover as "The Lieutenant Takes the Air." The story inside was titled "The Lieutenant Takes the Sky."

B124.   **"Death Waits at Sundown."**   *Western Story Magazine*, Vol. 169, No. 1, Oct. 29, 1938: 46-56.

b.   Scheduled for publication in book form by Author Services, Inc., in Fall 1996. (See AA31.)

A hard-riding, two-fisted Texan isn't depriving the town of Pioneer of its necktie party—he just wants to substitute another victim.

B125.   **"Silent Pards."**   *Western Story Magazine*, Vol. 169, No. 4, Nov. 19, 1938: 54-61.

b.   Scheduled for publication in book form by Author Services, Inc., in Spring 1998. (See AA48.)

A couple of human rattlesnakes have Old Cherokee marked for their hungry fangs, but they overlook his two silent partners—his dog, Hardtack, and Joe the mule.

B126. **"Ruin at Rio Piedras."** *Western Story Magazine*, Vol. 170, No. 3, Dec. 24, 1938: 83-94.

b.   Scheduled for publication in book form by Author Services, Inc., in Winter 1998. (See AA45.)

Exile at Rio Piedras portends the worst for Tumbleweed Lowrie—but he captures the rustlers and saves the cattle and the ranch.

B127. **"Empty Saddles."** *Adventure Yarns*, Vol. 1, No. 2, Dec. 1938: 26-58.

b.   Los Angeles: Author Services, Inc., 1991, leather, 161p. (See A40.)

Having failed his command, and while awaiting court martial, U.S. cavalry major Lee Stuart deserts, pretends to join the band of outlaws who ambushed his men, helps to foil their attack on the fort, vanquishes their renegade leader and reclaims his reputation.

B128. **"Trouble on His Wings."** *Five Novels Monthly*, Vol. 45, No. 1, Jan. 1939: 8-41.

b.   as *Doden på Vingen*. [Death on the Wing] Nyckelbockerna #368, Göteborg: Romanförlaget, 1953. [Swedish]

c.   Los Angeles: Author Services, Inc., 1994, leather, 115p (See A72.)

Covering a rampaging forest fire, a burning ship, or war in China, it's all in a perilous day's work for ace photographer Johnny Brice—despite the boss's guileful daughter.

B129. **"Wings Over Ethiopia."** *Air Action*, Vol. 1, No. 2, Feb. 1939: 77-87.

b.   Scheduled for publication in book form by Author Services, Inc., in Fall 1995. (See AA20.)

The only weapon with which Larry Colter can elude pursuit planes and sharpshooters is a movie camera.

B130. **"The Ultimate Adventure."** *Unknown*, Vol. 1, No. 2, Apr. 1939: 9-62.

b.   in *L'uomo che non poteva morire*. Translated by Patrizio Dalloro. Urania No. 5, Milano: Mondadori, 1954, paper. (See A12.) [Italian]

c.   *Fear & The Ultimate Adventure*. New York: Berkley Medallion Books, 1970, 135-221. Collection. (See A17.)

d.   in *L'uomo che non poteva morire*. Translated by Manuela Fugenzi and Roberta Rambelli. Bologna: Libra Editrice, 1982, cloth. Collection. (See A12.) [Italian]

e.   Los Angeles: Author Services, Inc., 1992, leather, 129p. (See A50.)

A penniless young man, Stevie Jepson, undergoes an experiment by a malign scientist and journeys into a fantastic Arabian Nights land where a beautiful queen and her subjects are asleep, and an evil jinn nearly kills Jepson before he returns to the real world. Sent back by the scientist for jewels, Jepson rescues the queen from a usurper, shares her throne and then deals peremptorily with the scientist when he himself comes searching for the jewels.

Notes: Conventionally considered Hubbard's first published work of fantasy, and his first appearance in *Unknown* magazine, the preeminent all-fantasy companion to *Astounding Science Fiction*. But see "Dangerous Dimension" (B115), and Dream Makers Vol. II, op. cit. (L35) for Hubbard's views on "Dangerous Dimension" as his first work of fantasy. Also compare "The Death Flyer" (B57).

B131.   "The Falcon Killer."   *Five Novels Monthly*, Vol. 46, No. 1, Apr. 1939: 6-37.

b.   Scheduled for publication in book form by Author Services, Inc., in Fall 1994. (See AA7.)

War-torn China is again the setting for this swiftly-paced story of an ace free-lance fighter pilot, the spy he finally eliminates, and the meaning of the mark of a half dragon he bears on his shoulder.

B132.   "The Hurricane's Roar."   *Adventure Novels and Short Stories*, Vol. 1, No. 3, Apr. 1939: 10-27.

b.   *Wind-Gone-Mad & Hurricane's Roar.* Los Angeles: Author Services, Inc., 1992, leather, 73-149. (See A53.)

Hubbard's second story about the man the Chinese call "Feng-Feng" or "Wind-Gone-Mad"—actually pilot-adventurer Jim Dahlgren—and a conspiracy to incite a provincial war. (See "Wind-Gone-Mad" B41.)

B133.   "Danger in the Dark."   *Unknown*, Vol. 1, No. 3, May 1939: 59-74.

b.   *Unknown*, Vol. 1, No. 3, May 1939: 59-74. United Kingdom.

c.   Scheduled for publication in book form by Author Services, Inc., in Spring 1995. (See AA12.)

Billy Newman purchases a South Sea island, encounters its terrifying shark-god, Tadamona, and destroys the powerful spirit with brilliant flares of light.

B134.   "Slaves of Sleep."   *Unknown*, Vol. 1, No. 5, July 1939: 9+.

b.   Chicago: Shasta Publishing Company, 1948, cloth, 206p. First hardcover edition. (See A4.)

c.   as "Versklavte Seelen." *Utopia Zukunftsroman No. 381*, Part 1, 1964; Part 2, 1964. [German]

d.   New York: Lancer Books, 1967, paper, 176p.

e.   as *Versklavte Seelen.* Verlag Ullstein Buch #3517, *Visionen des Schreckens.* Frankfurt, Berlin, Vienna: Ullstein, 1978. [German]

f.   *Schiavi del Sonno & I Signori del Sonno.* Milano: Armenia Editore, 1978, cloth. Translation of the two novels "Slaves of Sleep" and "The Masters of Sleep." (See A4.) [Italian]

g.   New York: Dell Publishing Co., 1979, paper, 190p.

h.   with "Masters of Sleep." Los Angeles: Bridge Publications, Inc., 1993, cloth, 392p.

i. Scheduled for publication in book form by Author Services, Inc., in Winter 1998. (See AA47.)

When larcenous Professor Frobish opens businessman Jan Palmer's ancient copper jar, he releases Zongri, an enormous, angrily vengeful jinn who slices the professor in half, and condemns Palmer to eternal wakefulness. Arrested for murder and asleep in his cell, Palmer finds himself suddenly in a nightmare world ruled by the jinn, where he has taken on the identity of Tiger, a buccaneer and rogue. Transported magically between parallel worlds by the ring and seal of Sulayman, Palmer/Tiger vanquishes the jinn in the fantasy world, defeats his corporate enemies in the real world, and, exonerated, marries the girl of his dreams, Alice/Wanna.

Notes: With its sequel, "The Masters of Sleep" (B215), "Slaves of Sleep" develops strong interrelated themes of parallel worlds, myths and nightmares. Considered prototypical in its use of the theme of simultaneous coexistence in parallel worlds. See *The Science Fiction Encyclopedia*, passim (L22) and *The New Encyclopedia of Science Fiction*, op. cit., passim (L46).

B135. **"The Ghoul."** *Unknown*, Vol. 1, No. 6, Aug. 1939: 9+.

b. as "Il Ghoul." *Le Quattro Ore di Satana.* [collection] Milano: Libra Editrice, 1955, cloth. (See A13.) [Italian]

c. Los Angeles: Author Services, Inc., 1991, leather, 273p. (See A46.)

A maladroit bellhop opens a trunk left by a mysterious turbaned guest, but finds it empty. And then the voices begin . . .

B136. **"The Ranch That No One Would Buy."** *Western Yarns*, Vol. 2, No. 3, Oct. 1939: 37-48.

b. Scheduled for publication in book form by Author Services, Inc., in Spring 1995. (See AA13.)

When a fearful young man comes to town, and is challenged to a gun fight for cheating by the local bully, the outcome of the six-gun showdown seems sadly predictable. Until the young man's true identity is revealed.

B137. **"The Professor Was a Thief."** *Astounding Science Fiction,* Vol. 24, No. 6, Feb. 1940: 130-156.

b. *Astounding Science Fiction,* Vol. 24, No. 6, Feb. 1940: 77-96. United Kingdom.

c. as "El Professor era un Ladron," *Los Cuentos Fantasticos,* Vol. 3, No. 15, June 1949. [Spanish]

d. in *My Best Science Fiction Story.* New York: Merlin Press, Inc., 1949: 249-284. Anthology, edited by Leo Margulies and Oscar J. Friend. An anthology of science fiction stories, each chosen by the story's author. In Hubbard's introduction to this story, he explained that he chose it because "it changed a trend."

e. Scheduled for publication in book form by Author Services, Inc., in Summer 1997. (See AA41.)

After the Empire State Building, Grant's Tomb, a taxi and an apartment building disappear, an elderly newspaper reporter discovers that they are actually being miniaturized by an ordinary cigarette lighter that has been transformed into an atomic accelerator.

Notes: Dramatized in a radio version by NBC radio Nov. 5, 1950. (See E1.)

B138. **"The Small Boss of Nunaloha."** *South Sea Stories Magazine,* Vol. 1, No. 2, Feb. 1940: 98+.

b. Scheduled for publication in book form by Author Services, Inc., in Fall 1999. (See AA66.)

A man short in stature but large in courage, beaten by a brutal South Seas pirate, finally defies and vanquishes him.

B139. **"If I Were You."** *Five Novels Monthly,* Vol. 50, No. 2, Feb. 1940: 34-59.

b.   Scheduled for publication in book form by Author Services, Inc., in Winter 1997. (See AA35.)

A circus midget named Little Tom Little learns from a set of ancient books on black magic how to switch bodies. But when he exchanges bodies with the lion tamer and finds himself suddenly face to face with the big cats, he discovers—almost too late—that having someone else's body and clothes is not the same as having their attributes of courage or ability.

B140.   "Death's Deputy."   *Unknown*, Vol. 2, No. 6, Feb. 1940: 9-162.

b.   "Death's Deputy." *Unknown*, Vol. 2, No. 6, Feb. 1940. United Kingdom.

c.   Los Angeles: Fantasy Publishing Co. Inc., 1948, paper, 167p. Illustrated by Lou Goldstone.

d.   in *From Death to the Stars*. Los Angeles: Fantasy Publishing, 1950, cloth, 11-167. Collection. (See A9.)

e.   as *Le Bras Droit de la Mort*. Trans. Igor B. Maslowski. Collection Enigme - Romans Extraordinaires. Paris: Librairie Hachette, 1951, paper. [French]

f.   as "L'ereditiera della morte." Part 1 *Urania No. 5* (Mondadori) Mar. 1953: 142+; Part 2 *Urania No. 6* (Mondadori) Apr. 1953: 154+. [Italian]

g.   as "L'uomo che non poteva morire." *Urania No. 37*, Translated by Patrizio Dalloro. Milano: Arnoldo Mondadori Editore, 1954, paper. (See A12.) [Italian]

h.   Hollywood: Leisure Books, 1970, paper, 158p.

i.   as *Bote des Grauens. Vampir-Roman #26*, Rastatt: Erich Pabel Verlag, Aug. 1973. [German]

j.   *L'uomo che non poteva morire*. Trans. Manuela Fugenzi & Roberta Rambelli. Bologna: Libra Editrice, 1982. Contains "Death's Deputy" and "The Ultimate Adventure." [Italian]

k.   as *Shi No Dailinin*. Tokyo: New Era Publications Japan, 1992, cloth, 241p. [Japanese]

l. as *Shi No Dailinin.* Copenhagen: New Era Publications ApS., 1994, paper, 271p. [Japanese]

m. Scheduled for publication in book form by Author Services, Inc., in Winter 1996. (See AA23.)

When people mysteriously begin to die around Clayton McLean, he knows that their deaths are inexplicably linked to him.

B141. **"The Indigestible Triton."** (Rene Lafayette) *Unknown*, Vol. 3, No. 2, Apr. 1940: 9-80.

b. "The Indigestible Triton." *Unknown Fantasy Fiction*, Vol. 3, No. 2, Apr. 1940. United Kingdom.

c. as *Triton.* Los Angeles: Fantasy Publishing, 1949: 9-53. Hardcover and softcover edition. Also contains the short story "Battle of Wizards." (See A5.)

d. in *Quintette.* Los Angeles: Fantasy Publishing, 1950, 9-53. Science fiction and fantasy anthology.

e. as "Il tritone indigesto." *Le Quattro Ore di Satana* Milano: Libra Editrice, 1955, paper. Collection. (See A13.) [Italian]

f. *Oscar Mondadori No. 849.* Milano: Arnoldo Mondadori Editore, 1978, paper. [Italian]

g. as *Il segno del tritone.* Collano Sirio #1, Milano: Edizioni Onda TV Srl, 1980, paper. (See A5.)   [Italian]

h. Bologna: Libra Editrice, 1981, cloth. [Italian]

i. Los Angeles: Author Services, Inc., 1993, 225p., leather. (See A5.)

Bill Grayson, on a brief fishing trip, hooks a formidable fish that turns out to be Trigon, the Triton, great-grandson to Neptune, ruler of the sea. Triton enters Bill's body, shares a sanitarium cell with him and escapes into the sea with Bill who is now able to breathe under water and communicate with the fish. At Neptune's palace, Bill threatens to use his hypnotic powers, and is permitted to go ashore with a wealth of treasure.

B142. **"Final Blackout."** *Astounding Science Fiction*, Part 1, Vol.

25, No. 2, Apr. 1940: 9-37; Part 2, Vol. 25, No. 3, May 1940: 121-47; Part 3, Vol. 25, No. 4, June 1940: 113-51.

b.   East Providence: Hadley Publishing, 1948, cloth, 154p. First hardcover edition. (See A2.)

c.   as "L'ultimo vessillo." Translated by Ugo Malaguti. La Tribuna Editrice Piacenza, Galassia No. 57, Sept. 1, 1965: 7+. [Italian]

d.   Hollywood: Leisure Books, 1970, paper, 191p.

e.   Apollo Science Fiction, Issue #6, 1972. The Netherlands and Belgium.

f.   New York: Garland Publishing, 1975, cloth, 191p.

g.   as *Il tenente*. Translated by Maria Benedetta de Castiglione. *Urania No. 701,* Milano: Mondadori, 1976, paper. [Italian]

h.   as "L'ultimo vessillo." Translated by Ugo Malaguti. Bologna: Libra Editrice, 1982. [Italian]

i.   as "Il tenente." Classici Urania #98. Milano: Arnoldo Mondadori Editore, 1985. [Italian]

j.   Los Angeles: Bridge Publications, Inc., 1989, cloth, 184p. Introduction by Algis Budrys.

k.   Los Angeles: Bridge Publications, Inc., 1992, paper, 218p. Introduction by Algis Budrys.

l.   Garden City, NY: Doubleday, Science Fiction Bookclub, 1992, cloth. Illustrated by Sergei Poyarkov. Introduction by Algis Budrys.

m.   Paris: Presses de la Cité, New Era Publications, 1992, paper. [French]

n.   Norwalk, CT: The Easton Press, 1994, leather, 218p. Introduction by Algis Budrys. Illustrated by Sergey V. Poyarkov.

o.   Scheduled for publication in book form by Author Services, Inc., in Spring 1997. (See AA40.)

In a Europe ravaged by 30 years of incessant war, devastating plague, and a blight of crop-devouring insects, small bands of soldiers are left to wander over the desolate face of the Continent. One such group of survivors is led by a man of extraordinary courage, resourcefulness, and personal magnetism—identified in the novel only as the Lieutenant. Ordered to surrender his command, he subdues his headquarters garrison, then augments his troop and heads for England. There, he attacks the Tower of London and seizes the shattered remnants of government in a chaotic country. Two years later, with England's productivity and internal unity restored, he defies the interference of a decadent but powerful United States by killing the men appointed to replace him—at the sacrifice of his own life. His act of ultimate valor preserves the essential integrity of both command and government—and the symbol of these verities, the Lieutenant's Flag of Command, continues to fly above the Byward Gate on Tower Hill. In the elegiac final words of the novel:

"That flag still flies, and on the plaque below are graven the words: 'When that command remains, no matter what happens to its officer, he has not failed.'"

Notes: Consistently ranked as one of the ten greatest novels of "The Golden Age of Science Fiction" and arguably Hubbard's most famous and most controversially apocalyptic science fiction novel before *Battlefield Earth* (A27). Distinguished stylistically by its visceral symbolism: the Lieutenant, e.g., deliberately identified in the text only by his rank, personifies courage or leadership; abstract qualities of command and government are objectified in the Lieutenant's flag. *Final Blackout* is also widely seen by contemporary critics as Hubbard's defining classic of "survivalist" fiction—paradigmatic for that genre in concept and intensity of characterization—before *Battlefield Earth*. (See *The World of Science Fiction*, pg. 386 (L 24) and *The New Encyclopedia of Science Fiction*, op. cit., passim (L 46). See also A2.)

B143.   **"On Blazing Wings."** *Five Novels Monthly*, Vol. 51, No. 2, May 1940: 60-91.

b.   *Roda Vingar.* [Red Wings] Nyckelbockerna #399, Göteborg: Romanförlaget, 1954. [Swedish] (See A10.)

c.   Scheduled for publication in book form by Author Services, Inc., in Fall 1996. (See AA32.)

David Duane, artist, adventurer and air ace learns his destiny in a mystery-shrouded city of golden minarets. Then, during an aerial dogfight, he decisively—and heroically—changes that destiny by flying headlong into a bomb-filled enemy aircraft.

B144.   **"Shadows from Boothill."**   *Wild West Weekly,* Vol. 137, No. 3, June 1, 1940: 55-72.

b.   Scheduled for publication in book form by Author Services, Inc., in Spring 1998. (See AA48.)

A hired gunman acquires two sinister shadows, then loses them—and his own—in a final gunfight.

Notes: Hubbard's only known Western fantasy.

B145.   **"Inky Odds."**   *Five Novels Monthly,* Vol. 51, No. 3, June 1940: 126-59.

b.   Los Angeles: Author Services, Inc., 1992, leather, 129p. (See A47.)

The best newspaper correspondent in China and an ambitious new correspondent, who beats him to the "scoop," cross paths in the war-ravaged country.

B146.   **"The Iron Duke."**   *Five Novels Monthly,* Vol. 52, No. 1, July 1940: 116-45.

b.   Scheduled for publication in book form by Author Services, Inc., in Fall 1994. (See AA8.)

Blackie Lee's outrageous impersonation of the drunken Archduke of Aldoria—with the secret collaboration of the prime minister—leads to unexpected political and personal consequences.

B147.   **"Fear."**   *Unknown Fantasy Fiction,* Vol. 3, No. 5, July 1940: 9-84.

b.   *Unknown*, Vol. 3, No. 5, July 1940: 2-57. United Kingdom.

c.   *Fear/Typewriter in the Sky*. NY: Gnome Press, 1951, cloth, 135-256. (See A15.)

d.   *Fear/Typewriter in the Sky. Fantasy Books*, Kemsley Newspapers, 1951, paper, 100-190.

e.   as "La paura" in *Le quattro ore di Satana*. [The Four Hours of Satan] Translated by Tom Arno. Urania #89, Milano: Arnoldo Mondadori Editore, 1955. [Italian]

f.   as "Angst." *Fanzine Pioneer Magazine No. 10*, Part 1, May-June 1962; *Fanzine Pioneer Magazine No. 11*, Part 2, July-Aug. 1962. [German]

g.   *Fear & The Ultimate Adventure*. Berkley Medallion Books, Mar. 1970, paper, 9-131. (See A17.)

h.   *Dodens Timer*. (The Hour of Death) Translated by Frits Remar. Iskolde Gys #6, Copenhagen: Winther Forlag, 1973, paper. [Danish]

i.   as *Omansklig Fasa*. Kalla Karar #17, Stockholm: B. Wahlstroms Bokforlag, 1973, paper. [Swedish]

j.   as "Opfer der Damonen." *Vampir-Horror Roman Magazine #69*, Rastatt: Erich Pabel Verlag, June 1974. [German]

k.   *Fear & Typewriter in the Sky*. New York: Popular Library, 1977, paper, 157-286. (See A8.)

l.   as *Omansklig Fasa*. Stockholm: B. Wahlstroms Bokforlag, 1980, paper. [Swedish]

m.   in *Le quattro ore di Satana*. Bologna: Libra Editrice, 1981, cloth. [Italian]

n.   Los Angeles: Bridge Publications, Inc., 1991, cloth, 188p. Illustrated by Derek Hegsted. (See A15.)

o.   Redhill, Surrey, England: New Era Publications, Ltd., 1991, cloth.

p.   as *Au Bout de Cauchemar*. Paris: Presse de la Cité, 1991, paper. [French]

q.   as *Miedo*. Madrid: Nueva Era Dinámica, S.A., 1991, paper. [Spanish]

r.   as *Retteges*. Budapest: Phoenix, 1992, cloth, 201p. [Hungarian]

s.   as *CTRAX*. Moscow: Image, 1992, cloth, 183p. [Russian]

t.   as *KYOUFU*. Tokyo: New Era Publications Japan, 1992, cloth, 210p. [Japanese]

u.   with "Borrowed Glory." Los Angeles: Bridge Publications, Inc., 1992, paper, 1-205. (See A15.)

v.   as *CTRAX*. Sofia: Pero, 1993, cloth, 161p. [Bulgarian]

w.   as *Des*. Svoboda, 1993, paper, 102p. [Czechoslovakian]

x.   Scheduled for publication in book form by Author Services, Inc., in Summer 1994. (See AA16.)

James Lowry, professor of ethnology at Atwater College, having publicly denied the existence of demons and devils, unexpectedly finds himself outside the house of an academic colleague. It is a quarter of three in the afternoon of a bright spring day, brushed with ominous gusts of a cold, dark wind. Then, suddenly it is a quarter of seven in the evening. Professor Lowry has lost four hours of his life, and his hat, and has begun a descent into a macabre world of night without day; of strange figures out of time; of "hats and bats and cats," of graves and murder in cold blood.

Notes: Prototype novel of modern horror fiction, esp. in its imaginative use of the prosaic: the ordinary individual in ordinary circumstances experiencing extraordinary or bizarre (but not necessarily supernatural) events as a theme, and the inconspicuously "normal" small town as a setting. Notable, as well, for its use of a strongly metrical prose style, principally alliteration and assonance—to achieve mounting effects of both "psychological suspense and phantasmagoric horror." (See the Introduction to the Bibliography, the Introduction to the novel itself [A15], and *The Science Fiction Encyclopedia*, op. cit., passim [L22.])

See also Gail Regier's exegetical review, "A Metaphysical Unease" (*The World & I*, L55), for its original examination of "Fear" on several levels: Hubbard's archetypical themes and techniques in transforming mundane effects, characters and *mise en scène*—gradually and credibly— into the frighteningly macabre; his use of solipsism—"the problem of other minds"—and its plural perceptions of reality ("no one has dramatized it as effectively" in the literature of the genre); Hubbard's deliberate evocation of a single emotion, the "Fear" of the book's title; and the novel's classic literary and filmic analogues, seen by Regier, in various aspects of the work, to include Henry James, Kafka, Poe and a "fusion of Lovecraft and Alfred Hitchcock."

B148. **"The Idealist."** (Kurt von Rachen) *Astounding Science Fiction*, Vol. 25, No. 5, July 1940: 94-107.

b. *Astounding Science Fiction*, Vol. 25, No. 5, July 1940: 41-50. United Kingdom.

c. as "L'idealista" in *I ribelli dell'universo*. (The Rebels of the Universe) Bologna: Libra Editrice, 1980, paper. Collection. (See Λ24.) [Italian]

d. *Kilkenny Cats Series*. Los Angeles: Author Services, Inc., 1992, leather, 1-37. Collection. (See A48.)

The year is 2893, and the world is ruled by the despot Fagar the Deliverer, who is determined to obliterate his opposition. But the captive legal system decides, virtually as a joke, to send the two principal dissident groups—the scientists and the longshoremen—to colonize the planet Sereon, confident the rival groups will destroy each other. Along with them go the dissident "Idealist" Colonel Stephen Galbraith and the rebellious Vicky Stalton. Galbraith determines during the trip to Sereon to overthrow Fagar.

Notes: The first of five stories collectively called "The Kilkenny Cats"; only the second story in the series bears this specific title. Other stories in the series are: "The Kilkenny Cats" (B150); "The Traitor" (B154); "The Mutineers" (B156), and "The Rebels" (B162).(Also see Q3.)

B149.   **"Sabotage in the Sky."** *Five Novels Monthly*, Vol. 52, No. 2, Aug. 1940: 6-34.

   b.   as "Sabotage i Luften." *Detektivmagasinet*, Vol. 20, No. 10, Göteborg: Romanförlaget, 1954. [Swedish]

   c.   Scheduled for publication in book form by Author Services, Inc., in Spring 1994. (See AA2.)

   None of the fighter planes test pilot Bill Trevillian flies are hotter than the BCA 41 pursuit ship, so he takes it up. But someone has deliberately rigged it for failure and destruction—and for Trevillian's death.

B150.   **"Kilkenny Cats."** (Kurt von Rachen) *Astounding Science Fiction*, Vol. 26, No. 1, Sept. 1940: 98-116.

   b.   *Astounding Science Fiction*, Vol. 26, No. 1, Sept. 1940: 42-54. United Kingdom.

   c.   as "I lupi di sirio" in *I Ribelli dell'universo*. (The Rebels of the Universe) Bologna: Libra Editrice, 1980, paper. Collection. (See A24.) [Italian]

   d.   *Kilkenny Cats Series*. Los Angeles: Author Services, Inc., 1992, leather, 41-85. Collection. (See A48.)

   A sequel to "The Idealist": two rival groups—scientists and longshoremen—that have been exiled together on the planet Sereon discover that Fagar's plan to help them to destroy each other includes an unequal distribution of supplies. One has food, the other, water and weapons. But "Idealist" Steve Gailbraith and his rebel companion, Vicki, unite the warring groups to face a common enemy: ravenous wolves.

   Notes: Second in the "Kilkenny Cats" series. (See Q3.)

B151.   **"The Devil's Rescue."** *Unknown Fantasy Fiction*, Vol. 4, No. 2, Oct. 1940: 99-113.

   b.   *Unknown Fantasy Fiction*, Vol. 4, No. 2, Oct. 1940: 61-69. United Kingdom.

   c.   in *Hell Hath Fury*. (Anthology, edited by George Hay.) London: Neville Spearman, 1963, 175-96.

   d.   in *Sea Tales of Terror*. (Anthology, edited by J. J.

Strating.) Glasgow: Fontana Books, 1974, 29-46.

e.   *Fantasy Book Magazine*, Vol. 1, No. 5, Aug. 1982.

f.   *Fantasy Short Stories, Vol. 2.* Los Angeles: Author Services, Inc., 1993, 51-88, leather. (See A68.)

When the crew of a spectral old clipper ship rescues Lanson from his drifting lifeboat, he discovers that they are faceless—except for the captain. When a special guest, the Dark One, appears, as he does every seven years, the captain—seeking release from endless wandering—plays a game of dice with the visitor and loses, once again. Lanson then plays and wins and is instantly plunged back into the sea—but finds his lifeboat.

B152.   "One Was Stubborn."   (Rene Lafayette) *Astounding Science Fiction*, Vol. 26, No. 3, Nov. 1940: 82-95.

b.   *Astounding Science Fiction*, Vol. 26, No. 3, Nov. 1940: 59-68. United Kingdom.

c.   *Ad Astra Issue 12*, Vol. 2, No. 6, Oct. 1980: 27+.

d.   as "Just Imagine." *International Comm Line*, Vol. 2, Issue 11, Sept. 1982: 4-7.

e.   Scheduled for publication in book form by Author Services, Inc., in Summer 1995. (See AA17.)

When an old man discovers that the world keeps disappearing around him, he checks first with his eye doctor, then with an enigmatic man named George Smiley. Finally, he realizes that things vanish as soon as he stops thinking about them. When he finds someone else with the same ability, they collaboratively begin to reassemble the world as we know it.

B153.   "Typewriter in the Sky."   *Unknown Fantasy Fiction*, Part 1, Vol. 4, No. 3, Nov. 1940: 9-67; Part 2, Vol. 4, No. 4, Dec. 1940: 127-162.

b.   *Typewriter in the Sky/Fear.* New York: Gnome Press, 1951, 9-134. (See A8.)

c.   *Fear/Typewriter in the Sky.* London: Fantasy Books,

Kemsley Newspapers, 1951, 7-99. (See A8.)

d. as "La trama tra le nubi." *Urania No. 105*, Mondadori, Nov. 17, 1955, paper. (See A14.) [Italian]

e. *Fear & Typewriter in the Sky*. New York: Popular Library, 1977, 9-153. (See A15.)

f. as "La trama tra le nubi," [collection] Bologna: Libra Editrice, 1980, cloth. (See A14.) [Italian]

g. Los Angeles: Author Services, Inc., leather, 1994. (See A8.)

A piano player suddenly finds himself part of an adventure novel being written by his friend Horace Hackett. Not only is he in the novel, but he is the villain and destined to die. Frustrated by his boredom when Horace ignores him to concentrate on other characters in the novel, and trapped by Horace's poorly researched plot and characterization, the piano player alternates between enjoying the drama and wanting to murder Horace. As the story proceeds he becomes more and more concerned about his imminent death.

The novel's final lines appear to reflect Hubbard's own, wry characterization of the creative process: as the piano player looks up at the sky, he sees upon the fleecy clouds an image not unlike Horace Hackett and thinks: "Up there— God? In a dirty bathrobe?"

Notes: Considered [with "Slaves of Sleep" (B134) and "Masters of Sleep" (B215)] his most celebrated and seminally influential fantasy: the prototypical "journey into the mind" story of modern fantastic fiction (cf. "Fear" B147). See *The New Encyclopedia of Science Fiction*, op. cit., passim (L 46). See also *The Encyclopedia of Science Fiction (Clute and Nicholls*, 2nd ed.) for its discussion of Hubbard's early, seminal use of virtual reality as a central theme in Typewriter in the Sky (L60).

B154. **"The Traitor."** (Kurt von Rachen) *Astounding Science Fiction*, Vol. 26, No. 5, Jan. 1941: 74-89.

b. *Astounding Science Fiction*, Vol. 2, No. 5, Jan. 1941: 39-

48. United Kingdom.

c.   as "La febbre verde" in *I Ribelli dell'universo*. (The Rebels of the Universe) Bologna: Libra Editrice, 1980, paper. Collection. (See A24.) [Italian]

d.   *The Kilkenny Cats Series*. Los Angeles: Author Services, Inc., 1992, leather, 89-130. Collection. (See A48.)

The feuding exiles on Sereon, scientists and longshoremen, are beset by a green plague. A spacecraft, the *Fury*, is readied for an escape from the inhospitable planet. And once more, "Idealist" Steve Gailbraith, still intent on toppling Fagar the Deliverer, placates the rival factions.

Notes: Third in the "Kilkenny Cats" series. (See Q3.)

B155.   **"The Crossroads."**   *Unknown*, Vol. 4, No. 5, Feb. 1941: 71-86.

b.   *Unknown Worlds Magazine*, Vol. 4, No. 5, Winter 1949: 12-22. United Kingdom.

c.   *Fantasy Short Stories,* Vol. 2, Los Angeles: Author Services, Inc., 1993, 1-51, leather. (See A68.)

Farmer Eben Morse sets out to sell his crops in the big city, but encounters a strange crossroads in time. He follows each of the roads to its destination—each a different culture—and having scattered havoc in all of them, wearily sets off for home.

B156.   **"The Mutineers."**   (Kurt von Rachen) *Astounding Science Fiction*, Vol. 27, No. 2, Apr. 1941: 127-154.

b.   as "Gli ammutinati del cielo" in *I ribelli dell'universo*. (The Rebels of the Universe) Bologna: Libra Editrice, 1980, paper. Collection. (See A24.) [Italian]

c.   *The Kilkenny Cats Series*. Los Angeles: Author Services, Inc., 1992, leather, 135-188. Collection. (See A48.)

The chief scientist seizes the *Fury* and heads for the planet New Terre. The "Idealist" Steve Gailbraith wrests control from him, lands and is confronted by a race of giants. They submit when Gailbraith intimidates them with the illusion of a massive armed force in space.

Notes: Fourth in the "Kilkenny Cats" series. (See Q3.)

B157.   "The Case of the Friendly Corpse." *Unknown Fantasy Fiction*, Vol. 5, No. 2, Aug. 1941: 9-80.

   b.   *Unknown Worlds Magazine*, Vol. 3, No. 9, Spring 1947: 2-34. United Kingdom.

   c.   in *Le quattro ore di satana*. Bologna: Libra Editrice, 1981.

   d.   Los Angeles: Author Services, Inc., 1991, leather, 199p. (See A41.)

A young college student who switches places with a mighty wizard, is inducted into the Order of Necromancers. When he dispenses to a dead sultan a "revivification potion" that has been accidently mixed with the potion for making friends, he has on his hands a "friendly corpse."

B158.   "Borrowed Glory." *Unknown Worlds Magazine*, Vol. 5, No. 3, Oct. 1941: 85-91.

   b.   in *Fear*. Los Angeles: Bridge Publications, Inc., 1992, paper, 209-238. (See A15.)

   c.   Scheduled for publication in book form by Author Services, Inc., in Fall 1998. (See AA55.)

For a single glimmering day of youth and infinite promise, and the settlement of a small dispute about truth among the immortals, a life—or two—may be a satisfactory price to pay.

B159.   "The Last Drop."   (with L. Sprague de Camp) *Astonishing Stories*, Vol. 3, No. 2, Nov., 1941: 87-95.

b.	*Astonishing Stories*, Vol. 1, No. 1, Jan. 1942: 56-64. Canada.

c.	Scheduled for publication in book form by Author Services, Inc., in Fall 1998. (See AA55.)

A special elixir from Borneo that grows or shrinks you reduces a bartender and a mobster to combat in miniature.

B160.	**"The Invaders."**	[aka "Behind the Black Nebula"] *Astounding Science Fiction*, Vol. 28, No. 5, Jan. 1942: 62-75.

b.	*Astounding Science Fiction*, Vol. 28, No. 5, Jan. 1942, 51-64. United Kingdom.

c.	in *The Kingslayer*. [collection] Los Angeles: Fantasy Publishing Co., 1949, cloth, 163-208. (See A6.)

d.	in *From Death to the Stars*. [collection] Los Angeles: Fantasy Publishing Co., 1950, cloth, 163-208. (See A9.)

e.	as "Behind the Black Nebula" in *Tales from Outer Space*. (Anthology, edited by Donald A. Wollheim.) New York: Ace Books, paper, 1954, 111-140.

f.	*Seven Steps to the Arbiter*. Chatsworth CA: Major Books, 1975, paper, 149-92. Collection. (See A18.)

g.	as "Derriere la Nebouleuse Noire" in *Les Pieges de l'Espace*. (Anthology edited by Marianne LeConte.) Le Masque Science Fiction #43. Paris: Librairie des Champs-Elysees, 1977. [French]

h.	as "Altraterra, 2204: La nascita dell'Impero" in *L'impero dei mille soli*. [collection] Bologna: Libra Editrice, 1981. (See A25.) [Italian]

i.	*Science Fiction Short Stories, Vol. 1*. Los Angeles: Author Services, Inc., 1993, 1-59, leather. (See A65.)

Far in the future, criminals are condemned to the Crystal Mines of the Black Nebula. When the mines are assaulted by a legion of monstrous forms, a science corps technician makes a monumental discovery: the nebula is a warp in space, and the mines are inside the macrocosmic viscera of a worm.

Notes: See *The Science Fiction Encyclopedia*, "cosmology," p. 141 (L22).

B161. **"He Didn't Like Cats."** *Unknown Worlds*, Vol. 5, No. 5, Feb. 1942: 83-90.

b. *Unknown Worlds*, Vol. 5, No. 5, Mar. 1942: 13-20. United Kingdom.

c. in *Zacherley's Vulture Stew*. (Anthology) New York: Ballantine Books, 1960, 7-22.

d. in *Supernatural Cats*. (Anthology, edited by Claire Necker.) Garden City: Doubleday & Company, 1972, 368-385.

e. *Supernatural Cats*. New York: Warner Books, 1974.

f. Scheduled for publication in book form by Author Services, Inc., in Summer 1997. (See AA41.)

The small man has one large aversion—cats. A mousy little fellow ordinarily, he insensitively sends one large and ownerless alley cat to its fate under the wheels of a passing car. The cat, however, comes back in the form of an endlessly recurring nightmare.

B162. **"The Rebels."** (Kurt von Rachen) *Astounding Science Fiction*, Vol. 28, No. 6, Feb. 1942: 49-61.

b. *Astounding Science Fiction*, Vol. 28, No. 6, Feb. 1942: 42-54. United Kingdom.

c. as "Attacco al planeta" in *I ribelli dell'universo*. (The Rebels of the Universe) Bologna: Libra Editrice, 1980, paper. Collection. (See A24.) [Italian]

d. *The Kilkenny Cats Series*. Los Angeles: Author Services, Inc., 1992, leather, 193-243. Collection. (See A48.)

When Steve Gailbraith begins faltering in his resolve to overthrow Fagar the Deliverer, the head of the longshoremen's faction conspires with the dictator to send a fleet to conquer New Terre and dispose of the "Idealist." Gailbraith substitutes a potent intoxicant for the flagship's water supply, seizes the spacecraft, disables the rest of the Earth's ships, then takes off with his crew to deal finally with Fagar.

Notes: Fifth and final story in the "Kilkenny Cats" series. (See Q3.)

B163.   **"Strain."**   *Astounding Science Fiction*, Vol. 29, No. 2, Apr. 1942: 72-77.

b.   Scheduled for publication in book form by Author Services, Inc., in Winter 1997. (See AA33.)

Two Earth intelligence officers, shot down by Saturnians, are subjected unsuccessfully to brutal interrogation.

B164.   **"The Room."**   *Unknown Worlds Magazine*, Vol. 5, No. 6, Apr. 1942: 93-99.

b.   *Unknown Worlds Magazine*, Vol. 6, No. 1, June 1942: 58+. United Kingdom.

c.   *Fantasy Short Stories,* Vol. 2, Los Angeles: Author Services, Inc., 1993, 89-120, leather. (See A68.)

The country doctor's room is his private den—a den filled with strange souvenirs with even stranger properties. The bottle of excellent liquor, for instance. It pours but it never empties. And one day the doctor's son opens the door to find a land with camels and a green sea.

B165.   **"The Slaver."**   *Astounding Science Fiction*, Vol. 29, No. 4, June 1942: 31-38.

b.   *Astounding Science Fiction*, Vol. 29, No. 4, Aug. 1942: 43-51. United Kingdom.

c.   Scheduled for publication in book form by Author Services, Inc., in Winter 1997. (See AA33.)

Captured by space slave traders, befriended by a slave girl, Kree Lorin outwits his captors, frees the girl, and regains his spaceship.

B166. **"Space Can."** *Astounding Science Fiction*, Vol. 29, No. 5, July 1942: 71-77.

    b.   Scheduled for publication in book form by Author Services, Inc., in Winter 1997. (See AA33.)

If your ship is riddled with holes, on fire, unable to maneuver, and is an obvious hopeless wreck in the midst of a space battle, there's only one way out: take over the heavier enemy ship.

B167. **"The Beast."** *Astounding Science Fiction*, Vol. 30, No. 2, Oct. 1942: 100-107.

    b.   *Astounding Science Fiction*, Vol. 30, No. 2, Jan. 1943: 40-47. United Kingdom.

    c.   in *The Kingslayer*. Los Angeles: Fantasy Publishing, 1949, cloth, 135-160. Collection includes "The Kingslayer," "The Beast," and "The Invaders." (See A6.)

    d.   *From Death to the Stars*. Los Angeles: Fantasy Publishing, 1950, cloth, 163-208. Collection includes: "Death's Deputy," "The Kingslayer," "The Beast," and "The Invaders." (See A9.)

    e.   *Seven Steps to the Arbiter*. Chatsworth, CA: Major Books, 1975, 125-148. Collection includes "The Kingslayer," "The Beast," and "The Invaders." (See A18.)

    f.   *Science Fiction Short Stories,* Vol. 1, Los Angeles: Author Services, Inc., 1993, 60-91, leather. (See A65.)

In the jungles of Venus, the mysterious Beast has to be killed—not only because it has murdered, but because it has stolen something Ginger Cranston can't live without—an intangible, absolutely necessary thing: Cranston's courage.

B168. **"The Great Secret."** *Science Fiction Stories*, Vol. 3, No. 4, Apr. 1943: 81-85.

b.   Scheduled for publication in book form by Author Services, Inc., in Fall 1997. (See AA44.)

Under the searing rays of the world's double sun, Fanner Marston, wracked with thirst and exhaustion, pushes on toward his goal. Parva, city of the erstwhile master race of the universe, is here; and here Marston will find the secret which can make him lord of creation, ruler of the very stars.

B169.   **"The Chee-Chalker."**   *Five Novels Monthly*, Vol. 65, No. 15, July-Aug. 1947: 84-113.

b.   Los Angeles: Author Services, Inc., 1992, leather, 129p. (See A52.)

The heiress to a bankrupt halibut fishing fleet, a missing government man, an FBI agent and a string of corpses which are dismissed as "accidental drownings," lead to a murderous heroin smuggling ring.

B170.   **"The End is Not Yet."**   *Astounding Science Fiction*, Part 1, Vol. 39, No. 6, Aug. 1947: 6-55; Part 2, Vol. 40, No. 1, Sept. 1947: 110-62; Part 3, Vol. 40, No. 2, Oct. 1947: 107-62.

b.   as *I guerrieri del tempo*. Bologna: Libra Editrice, 1982, cloth. [Italian] (See A26.)

c.   Scheduled for publication in book form by Author Services, Inc., in Spring 1999. (See AA62.)

In a dangerous post-atomic world, a conspiracy to provoke a nuclear war between the superpowers is opposed, and ultimately defeated, by a coalition of nuclear scientists led by Charles Martel and his closest allies, his own son, and Le Chat a Faim (the Cat Is Hungry), the writer and adventurer who tells the story.

B171.   **"Killer's Law."**   *New Detective Magazine*, Vol. 10, No. 3, Sept. 1947: 96+.

b.   Scheduled for publication in book form by Author Services, Inc., in Summer 1994. (See AA3.)

A straight-shooting Nevada sheriff mysteriously finds badlands in the middle of Washington, D.C.—when a senator is killed and the sheriff is accused of his murder.

B172. **"Ole Doc Methuselah."** (Rene Lafayette) *Astounding Science Fiction*, Vol. 40, No. 2, Oct. 1947:

b. *Astounding Science Fiction*, Vol. 6, No. 6, Oct. 1948: 2-18. United Kingdom.

c. as "Gamle Doktor Methusalem." *Häpna!* Vol. 2, No. 5. Jönköping: Grafiska Forloget, paper, May 1955. [Swedish]

d. *Ole Doc Methuselah*. Austin: Theta Press, 1970, 1-35. First hardcover edition. Collection includes: "Ole Doc Methuselah," "Her Majesty's Aberration," "The Expensive Slaves," "The Great Air Monopoly," "Plague," "A Sound Investment," and "Ole Mother Methuselah." (See A16.)

e. *Ole Doc Methuselah*. New York: Daw Books, 1970, paper, 7-43. Collection.

f. *Ole Doc Methuselah*. Los Angeles: Bridge Publications, Inc., 1992, cloth, 1-52. Collection.

g. East Grinstead: New Era Publications, Ltd., United Kingdom, 1993, cloth, 270p.

h. London: Book Club Associates, 1993, cloth, 270p.

i. as *Doc Mathusalem*. Paris: Presses de la Cité and New Era Publications International ApS, paper, 1993. Collection. [French]

j. Scheduled for publication in book form by Author Services, Inc., in Summer 1997. (See AA39.)

Ole Doc Methuselah is one of 600 elite, Soldier of Light Immortals, who have dedicated themselves to the preservation of mankind, combatting disease, corruption, and desperate perversities of human behavior along the intergalactic spaceways. With his devoted companion, the four-armed, one-meter-high, gypsum-eating, book-reading Hippocrates, Doc lands on the planet Spico, initially to do some fishing. But instead—ignoring the codes of authority under which he operates—Doc finds himself administering summary justice to a man who has heartlessly swindled the inhabitants of the city. When a girl discovers that Ole Doc is 700 years old, her infatuation with him ends abruptly, and Doc and Hippocrates decamp for a new destination.

Notes: First in a series of seven stories about the most famous Soldier of Light, collectively entitled "Ole Doc Methuselah." Only the first story in the series carries that specific name. The other stories are: "The Expensive Slaves" (B173); "Her Majesty's Aberration" (B174); "The Great Air Monopoly" (B178); "Plague" (B185); "A Sound Investment" (B190), and "Ole Mother Methuselah" (B203). (Also see Q4.)

B173. **"The Expensive Slaves."**   (Rene Lafayette) *Astounding Science Fiction*, Vol. 40, No. 3, Nov. 1947: 63-75.

b.   as "De Dyrbara Slavarna." *Hapna!* Vol. 2, No. 10, Oct. 1955: 81-93. [Swedish]

c.   *Ole Doc Methuselah.* Austin: Theta Press, 1970, 52-65. Collection. (See A16.)

d.   *Ole Doc Methuselah.* New York: Daw Books, 1970, paper, 61-74. Collection.

e.   as "Gefährliche Sklaven," in *Doktor Methusalem*, Terra Astra No. 135, Pabel Verlag, Mar. 1974. Collection. [German]

f.   *Ole Doc Methuselah.* Los Angeles: Bridge Publications, Inc., 1992, cloth, 79-100. Collection.

g.   as *Doc Mathusalem.* Paris: Presses de la Cité and New Era Publications International ApS, 1993. Collection.

h.   East Grinstead: New Era Publications, Ltd., United Kingdom, 1993, cloth, 270p.

i.   London: Book Club Associates, 1993, cloth, 270p.

j.   Scheduled for publication in book form by Author Services, Inc., in Summer 1997. (See AA39.)

When Ole Doc Methuselah and his assistant,

Hippocrates, receive a message that the population of Dorab is being destroyed by a mysterious disease, they land on the planet. Doc discovers that George Arlington, an empire builder, has brought 900 workers from the planet Sirius 68, and their arrival heralded the onset of the fatal disease. He discovers that at their biannual festivals, the Sirians feast on a substance called Kufra, and sickness is unknown among them. Doc examines the tissues of the Dorab dead, then tells the empire builder they must send the Kufra eaters back to their home planet. Arlington at first resists—but faced with planetary quarantine, he relents. The inhabitants of Dorab are dying of cancer, induced by radiation from the Kufra eaters. Kufra, Doc reveals, is plutonium.

Notes: Second in the "Ole Doc Methuselah" series. (See Q4.)

B174.   "Her Majesty's Aberration."   (René Lafayette) *Astounding Science Fiction*, Vol. 50, No. 1, Mar. 1948: 126-40.

  b.   as "Doktorn och Hennes Majestat." *Hapna!* Vol. 2, No. 12, Dec. 1955: 3-19. [Swedish]

  c.   *Ole Doc Methuselah.* Austin: Theta Press, 1970, 36-51. Collection. (See A16.)

  d.   *Ole Doc Methuselah.* New York: DAW Books, 1970, paper, 44-60. Collection.

  e.   as "Die Rache einer Konigin," in *Doktor Methusalem*, Terra Astra No. 135, Pabel Verlag, Mar. 1974. Collection. [German]

  f.   *Ole Doc Methuselah.* Los Angeles: Bridge Publications, Inc., 1992, cloth, 53-77. Collection. (See A16.)

  g.   as *Doc Mathusalem.* Paris: Presses de la Cité and New Era Publications International ApS, 1993, paper. Collection. [French]

  h.   East Grinstead: New Era Publications, Ltd., United Kingdom, 1993, cloth, 270p.

  i.   London: Book Club Associates, 1993, cloth, 270p.

  j.   Scheduled for publication in book form by Author Services, Inc., in Summer 1997. (See AA39.)

When Ole Doc Methuselah lands on the planet Dorcon, he finds murderously hostile inhabitants, a mad queen with a face disfigured by an assassin's bomb, and her deposed tubercular son—the true king—and his wife and child imprisoned in the palace dungeon. Ole Doc restores the old queen's beauty and sanity, and puts the son back on his rightful throne.

Notes: Third in the "Ole Doc Methuselah" series. (See Q4.)

B175.   **"The Obsolete Weapon."**   *Astounding Science Fiction,* Vol. 41, No. 3, May 1948, 48-63.

b.   *Astounding Science Fiction,* Vol. 6, No. 9, Apr. 1949. United Kingdom.

c.   Scheduled for publication in book form by Author Services, Inc., in Summer 1994. (See AA4.)

An American soldier in modern Rome finds himself jailed for desertion after an "obsolete" fountain pen-like device that alters time transports him back to the Rome of Nero as a gladiator in the Colosseum.

B176.   **"The Magic Quirt."**   *The Rio Kid Western Magazine,* Vol. 16, No. 3, June 1948: 68-78. Canada.

b.   Scheduled for publication in book form by Author Services, Inc., in Fall 1995. (See AA19.)

When a ranch cook saves an Aztec family from bandits, they give him a silver quirt with magical properties that enable him to perform extraordinary deeds of courage. It's only later—after his heroics—that he discovers the quirt is just a souvenir, worth $2.50.

B177.   **"When Shadows Fall."**   *Startling Stories,* Vol. 17, No. 3, July 1948: 83-92.

b.   as "Cuando Caen Las Sombras." *Los Cuentos Fantasticos Magazine,* Vol. 1, No. 2, July 15 1948. [Spanish]

c.   in *Men Against The Stars.* (Anthology, edited by Martin Greenberg.) New York: Gnome Press, 1950, 335-351.

d.　in *Men Against The Stars.* London: Grayson & Grayson, 1951, 237-253.

e.　in *Men Against The Stars.* New York: Pyramid Books, 1957, 180-191.

f.　in *Men Against The Stars.* New York: Pyramid Publications, 1963, 180-191.

g.　*Science Fiction Yearbook No. 4.* New York: Popular Library, 1970, 55+.

h.　*Histoires Galactiques.* France: Le Livre de Poche, 1974. [French]

i.　as "Altraterra, 2499: Il crepuscolo dell'impero." *L'impero dei Mille Soli.* Bologna: Libra Editrice, 1981, cloth. Collection. (See A25.) [Italian]

j.　Scheduled for publication in book form by Author Services, Inc., in Summer 1999. (See AA63.)

Far in the future, the earth faces the prospects of slow environmental death, or more immediate destruction from the fleets of the myriad colonial civilizations spawned by Earth among the galaxies. Three missions are dispatched to solicit help for the home planet from these new worlds; two out of the three missions return with grimly pessimistic reports. But when the colonial fleets do land, they come with a braver purpose:

"So we have come here, these combined forces, to make the land green again, to replace the oceans, to rebuild the atmosphere, to make the rivers run, to put fish in the streams, and game in the hills."

Notes: The first in a "Future History" cycle of nine stories collectively titled "The Conquest of Space." The other stories in the series include: "Forbidden Voyage" (B181); "The Magnificent Failure" (B183); "The Incredible Destination" (B188); "The Unwilling Hero" (B191); "Beyond the Black Nebula" (B194); "The Emperor of the Universe" (B199); "The Last Admiral" (B206), and "Tough Old Man" (B216). (See also Q1.)

B178. **"The Great Air Monopoly."** (Rene Lafayette) *Astounding Science Fiction*, Vol. 42, No. 1, Sept. 1948: 71-99.

b. *Astounding Science Fiction*, Vol. 6, No. 8, Feb. 1949: 34-48. Great Britain.

c. *Ole Doc Methuselah.* Clearwater, FL: Theta Press, 1970, 66-97. Collection. (See A16.)

d. *Ole Doc Methuselah.* New York: Daw Books, 1970, paper, 75-108. Collection.

e. as "Das Luftmonopol," in *Doktor Methusalem*, Terra Astra No. 135, Pabel Verlag, Mar. 1974. Collection. [German]

f. *Ole Doc Methuselah.* Los Angeles: Bridge Publications, Inc., 1992, 101-148. Collection.

g. as *Doc Mathusalem.* Paris: Presses de la Cité and New Era Publications France ApS, 1993. Collection. [French]

h. New Era Publications, United Kingdom, Ltd., 1993, cloth, 270p.

i. Book Club Associates London: 1993, cloth, 270p.

j. Scheduled for publication in book form by Author Services, Inc., in Summer 1997. (See AA39.)

Ole Doc Methuselah and his companion, Hippocrates, discover that a man named Tolliver has monopolized the air on the planet Arphon, taxing the inhabitants tyrannically for making the air breathable. The Soldier of Light uncovers the truth—an atmosphere contaminated with ragweed—and exposes Tolliver's scheme to control the planet.

Notes: Fourth in the "Ole Doc Methuselah" series. (See Q4.)

B179. **"240,000 Miles Straight Up."** *Thrilling Wonder Stories*, Vol. 33, No. 2, Dec. 1948: 42-57.

b. in *Fantasy Short Stories,* Vol. 1, Los Angeles: Author Services, Inc., 1993, leather, 1-62. (See A62.)

A renegade Russian general seizes the moon—"240,000 miles straight up"—for a potential military base, menacing the United States. First Lieutenant Cannon Gray, in defiance of presidential directives, successfully thwarts the general's plot and defeats him in a final battle.

B180.   **"Stacked Bullets."**   *Famous Western Magazine,* Vol. 9, No. 6, Dec. 1948: 30-39.

b.   Scheduled for publication in book form by Author Services, Inc., in Fall 1995. (See AA19.)

Charley Montgomery has the only land around with water on it. When he sells it for needed cash only to lose the money in a fixed poker game and the new owners start charging the other ranchers for water, Charley takes appropriate steps to rectify the situation in a shootout, and to recover his lost poke.

B181.   **"Forbidden Voyage."**   (Rene Lafayette) *Startling Stories,* Vol. 18, No. 3, Jan. 1949: 142-50.

b.   *Future Science Fiction Magazine,* Vol. 1, No. 2, Nov. 1953: 55-66. Australia.

c.   as "Altraterra, 1953: La conquista della luna." *L'impero dei Mille Soli.* Bologna: Libra Editrice, 1981. Italy. Collection. (See A25.) [Italian]

d.   Scheduled for publication in book form by Author Services, Inc., in Summer 1999. (See AA63.)

George Carlyle knows how to get to the moon—but conscientious folk in authority do their best to prevent him. When he does make it there and back, his feat goes unheralded.

Notes: The second in "The Conquest of Space" series. (See Q1.)

B182.   **"Gunman!"**   *Famous Western Magazine,* Vol. 10, No. 1, Feb. 1949: 8-28.

b.   Scheduled for publication in book form by Author Services, Inc., in Spring 1998. (See AA48.)

With three days left to save his badge, the marshal of Deadlight cleverly prevents the bank from being robbed.

B183. **"TheMagnificentFailure."** (Rene Lafayette) *Startling Stories*, Vol. 19, No. 1, Mar. 1949: 104-114.

b. as "Altraterra, 1981: La conquista di marte." *L'impero dei mille soli.* Bologna: Libra Editrice, 1981, cloth. Collection. (See A25.) [Italian]

c. Scheduled for publication in book form by Author Services, Inc., in Summer 1999. (See AA63.)

Jonathan Bates, the legendary "Father of Exploration," reaches the moon, discovers George Carlyle has preceded him, then takes off for Mars and Venus and successfully returns. When subsequent spaceflights end disastrously, Bates builds a bigger ship, takes on a little boy and his dog as companion voyagers, and leaves Earth, never to return.

Notes: Third in "The Conquest of Space" series. (See Q1.)

B184. **"The Gunner from Gehenna."** *Giant Western*, Vol. 3, No. 2, Apr. 1949: 149-59.

b. Scheduled for publication in book form by Author Services, Inc., in Summer 1998. (See AA53.)

The renegade "Gunner" returns, steals the miners' gold and vanishes into the desert with the deputy sheriff in angry pursuit.

B185. **"Plague!"** (Rene Lafayette) *Astounding Science Fiction*, Vol. 43, No. 2, Apr. 1949: 6-33.

b. *Astounding Science Fiction*, Vol. 6, No. 11, Sept. 1949: 3-18. United Kingdom.

c. as "Farsoten." *Hapna!* Vol. 4, No. 3, Apr. 15 1957. [Swedish]

d. as "Die Kampfer des Lichts." *Terra Utopische Romane No. 512.* Rastatt: Moewig Verlag, 1967. Collection. [German]

e. *Ole Doc Methuselah.* Austin: Theta Press, 1970, 98-125. Collection. (See A16.)

f.   *Ole Doc Methuselah.* New York: Daw Books, 1970, paper, 109-138. Collection.

g.   as "L'epidemia." *Nova SF No. 40*, Bologna: Libra Editrice, July 1979, and Feb. 1980, paper. (See A22.) [Italian]

h.   *Ole Doc Methuselah.* Los Angeles: Bridge Publications, Inc., 1992, 149-190. Collection.

i.   East Grinstead, New Era Publications Ltd., United Kingdom, 1993, cloth, 270p.

j.   London: Book Club Associates, 1993, cloth, 270p.

k.   as *Doc Mathusalem.* Paris: Presses de la Cité and New Era Publications France, 1993. Collection. [French]

l.   Scheduled for publication in book form by Author Services, Inc., in Summer 1997. (See AA39.)

A spaceship, with an epidemic aboard, is ordered back into space, and ultimately lands on the third habitable planet of Sirius, communicating the "plague" to the local inhabitants. Ole Doc Methuselah saves the ship and its environs from being destroyed, and identifies the "plague" as an ancient—but totally unfamiliar—disease: measles.

Notes: Fifth in the "Ole Doc Methuselah" series. (See Q4.)

B186. **"Gun Boss of Tumbleweed."** *Thrilling Western*, Vol. 59, No. 1, Apr. 1949: 13-34.

b.   *Thrilling Western,* Autumn 1949: 13-34. United Kingdom.

c.   Scheduled for publication in book form by Author Services, Inc., in Spring 1997. (See AA36.)

Forced to act as a gunhawk for the man he hates bitterly, Mart Kincaid brings matters to a fiery Colt showdown.

B187. **"The Conroy Diary."** (Rene Lafayette) *Astounding Science Fiction*, Vol. 43, No. 3, May 1949: 134-43.

b.   *Astounding Science Fiction*, Vol. 7, No. 1, Jan. 1950:

59+. United Kingdom.

Mallory Fitz explores new worlds to open up the universe for mankind. When he writes a book about his travels, which becomes an instant bestseller, he's hit with a fraud case—and a gigantic tax bill!

B188. **"The Incredible Destination."** (Rene Lafayette) *Startling Stories*, Vol. 19, No. 2, May 1949: 96-115.

b.   as "Altraterra 2001: Oltre i confini del sistema solare." *L'impero dei mille soli*. Bologna: Libra Editrice, 1981, cloth. Collection. (See A25.) [Italian]

James Dolan, using a magnetic space drive, reaches a distant solar system, returns to Earth with proof in the form of photos—unfortunately damaged—and mineral samples that are dismissed as laughable. Though his claims are discredited, Dolan in fact finds a way to the distant stars long before mankind begins to make the same journey.

Notes: Fourth in "The Conquest of Space" series. (See Q1.)

B189. **"Battle of Wizards."** *Fantasy Book Magazine*, Vol. 1, No. 5, 1949: 4-13.

b.   in *Triton*. Los Angeles: Fantasy Publishing Co., 1949, 157-172. (See A5.)

c.   *Quintette*. (Anthology.) Los Angeles: Fantasy Publishing Co., 1949, 157-172.

d.   *Spaceway Stories of the Future*, Vol. 1, No. 2, Feb. 1954: 90-107.

e.   *Spaceway Stories of the Future*, Vol. 1, No. 3, Feb. 1954: 93-103. United Kingdom.

f.   *Spaceway Science Fiction*, Vol. 4, No. 2, May-June 1969: 35-47.

g.   in *Wizards and Warlocks*. (Anthology, edited by Vic Ghidalia.) New York: Manor Books, 1972, 61-73.

h.   Scheduled for publication in book form by Author Services, Inc., in Spring 1995. (See AA12.)

The Mineralogy Service wants to mine the fuel catalyst crystals on Deltoid, but the primitive natives object. With the issue to be resolved in a battle of magic between resourceful civil officer Angus McBane and the natives' great wizard, McBane resorts—with mystifying success—to a ruse of robotry.

B190.   **"A Sound Investment."**   (Rene Lafayette) *Astounding Science Fiction*, Vol. 43, No. 4, June 1949: 36-57.

　　b.   *Astounding Science Fiction*, Vol. 6, No. 12, Oct. 1949: 15-26. United Kingdom.

　　c.   as "Die Kampfer Des Lichts." *Terra Utopische Romane No. 512*. Rastatt: Moewig-Verlag, 1967. [German]

　　d.   *Ole Doc Methuselah*. Austin: Theta Press, 1970, 126-149. Collection. (See A16.)

　　e.   *Ole Doc Methuselah*. New York: Daw Books, 1970, paper, 139-163. Collection.

　　f.   as "La macchina infernale." *Nova SF No. 41*. Bologna: Libra Editrice, 1980, paper. (See A23.) [Italian]

　　g.   *Ole Doc Methuselah*. Los Angeles: Bridge Publications, Inc., 1992, 191-226. Collection.

　　h.   East Grinstead: New Era Publications, Ltd., United Kingdom, 1993, cloth, 270p.

　　i.   London: Book Club Associates, 1993, cloth, 270p.

　　j.   as *Doc Mathusalem*. Paris: Presses de la Cité and New Era Publications France, 1993. Collection. [French]

　　k.   Scheduled for publication in book form by Author Services, Inc., in Summer 1997. (See AA39.)

The Soldier of Light summarily fires Hippocrates for carelessness, discovers a plot to destroy all life in the Fomalton planetary system, the man behind the plot, and a subsonic weapon that kills by inducing lethally paralyzing fear. Ole Doc Methuselah reduces the plotter to pulpy helplessness in a fistfight, and takes Hippocrates back.

Notes: Sixth in the "Ole Doc Methuselah" series. (See

Q4.)

B191. **"The Unwilling Hero."** (Rene Lafayette) *Startling Stories*, Vol. 19, No. 3, July 1949: 98-124.

b. as "Altraterra 2099: Al di la del centauro." *L'impero dei mille soli.* Bologna: Libra Editrice, 1981. Collection. (See A25.) [Italian]

c. Scheduled for publication in book form by Author Services, Inc., in Summer 1999. (See AA64.)

It's not hunger for personal glory or adventure that propels Vic Hardin into the far reaches of outer space on a daring rescue mission: he's been ordered out there by his editor.

Notes: Fifth in "The Conquest of Space" series.

B192. **"Johnny, the Town Tamer."** *Famous Western Magazine*, Vol. 10, No. 4, Aug. 1949: 39+.

b. *Western Short Stories, Vol. 3.* Los Angeles: Author Services, Inc., 1993. leather. (See A66.)

Texas Johnny frustrates an attempt to kill him, and runs off the man who tried to do it.

B193. **"A Matter of Matter."** *Astounding Science Fiction*, Vol. 43, No. 6, Aug. 1949: 59-72.

b. *Astounding Science Fiction*, Vol. 7, No. 6, Oct. 1950: 53-60. United Kingdom.

c. Scheduled for publication in book form by Author Services, Inc., in Summer 1995. (See AA17.)

There have been small-time real estate swindlers, but in a galactic economy, the man who sells planets does it on a stupendous scale: like selling the unwary customer a planet he can't even sit down on. It's all a matter of negative matter.

B194. **"Beyond the Black Nebula."** *Startling Stories*, Vol. 20, No. 1, Sept. 1949: 126-36.

b. Scheduled for publication in book form by Author Services, Inc., in Summer 1999. (See AA64.)

Writer Anthony Twain—accused of being a charlatan—

can restore his reputation only by going where no man has gone before: through the forbidding Coal Sack in space.

Notes: Sixth in "The Conquest of Space" series. (See Q1.)

B195. **"Guns of Mark Jardine."**   *Western Action Magazine*, Vol. 13, No. 6, Sept. 1949: 6-65.

    b.   Sydney: Malian Press Pty, Ltd., ca. 1950, cloth. Australia.

    c.   Los Angeles: Author Services, Inc., 1991, 225p. leather. (See A7.)

Young Mark Jardine returns to the Arizona Territory to avenge the torture and death of his close friend, a landowner ambushed after striking gold. Faced with the task of single-handedly tracking down the unknown killers—and protecting the life of the landowner's beautiful daughter— Jardine sets out on a lone, perilous course of retributive justice.

B196. **"Blood on His Spurs."**   *Thrilling Western*, Vol. 60, No. 3, Sept. 1949: 32-42.

    b.   *Western Short Stories,* Vol. 4, Los Angeles: Author Services, Inc., 1993, 111-52, leather. (See A69.)

Two old antagonists—Bates and McLean—bury their feud long enough to save McLean's son and wipe out a band of rustlers.

B197. **"The Automagic Horse."**   *Astounding Science Fiction*, Vol. 44, No. 2, Oct. 1949: 75-111.

    b.   Los Angeles: Bridge Publications, Inc., 1994, cloth. Art by Scott E. Sutton.

    c.   Scheduled for publication in book form by Author Services, Inc., in Fall 1997. (See AA44.)

"Gadget" O'Dowd builds an "automagic" mechanical facsimile of the great racehorse *Man-of-War* for a movie, finally races it—and wins—at Santa Anita, then equips it with an anti-gravity device: all to deceive a beautiful accountant and conceal the secret building of a spaceship.

B198. **"The Planet Makers."** *Thrilling Wonder Stories*, Vol. 35, No. 1, Oct. 1949: 123-28.

b. Scheduled for publication in book form by Author Services, Inc., in Summer 1994. (See AA4.)

Sleepy McGee isn't too accomplished as a poker player —but he has an ace in the hole for building new planets.

B199. **"The Emperor of the Universe."** (Rene Lafayette) *Startling Stories*, Vol. 20, No. 2, Nov. 1949: 132-41.

b. as "Altraterra, 2284: L'imperatore dell'universo." *L'impero dei mille soli*. Bologna: Libra Editrice, 1981, cloth. Collection. (See A25.) [Italian]

c. Scheduled for publication in book form by Author Services, Inc., in Summer 1999. (See AA64.)

When Erskine encounters "The Emperor of the Universe," again, the old man is dead, lying within yards of his disreputable old spacecraft and its extraordinary cargo— the seeds the "Emperor" has been sowing among the barren planets in preparation for man's coming among the distant stars.

Notes: Seventh in "The Conquest of Space" series. (See Q1.)

B200. **"Man for Breakfast."** (Winchester Remington Colt) *Texas Rangers Magazine*, Vol. 36, No. 3, Nov. 1949: 76-82.

Being robbed, almost hung, dry-gulched and wounded, is all in a day's work for young Johnny Purcell. (See A69.)

B201. **"Stranger in Town."** *Famous Western Magazine*, Vol. 10, No. 6, Dec. 1949: 46+.

b. *Western Short Stories Vol. 1*. Los Angeles: Author Services, Inc., 1992, leather, 29-58. (See A56.)

New in Dry Creek himself, Zeke Tomlin knows someone will ride in one day, looking for him. When the corrupt marshal arrives in pursuit, Zeke must deal with him and the town.

B202. **"A Can of Vacuum."** *Astounding Science Fiction*, Vol. 44, No. 4, Dec. 1949: 81-92.

b.   *Astounding Science Fiction*, Vol. 7, No. 3, May 1950: 30-35. United Kingdom.

c.   as "En burk vakuum." *Hapna!* Nov. 1958: 15-28. [Swedish]

d.   Scheduled for publication in book form by Author Services, Inc., in Fall 1998. (See AA55.)

A cosmic practical joke backfires when Bigby Pettigrew actually brings back the "rudey rays" he was sent out to get—as a joke.

B203.   "Ole Mother Methuselah."   (Rene Lafayette) *Astounding Science Fiction*, Vol. 44, No. 5, Jan.1950: 80-104.

b.   *Astounding Science Fiction*, Vol. 7, No. 5, Aug. 1950: 47-64. United Kingdom.

c.   as "Gamla Mor Metusalem." *Hapna!* Vol. 6, No. 5, May 1959. [Swedish]

d.   as "Mama Methusalem," in *Die Kampfer Des Lichts*, Terra Utopische Romane No. 512, Moewig Verlag, 1967. [German]

e.   *Ole Doc Methuselah*. Austin: Theta Press, 1970, 150-175. Collection. (See A16.)

f.   *Ole Doc Methuselah*. New York: Daw Books, 1970, paper, 164-190. Collection.

g.   as "Doc und der Kindergarten," in *Doktor Methusalem*, Terra Astra No. 135, Pabel Verlag, Mar. 1974. Collection. [German]

h.   as "L'ultima avventura del soldato della luce." [The Last Adventure of the Soldier of Light] *Nova SF No. 39*, Bologna: Libra Editrice, 1978, paper. (See A21.) [Italian]

i.   *Ole Doc Methuselah*. Los Angeles: Bridge Publications, Inc., 1992, 227-270. Collection.

j.   East Grinstead: New Era Publications, Ltd., United Kingdom, 1993, cloth, 270p.

k.   London: Book Club Associates, 1993, cloth, 270p.

l.   as *Doc Mathusalem*. Paris: Presses de la Cité and New Era Publications France, 1993. Collection. [French]

m.   Scheduled for publication in book form by Author Services, Inc., in Summer 1997. (See AA39.)

It's one thing when lions are bred on planet Gorgon as an environmental measure to deal with the feral cat beast population, but when a shipment of human embryos mysteriously finds its way into the lion breeding vats, the result is a race of beings with superhuman strength and powers. Ole Doc Methuselah discovers the alien origin of the embryos, then induces an allergy in the superbeings that changes their cell structure and their behavior.

Notes: Seventh and last in the "Ole Doc Methuselah" series. (See Q4.)

B204.   **"Hoss Tamer."**   *Thrilling Western*, Vol. 66, No. 3, Jan. 1950: 109-16.

b.   *Western Short Stories, Vol. 1.* Los Angeles: Author Services, Inc., 1992, leather, 1-24. (See A56.)

An ex-circus horse trainer foils the Gopher Hole Gang's attempt to rob the Wells Fargo train by whistling at their horses.

Notes: See also F11 for 1958 adaptation of the story for "The Tales of Wells Fargo" television series.

B205.   **"Beyond All Weapons."**   *Super Science Stories*, Vol. 6, No. 2, Jan. 1950: 70-80.

b.   *Super Science Stories Vol. 6*, No. 2, Jan. 1950: 70-80. United Kingdom and Canada.

c.   as "Bortom Tid och Rum." [Beyond Time and Space] *Hapna!* Sept. 1961: 81+. [Swedish]

d.   in *Perry Rhodan #93: Vagabond of Space.* Anthology. New York: Ace Books, 1976 133-153.

e.   Scheduled for publication in book form by Author

Services, Inc., in Summer 1994. (See AA4.)

When fugitive colonists return to Earth from the stars to administer retributive justice to those who had driven them into exile, they find man's most pitiless enemy, time itself, has done their work for them.

Notes: Pioneer story in modern science fiction for its original use of Einstein's time dilation theory. Hubbard's explanation from "Beyond All Weapons":

"As mass approaches the speed of light . . . it approaches infinity. And, as mass approaches infinity, time approaches zero. It was only nine days back from Alpha. But in those nine days, six thousand years have passed by Earth."

See also, "To the Stars" (B207) for a fuller development of this theme.

B206. **"The Last Admiral."**   (Rene Lafayette) *Startling Stories*, Vol. 20, No. 3, Jan. 1950: 112-25.

   b.   as "Altraterra, 2175: La conquista dei grandi spazi." *L'impero dei mille soli.* Bologna: Libra Editrice, 1981, cloth. Collection. (See A25.) [Italian]

   c.   Scheduled for publication in book form by Author Services, Inc., in Summer 1999. (See AA64.)

The Admiral saves the Navy from extinction by intercepting a powerful pirate space vessel—at the sacrifice of his own life.

Notes: Eighth in "The Conquest of Space" series. (See Q1.)

B207. **"To the Stars."**   *Astounding Science Fiction,* Part 1, Vol. 44, No. 6, Feb. 1950: 5-45; Part 2, Vol. 45, No. 1, Mar. 1950: 78-123.

   b.   as *Return to Tomorrow.* New York: Ace Books, 1954, paper, 157p. (See A11.)

   c.   as *Gefangen in Raum und Zeit.* Utopia Spitzenklasse #612: Honne-Verlag N., 1956, paper. [German]

   d.   *Utyo Koro.* Translated by Yuichi Ohama. Tokyo: Gen Gen Sha, 1956. [Japanese]

e.   *Return to Tomorrow.* Glasgow: Hamilton & Co., Panther Book, 1957, cloth.

f.   as *Ritorno al domani.* Translated by Tom Arno. Urania #147, Milano: Arnoldo Mondadori Editore, 1957. [Italian]

g.   as *Retour a Demain.* Translated by A. Audiberti. Anticipation No. 98 Paris: Editions Fleuve Noir, 1957, paper. [French]

h.   as *Aterkomst Till Morgondagen.* Stockholm: Wennerbergs Förlaget AB, 1957, paper. [Swedish]

i.   *Gefangen in Raum und Zeit.* Terra No. 60. Moewig Verlag, Nov. 1958: 1+. [German]

j.   *Fremtiden Tur-Retur.* Translated by Jorgen Rothenburg. Rumfart Serien #1. Copenhagen: Winthers Forlag, 1958, paper. [Danish]

k.   as *Ritorno al domani.* Urania #394., Verona: Mondadori, 1965, paper. [Italian]

l.   as *Ritorno al domani.* Oscar Mondadori #512. Verona: Mondadori, 1974. [Italian]

m.   *Aterkomst Till Morgondagen.* Translated by Bengte Oste. Vannersborg: Delta Forlaget AB, 1974. [Swedish]

n.   *Return to Tomorrow.* New York & London: Garland Publishing, cloth, 1975, 157p.

o.   as *Ritorno al Domani.* Bologna: Libra Editrice, 1981, paper. [Italian]

p.   Scheduled for publication in book form by Author Services, Inc., in Winter 1995. (See AA9.)

They are the outcasts of time—space voyagers among the distant stars, rootless exiles from a world they left that has aged and passed away even as they remain young. Alan Conroy seeks understanding of his mission in life, in a world—unfamiliar, inhospitable—altered by the relative passage of time; at the end, he is the new commander of the symbolically named starship *Hound of Heaven.*

Notes: Hubbard's extended and searching exploration of the time dilation theme. Seminal in scope, technical depth and influence. See: "Beyond All Weapons" (B205); also entries for Faster Than Light, Spaceships, Time Travel, *The Science Fiction Encyclopedia*, passim, op. cit. (L22).

B208. **"Devil's Manhunt."** *Famous Western Magazine*, Vol. 11, No. 1, Feb. 1950: 8-23.

    b. Scheduled for publication in book form by Author Services, Inc., in Fall 1994. (See AA6.)

Jumped by a pair of bandits, Tim Beckdolt is forced to work his claim at gun-point, knowing when his work is done, his reward will be a bullet.

B209. **"The Kingslayer."** *Two Complete Science-Adventure Books*, No. 1, Winter 1950, 102-44.

    b. *The Kingslayer.* Collection. Los Angeles: Fantasy Publishing Co., 1949: 11-132.

    c. *From Death to the Stars.* Collection. Los Angeles: Fantasy Publishing Co., 1950, 11-132.

    d. as "Il regicida." in *La trama tra le nubi. Urania #105*, Mondadori, Nov. 17 1955, paper. (See A14.) [Italian]

    e. *Rebell der Milchstrasse.* Utopia Zukunftsromane #105. Rastatt: Erich Pabel Verlag, 1957. [German]

    f. *Seven Steps to the Arbiter.* Chatsworth, CA: Major Books, 1975, 7-24. Collection. (See A18.)

    g. Bologna: Libra Editrice, 1980, cloth. [Italian]

    h. *The Kingslayer.* Los Angeles: Author Services, Inc., 1991, 179p, leather. (See A6.)

A brilliant young engineer is kidnapped by a member of a revolutionary group, told of the existence of "The Arbiter," the person responsible for all the world's evil, and sent on a mission to find and destroy him. Discovery of the true identity of the Arbiter, and of the real purpose of the engineer's mission—and destiny—provides an ending of startling dimensions.

B210. **"Greed."** *Astounding Science Fiction*, Vol. 45, No. 2, Apr. 1950: 53-68.

    b.   Scheduled for publication in book form by Author Services, Inc., in Winter 1999. (See AA57.)

Far in the future, two Earth empires—separated physically by a weapon-projected "wall of space"—are poised for war. A space-navy lieutenant becomes a space raider, turns the weapon against the evil empire and destroys it.

B211. **"The No-Gun Man."** *Thrilling Western*. Vol. 62, No. 2, May 1950: 11-38.

    b.   *Thrilling Western*, Vol. 4, No. 3, Nov. 1950: 2-23. United Kingdom.

    c.   Scheduled for publication in book form by Author Services, Inc., in Fall 1995. (See AA19.)

Monte Calhoun returns to Superstition, uncovers his father's killer, survives a murderous assault, and brings the guilty man and his three sons to stern justice.

B212. **"Vengeance is Mine!"** *Real Western Stories*, Vol. 16, No. 1, June 1950: 34-44.

    b.   *Western Short Stories, Vol. 3*. Los Angeles: Author Services, Inc., 1993. (See A66.)

Whitney administers harsh vengeance, only to find, with cruel irony, that he has killed unjustly.

B213. **"Battling Bolto."** *Thrilling Wonder Stories*, Vol. 36, No. 3, Aug. 1950: 84-92.

    b.   *Science Fiction Yearbook*. Anthology. New York: Popular Library, 1971: 29+.

    c.   Scheduled for publication in book form by Author Services, Inc., in Fall 1997. (See AA44.)

When a strong man pretends to be a robot named Battling Bolto to sell fake robots, and discovers his "boss" is a robot pretending to be human, it touches off a series of curious events, including a prison stint in the mines for Battling Bolto.

B214. **"Final Enemy."** *Super Science Stories*, Vol. 7, No. 2, Sept. 1950: 119-26.

b. *Super Science Stories*, Vol. 7, No. 2, Sept. 1950: 119+. Canada.

c. *Super Science Stories*, Vol. 7, No. 2, Sept. 1950: 60+. United Kingdom.

d. as "Der Feind." *Utopia SF Magazine No. 8*. Pabel Verlag, 1957: 40-47. [German]

e. Scheduled for publication in book form by Author Services, Inc., in Winter 1999. (See AA57.)

The threat of the mysterious invaders that have wiped out millions of people on two planets unites the nations of Earth and spurs collective space exploration. The invaders, paradoxically, prove to be from Earth, itself.

B215. **"The Masters of Sleep."** *Fantastic Adventures*, Vol. 12, No. 10, Oct. 1950: 6-83.

b. *Fantastic Adventures*, No. 5, ca. Jan. 1951: 6-83. United Kingdom.

c. *Fantastic Adventures Quarterly Reissue*, Vol. 9, No. 1, Spring 1951: 6-83.

d. *Schiavi del sonno & I signori del sonno. Slaves of Sleep and The Masters of Sleep.* Armenia Editrice, 1978, cloth. (See A20.) [Italian]

e. with "Slaves of Sleep." Los Angeles: Bridge Publications, Inc., 1993, cloth, 392p.

f. Scheduled for publication in book form by Author Services, Inc., in Summer 1998. (See AA52.)

An older Jan/Tiger and Alice/Wanna rediscover adventure and each other, and Jan/Tiger finally merges into a single entity—master of day and night, of the parallel worlds of sleep and waking.

Notes: Sequel to "Slaves of Sleep" (B134).

B216. **"Tough Old Man."** *Startling Stories*, Vol. 22, No. 2, Nov. 1950: 116-129.

    b. *Space Police*. Anthology, edited by Andre Norton. Cleveland and New York: World Press, 1956: 151-172.

    c. as "Altreterra, 2352: Nel fulgore dell'impero." *L'impero dei mille soli*. Bologna: Libra Editrice, 1981, cloth. Collection. (See A26.) [Italian]

    d. Scheduled for publication in book form by Author Services, Inc., in Spring 1995. (See AA12.)

Moffat is sent for final training under the Senior Constable of the Frontier Patrol, old Keno. When Moffat—subjected to severe tests—discovers why Keno doesn't feel extreme cold or heat, and never seems to eat, he succeeds the old policeman as senior constable.

Notes: Ninth and last story in "The Conquest of Space" series. (See Q1.)

B217. **"The Were-Human."** *Fantasy Book Enterprises Magazine*, Vol. 1, No. 1, Oct. 1981: 42-44.

    b. *Fantasy Short Stories*, Vol. 1, Los Angeles: Author Services, Inc., 1993, leather. (See A62.)

The metamorphosis of a human being into a "were-human"—a creature of murderous hate, not unlike a werewolf, that was human but is now something else. The title is a conscious play-on-words.

B218. **"He Found God."** *Meta SF Magazine*, Vol. 1, No. 1, Sept. 1982: 5-9.

    b. *Fantasy Short Stories*, Vol. 1. Los Angeles: Author Services, Inc., 1993, leather. (See A62.)

When Dr. Joshua Reynolds, the evangelist with an enormous galactic following, finds God, the corrupt and decadent galactic empire is doomed.

B219. **"Mariner's Mate."** *Ron: The Master Mariner*, Issue 1, Los

Angeles: Bridge Publications, Inc., June 1991: 15-33.

The captain of a disabled freighter and his only passenger—the obnoxiously spoiled daughter of the ship's owner—battle a torrential South Pacific typhoon together. (Previously unpublished.)

B220. **"Model Gentleman."** *Legacy*, Premiere issue, 1992. Los Angeles: Author Services, Inc.: 7-8.

When Sheila O'Mara tries to use a model gentleman of the theatre to help smooth away her boxer boyfriend's social rough-edges, she discovers to her delight that the gentleman is also a man of unexpectedly decisive action. (Previously unpublished.)

B221. **"Hired Assassin."** *Legacy*, Issue 2, 1992. Los Angeles: Author Services, Inc.: 7-8.

A sharpshooting old sheriff shrewdly—and terminally—turns the tables on three New York gangsters who unwittingly hire him to assassinate himself. (Previously unpublished.)

B222. **"Gift From Heaven."** *Ron: The Writer*, Issue 2, Bridge Publications, Inc., 1992: 18-37.

Two well-intentioned but cheerily intoxicated old space pirates—commandeering a space tug that can move asteroids around—decide to present Earth with another moon; but in the process, almost remove their beloved home planet from the solar system. (Previously unpublished.)

B223. **"The Secret of Skeleton Creek."** *Legacy*, Issue 3, 1993. Los Angeles: Author Services, Inc.: 7-10.

An old prospector's shack and the waters of Skeleton Creek conceal a secret that spells wealth for a desperate rancher, and defeat for his adversary, the ruthless boss of Gunsmoke. (Previously unpublished.)

BB. UNPUBLISHED FICTION

(Arranged alphabetically by genre and then by title. Dates are indicated only where verified.)

ADVENTURE

BB1. **"The Ace of Alcazar."** (a.k.a. **"War Correspondent"**)

Unable to get his news dispatches out of the war-torn city of Toledo, Spain, a war correspondent discovers after the battle that he himself has become headline news around the world.

BB2. **"At the Front."**

A war correspondent believes he has sent out an incorrect story about the outcome of a major battle, only to discover when he reaches the scene of the battle to verify it personally, that his version of the fray was right all along.

BB3. **"Banana Oil."**

A man deceptively puts oil on his property to make it more attractive to a prospective buyer—but the buyer isn't interested.

BB4. **"Banners of the Brave."**

An army private, bravely confused about what makes a hero, defeats the enemy in a single-handed encounter, getting and then happily losing a girl in the process.

BB5. **"Beating the Broadcasters."**

A banjo player convinces a radio station to let him play his music on the air for nothing. A scheme to ensure that people call in with requests goes awry—but real listeners call in anyway and he gets the job.

BB6. **"The Boat from Nowhere."**

An adventurer encounters a corpse, a private yacht, a fierce tiger, an equally fierce knife-wielding bearded man, and a cargo hold filled with wild animals, before rescuing the captain and his crew.

BB7. **"Clipped Wings."** (Holograph manuscript)

An aerial dogfight, in a European combat setting, is recounted by a pilot blinded during the battle.

BB8. **"Death's Lieutenant."**

A legionnaire in North Africa, deceived by the death of his friend into deserting his post, striking an officer and fleeing to the enemy, foils a plot to disgrace him and is vindicated.

BB9. **"Diamonds are Dangerous."**

Unjustly accused, an American fugitive in Africa stumbles across a dying man, a cache of what he erroneously believes are diamonds and a wanted murderer who pursues him to get possession of the stones.

BB10. **"The Diplomat of Taranpang."** (a.k.a. **"Taranpang"**)

A U.S. Army engineer in the Philippines turns into an adroit diplomat when a reckless killing angers the local tribespeople.

BB11. **"Elephants on Wheels."**

A soldier of fortune helps the local inhabitants defeat the tanks—"elephants on wheels"—of an invading army.

BB12. **"Forest Fire."** (See also **"Forest Fire Fighter,"** BB13.)

A young man, who has run away from home because he has accidentally damaged the family car, helps put out a raging forest fire and earns enough money to pay for the automobile's damaged fender.

BB13. **"Forest Fire Fighter."**

This is a revision of "Forest Fire" above, BB12.

BB14. **"Fortress of the Dead."**

A daring, self-employed commercial pilot in North Africa, a fellow American and his pretty niece in grave danger, and precious gold hidden in a castle-fortress, lead to romance and a hair-raising escape by plane.

BB15. **"From the Seas!"**

A mutinous seaman and the crew of a merchant vessel turn pirate and capture a sloop, but are vanquished by its navigator and brought to justice.

BB16. **"Frozen Blood."** (a.k.a. **"The Golden Totem"**)

Falsely accused of murdering a miner for his gold, hounded by the real culprit, and near death from the cold and the snow, Ken Morane turns on his pursuer, then is freed by the Mounties for disposing of a wanted killer.

BB17. **"Ghost Gotha."**

An American fighter ace in World War I, taking to the air against a mysterious, giant Gotha bombing plane that can apparently hit targets with deadly accuracy in the dark, unravels an intricate plot and captures the "Ghost" ship and its supposedly dead pilot.

BB18. **"Ghosts of the Mitumbas."**

A river steamer captain and his hulking sidekick, a beautiful heiress who temporarily loses her sight, and a sinister army officer come together on a dangerous safari to write a new ending to an old Bantu legend.

BB19. **"The Great Wall of China."**

Seated in a watch tower on the Great Wall of China, the author lets his imagination play across great moments in the history of the wall.

BB20. **"Guns for Kiang."**

An adventurer in war-torn China rescues an American girl from enemy troops and two feuding warlords. They escape to freedom on his tramp steamer.

BB21. **"Hard-boiled Marine."**

A young marine complains loudly about a tough marine officer he has heard of but never met. To his chagrin—and deep regret—the man he is complaining to turns out to be the very officer he is complaining about.

BB22.   "He Didn't Come Back."

A dead fighter pilot is mourned in different ways by fellow fliers, friends and family.

BB23.   "High Danger."

A famed adventurer-pilot seeks both to regain the South American diamond mines once wrested from his father and to rescue the young woman he loves from an unwanted marriage.

BB24.   "The Last Frontier."

An engineer sent to his home town to complete the building of a dam succeeds in bringing needed water to the parched cattle country he grew up in, despite bitter opposition even from his own family.

BB25.   "Last Laughter."

Bert Colorado pursues practical joker Tommy Jackson for having stolen his beautiful girlfriend, only to discover that someone else has won the girl in the end.

BB26.   "The Lion Tamer."

A scheme to embarrass a lion tamer by pacifying his lion with a perfume-scented handkerchief backfires when the audience loves it, and the lion tamer and his act end up with star billing.

BB27.   "Meteors of Death."

World War I fighter pilot Bart Austin, after a bloody scuffle with his own commanding officer, goes after the enemy squadron that wiped out his wingmates with murderous incendiary bullets.

BB28.   "No Quarter."

A ruthless mercenary pilot is taught a powerful lesson in mercy by the flier he has shot down.

BB29.   "Once a Turkey Short."

Old Daniel outfoxes the canny, covetous, cantankerous Mr. Noah—and saves his small plot of land in the bargain —when a flock of turkeys comes up one gobbler short.

BB30. **"Patent Medicine."**

When a man offers a potion that heals dogs as a treatment for human ailments, the city first denounces then rewards him.

BB31. **"Peace."**

To earn the respect of the African villagers and win an ironic peace, Terry O'Flanning first has to beat his formidable native adversary.

BB32. **"Rat Trap."**

A World War I fighter pilot is suspected of fatally shooting his wingmate, until a fistfight with his commanding officer exposes the place in the wall where rats have cached his personal effects—and his dead wingmate's suicide note.

BB33. **"The Rendezvous."**

The town's most responsible citizen and only undertaker decides, at last, to renounce his humdrum life and follow his adventurous brother on a gold-seeking expedition to the Yucatan. But when a telegram arrives from there, the message is unexpected—and shocking.

BB34. **"Revolt in the Plaza."**

When the newest, revolutionary Santo Dominican government comes to power, an unemployed American mining engineer unexpectedly finds himself appointed to the president's cabinet.

BB35. **"Schemes Everyone Can Use Shooting Celebrities."**

(See "Shooting Celebrities" below, BB37.)

BB36. **"Shades of Captain Kidd."**

A map to Captain Kidd's legendary treasure on Mona Island leads two U.S. engineers in Puerto Rico to a hidden cache of a vastly different—but dangerously valuable—kind.

BB37.   **"Shooting Celebrities."**

Longer version of "Schemes..." above, BB35. In both versions, the same news photographer photographs the wrong person.

BB38.   **"Sinner Take All."**

The painfully young third mate of a China steamer discovers that dice can be crooked, waterfront bars can be dangerous, and not all chief engineers are honest.

BB39.   **"Sky Trap."**

False landing lights lead an air mail pilot with a pouch of valuable government papers into peril on the wrong side of the border.

BB40.   **"Stowaway Deluxe."**

A personable, quick-thinking young man charms his way aboard an ocean liner, outwits a bunch of gamblers trying to steal a set of pearls, and disembarks somewhat richer but as carefree as ever.

BB41.   **"Strategy."**

A dog enlists the help of other dogs to subdue the local canine bully.

BB42.   **"Strictly Confidential."**

A man buys up the land around the site of a proposed government dam, only to be duped into surrendering his claims.

BB43.   **"Suicide Preferred."**

Falsely accused of stealing a general's bankroll, faced with suicide or torture, a soldier of fortune in occupied China is exonerated when he captures the true culprit.

BB44.   **"Sultan O'Sullivan."**

An American soldier of fortune in North Africa and his reporter girlfriend become sultan and sultana when he uses disguise and a brilliant ruse to bring down a treacherous but powerful enemy.

BB45. **"Things That Pass in the Jungle."** (a.k.a. **"Completed Pass"**)

An injured, big-time professional football player saves the life of a fellow American and his own career, when he throws lethally accurate forward passes with coconuts, as if they were footballs, to drive off marauding bandits.

BB46. **"The Token of Torture."**

A resourceful reporter for the Oriental Press in China discovers the true identity of the Mysterious River Dragon, the man who has been ruthlessly robbing and then blowing up passenger ships.

BB47. **"The Typhoon Treasure."**

A hunt for a buried pirate treasure on Typhoon Island in the Philippines leads to rivalry, romance and sudden death.

BB48. **"War on Wheels."**

The decades-old "war on wheels"—violent accidents on the nation's highways—is the immediate issue in a brisk exchange of views between a powerful U.S. senator and an average American citizen with innovative ideas for solving problems.

BB49. **"Whispering Death."**

An American adventurer in the South Pacific overcomes deadly headhunters, poisonous snakes and a terrifying witch doctor to rescue his friend and retrieve a bag of precious pearls.

BB50. **"Winged Rescue."**

When a young woman pilot saves her father's cattle by flying food to them through a blinding snowstorm, she changes his mind about flying as a career.

BB51. **"The Wrecking Crew."**

A daredevil race car driver and his more cautious, safety-minded brother feud bitterly for years until a nearly-fatal accident during a dangerous crash test brings about a reconciliation.

MYSTERY/DETECTIVE

BB52. **"Brand of Cane."**

Convicted of crimes he did not commit, Bob Hoffman comes to grips with the man who framed him during a struggle in the deadly bowels of a sugar cane shredding machine.

BB53. **"Dash, the Reporter, Gets Fired."** (Holograph manuscript)

A cub reporter is duped by a rival into publishing the wrong story.

BB54. **"Death Caverns."**

A series of baffling cliffside murders is solved by a treasury agent.

BB55. **"A Demijohn Demon."** (Holograph manuscript)

Her superstitious dread of a witch doctor's grave frightens a woman to death.

BB56. **"Eye for an Eye."**

When John Masey takes final revenge on the hit-and-run driver who blinded him and crippled his young daughter, he makes a belated—and cruelly ironic—discovery.

BB57. **"Fangs of the Tiger."**

A bungling, corpulent police detective solves the mystery of the maharajah's missing false teeth and brings the most wanted criminal in New York City to justice.

BB58. **"Mixed Up Spies in China."** (Holograph manuscript)

Two British spies are duped by the man they are pursuing into unwittingly killing a fellow agent.

BB59. **"Murder at Pirate Castle."**

An FBI agent, posing as a private investigator, solves a series of mysterious "flame and blue smoke" murders at Pirate Castle and unmasks the pirate ghost of El Tiburon. Basis for the successful Columbia Pictures screen adaptation *Secret of Treasure Island.* (See F2.)

BB60. **"Murder for Murder."**

A priceless tapestry causes the strange deaths of three men.

BB61. **"Paper Traitor."** (See also **"A Paper Traitor,"** BB62.)

A belated pardon leads ironically to the recapture of an escaped convict.

BB62. **"A Paper Traitor."** (Holograph manuscript)

The convict in this, possibly earlier, version of "Paper Traitor," is a former gangster.

BB63. **"Passenger Fifty-One."**

Disguised as a passenger aboard a Zeppelin flight to New York, an American detective solves a murder, witnesses another, locates the missing documents he had been falsely accused of stealing, finds a fortune in stolen emeralds, parachutes from the dirigible, and is still in time for luncheon with his girlfriend at the Waldorf.

BB64. **"The Return of the Doomed."**

The electrocution of three convicted criminals becomes the key to a bizarre plot to destroy a district attorney.

BB65. **"Stunt Pilot."**

A strange crash, stolen money and the accidental death of a passenger leads a young airmail pilot to prison, then to a new career as a movie stunt flier who is threatened by the vengeful schemes of an unsuspected enemy.

BB66. **"The Tailor-made Spy."**

Disfigured in a crash, deliberately given a new face by plastic surgery in an enemy hospital, an American fighter pilot in World War I is mistaken for a German spy who looks just like him, and is sentenced to be shot.

BB67. **"Take a Poison from One to Ten."**

An insurance claims adjuster investigates the deaths of three members of the same family, all of whom had recently been heavily insured, apparently by the newly-wed wife of one of the victims.

BB68.   "Torch Murder."

When the reform candidate for mayor is torch murdered—and burned beyond recognition—an ace detective sets out to prove the guilt of the corrupt incumbent mayor, then makes a startling discovery.

BB69.   "Witch's Rocking Chair."

When the elderly woman the local town people had called a witch dies, she leaves an apparently haunted rocking chair and a valuable secret concealed in the stuffing of the chair.

ROMANCE

BB70.   "All South American."

Mistakenly believing that his girlfriend admires giant football players at an American school, a short-but-doughty Peruvian bullfighter proves he can play and win with the big boys, only to discover—to his delight—that his girlfriend's real passion is bullfighting.

BB71.   "A Bedtime Story."

Set in the sixteenth century, this charming historical romance tells the "bedtime story" of a beautiful young woman who, fleeing from parents who want her to wed a rich but ugly suitor, encounters a handsome nobleman, bests a rival, is rescued from wolves, and lives happily ever after.

BB72.   "He Had to Marry the Girl."

When a young man mistakes one sister for another, he comes uncomfortably close to losing both the one he really loves and a sizeable inheritance.

BB73.   "The Insignificant Obsession."

Believing the man she loves is dead, a woman falls in love with a second man, a painter, for whom she poses.

When the first man unexpectedly returns, she lies to him about her relationship with the painter and trouble ensues.

BB74. **"No Greater Love."**

When a young woman pilot braves adverse weather to fly emergency medical supplies to the scene of a mine disaster, she bests her movie star rival for the affections of an aviator boyfriend and earns the money to pay for needed surgery on her father's injured leg.

BB75. **"The Perfect Life."**

When a man and woman are rescued after being ship-wrecked together on a desert island, they separate and their lives take different directions. Reunited years later, they decide to return to the island.

BB76. **"The Price of Lust."**

When Sven masquerades as Griselda's dead brother to keep her near him, he risks losing her love forever, until an act of courage reveals the truth and reunites them.

BB77. **"Stormalong."**

Swashbuckling historical romance of the last days of the Spanish Main which follows the colorful exploits of the fiery buccaneer, Stormalong, as he defies the powerful English nobleman who has sworn to capture or kill him.

SCIENCE FICTION AND FANTASY

BB78. **"The Alkahest."**

A historian in the far distant future recounts the story of the long-vanished Earth (an area on astronomical charts now marked only as "Avoid—Dangerous") and of the Earthman who invented the "alkahest," the universal solvent that dissolved the Earth forever.

BB79. **"Cap of Doom."**

A judge puts on an extraordinary telepathic cap that persuades him—by showing him apparent memories of his own family's unsavory past—to free a young man unjustly accused of murder. The judge does not know that the memories are really not his, but those of the scientist operating the cap. But justice—despite bitter opposition even from his own family in a surprise story twist —has in fact been served.

BB80. **"Double Talk."**

A magic elixir brings a famous ventriloquist's equally famous dummy to life.

BB81. **"Due Process of Thought."**

The humdrum life of Henry Bronson is shattered forever when he invents a telepathic transmitter and discovers what his wife and son really think of him.

BB82. **"The Miseries of Mike."**

It's not the fillings in his teeth that are making Mike Williams say things he hadn't intended to say. He discovers he, himself, has become the receiver and the voice—the "mike"—for other people's thoughts.

BB83. **"The Soul of a Plane."** (Holograph manuscript)

Faced with the prospect of having his beloved plane carted off to a museum, a young flier watches as the plane mysteriously takes its fate into its own hands.

BB84. **"They Shall Inherit."**

A young man discovers after a serious illness that he is the last person left alive in the world, and that he has unwittingly helped the mean—not the meek—inherit the Earth.

BB85. **"Tickets."**

A fascinating "time-trap" fantasy that begins when a beautiful woman walks into a travel agency, pursued by a man with a gun. The travel agent—named Johnny Aldrich— shoots the pursuer with a gun he keeps under the counter for protection, then flees with the woman, first to Miami and then onto an ocean liner. Thrown overboard, Aldrich hurtles into nothingness, only to suddenly find himself back in the travel agency. A beautiful woman walks in, pursued by a man with a gun . . .

BB86. **"The Tombstone."**

All his life, Joshua Prout had done everything in a big way—the biggest house, the biggest fortune, the biggest car. But when Judgement Day comes and the dead are summoned from their graves, Joshua discovers his passion for bigness has followed him to the bitterest end—his tombstone is too big for him to move.

BB87. **"Unlucky Pistols."**

A ghost tells the ill-starred story of a pair of pirate pistols and a dying man's curse.

WESTERN

BB88. **"The Adventures of Bobby Mathews."**

(**Note:** L. Ron Hubbard's verifiably earliest story, written in 1921, at the age of ten. An accompanying handwritten note to his father establishes the date.)

Ten-year-old Bobby Mathews uses toy cap pistols instead of real guns to corral two renegade farm hands.

BB89. **"The Bandit and the Button."** (Holograph manuscript)

When a bandit fleeing from the law rescues a ten-year-old boy he affectionately calls "the button" from outlaws who had killed the boy's father, the bandit wins over a pursuing marshal.

BB90. **"The Black Rider."**

Disguise and mistaken identity play a near-fatal role in this lively yarn of two Damon-and-Pythias-type partners who wipe out the Black Rider and his gang of outlaws.

BB91. **"The Dead Man."**

As an old prospector, convinced that people are trying to cheat him of his gold, lies dying of thirst and hunger in the desert, the light of the moon reveals the ironic truth—the load of rock in his wagon contains gold nuggets after all.

BB92. **"Desert Mercy."**

A bankrupt ex-prospector, miraculously saved by cactus water from dying of thirst in the desert, helps his daughter and the son of his former partner stave off the guns of the town's ruthless sheriff and his gang of killers.

BB93. **"Dogged Vengeance."**

Kit McLean is saved from being hung for crimes he did not commit when his dog, Nugget, fearlessly attacks the real culprit, the town's crooked sheriff, just as evidence of Kit's innocence arrives in town.

BB94. **"The Galleon of Ghoul Mountain."**

In a search for treasure and a fabled Spanish galleon in the desert, a young man and his father encounter outlaws, subsequently capture them, and receive a real treasure—a $10,000 reward.

BB95. **"A Sheep in Wolf's Clothing."**

Mo Scanlon, a vagrant and a gifted liar, deceives everyone in town with his tall tale about how he captured the man who had stolen money from Wells Fargo, only to steal away with the money himself.

BB96. **"Signed with Lead."**

Okay Collins has to prove he is the real owner of the Thirty-Thirty Ranch and that he's not guilty of robbery and murder.

BB97. **"Tit for Tat."** (Holograph manuscript)

The man who saves a young preacher from a lynching turns out to be the same man who robbed the Wells Fargo stage—but the grateful preacher has already helped him escape the sheriff.

BB98. **"Two Guns from Texas."**

A sinister masquerade and a dangerous case of mistaken identity complicate the plot when a Texas cowboy and a range detective are sent by the Cattleman's Association to unmask a criminal.

BBC. INCOMPLETE STORIES AND FRAGMENTS

(Titles and special bibliophilic notes, only. Arranged alphabetically by genre, and then title.)

ADVENTURE

BBC1. **"Adventure: ideas and notes."** (holograph)

BBC2. **"Advertising."** (holograph, originally untitled)

BBC3. **"Automobiles."** (holograph)

BBC4. **"Babe, the Blue Ox."** (holograph)

BBC5. **"The Battle of the Swamp."**

BBC6. **"The Boys on the U.S.S. Zim."** (holograph, originally untitled)

BBC7. **"Brad and Spike."** (holograph, originally untitled)

BBC8. **"The Brass Monkey."**

BBC9. **"Chaos."**

BBC10. **"Characterizations."**

BBC11. **"China Story."** (holograph)

BBC12. **"Christmas Theme."**

BBC13. **"Collingsby, James A."** (originally untitled)

BBC14. **"Conductor."**

BBC15. **"CPO, U.S.N."** (synopsis)

BBC16. **"Dangerous Professions: ideas and notes."**

BBC17. **"Deserter."** (holograph, originally untitled)

BBC18. **"Double Indemnity."**

BBC19. **"The Elusive Emeralds."**

BBC20. **"Filibustero."** (two incomplete versions)

BBC21. **"Guam Story."** (holograph, originally untitled)

BBC22. **"Gunner's Mate."**

BBC23. **"Gun Runner."** (holograph, originally untitled)

BBC24. **"He Came Home."** (holograph, originally untitled)

BBC25. **"Hot Water."**

BBC26. **"How to Get and Keep Your Man."** (story outline)

BBC27. **"James, Medical Corpsman."** (originally untitled)

BBC28. **"Lords of the Roaring River."** (synopsis)

BBC29. **"Marietta Hits Red Eagle."**

BBC30. **"The Massacre of Dangerous Dan."** (holograph)

BBC31. **"Mr. Thornton in China."** (holograph, fragment)

BBC32. **"The Mysterious Pilot."** (synopsis)

BBC33. **"Oblivion."**

BBC34. **"A Painting."** (three versions, all holographs)

BBC35. **"Politics."** (originally untitled)

BBC36. **"The Promise."** (holograph, originally untitled)

BBC37. **"The Psychology of Flight."** (fragment)

BBC38. **"Rex."** (holograph, originally untitled)

BBC39. **"Sergeant Mahoney."** (originally untitled)

BBC40. **"So I Says to Neptune . . ."**

BBC41. **"Spike and Johnny, Sailors."** (holograph, originally untitled)

BBC42. **"Sword for Sale."** (holograph)

BBC43. **"Tide of Empire."** (holograph, synopsis, fragment)

BBC44. **"Writer, Not Engineer."** (originally untitled)

BBC45. **"Writer's Slang Story."** (originally untitled)

BBC46. **"Yellow Cargo."** (two versions)

MYSTERY/DETECTIVE

BBC47. "Death Warrant."

BBC48. "The Hoodoo Pilot."

BBC49. "Killer's Bride."

BBC50. "Mystery-Detective: ideas and notes."

BBC51. "Rocket Trescott." (letter, with synopsis)

BBC52. "Witch's Curse." (holograph, originally untitled)

SCIENCE FICTION/FANTASY

BBC53. "The Anatomy of Boredom."

BBC54. "Black Towers of Fear" a.k.a. "The Wizard of Wotung."
(two synopses)

BBC55. "The Brain Slayer."

BBC56. "The Comet, Space Master."

BBC57. "The Exiles."

BBC58. "The God and the Planet." (synopsis)

BBC59. "He Listens for His Name." (originally untitled)

BBC60. "The Hermit's Brain Children."

BBC61. "The Looting of Linden-Aoh." (fragment)

BBC62. "Science Fiction: ideas and notes." (holograph)

BBC63. "The Witch of Betelgeuze."

BBC64. "The Wolves Wept."

WESTERN

BBC65. "Buckeye, Politician."

BBC66. "The Devil's Backyard."

BBC67. "49."

BBC68. "The Parson Pays a Debt." (holograph)

BBC69. "Too Much Mine."

BBC70. **"Waldo, the Town-Tamer"** a.k.a. **"Waldo, Gunman."** (two versions)

BBC71. **"Western: ideas and notes."** (holograph)

C. Magazine Nonfiction

This section lists published nonfiction writings which are relevant to the author's fiction writing career, such as articles on writers and writing, aviation and deep-sea diving.

The entry format follows the same style as previous sections.

C. MAGAZINE NONFICTION

C1. **"Tailwind Willies."** *The Sportsman Pilot,* Vol. 7, No. 1, January, 1932: 21+.

C2. **"Sans Power."** *The Sportsman Pilot,* Vol. 8, No. 5, November, 1932: 20+.

C3. **"Washington's Langley Day."** *The Sportsman Pilot,* Vol. 9, No. 5-6, May-June, 1933: 16+. Includes photos by L. Ron Hubbard.

C4. **"Navy and Marine Pets Have Their Own Service Books."** *The Sunday Star,* Washington, D.C., August, 1933: 11+.

C5. **"Silhouettes."** *The Sportsman Pilot,* Vol. 10, No. 4, October, 1933: 20+.

C6. **"Music with Your Navigation."** *The Sportsman Pilot,* Vol. 10, No. 5, November, 1933: 16+.

C7. **"No Matter What You Call It, It Just Grins."** (a.k.a. "Whatever They Call It, It Just Grins.") *The Sportsman Pilot,* Vol. 10, No. 1, July, 1934: 26+.

C8. **"XC."** *The Sportsman Pilot,* Vol. 12, No. 3, September, 1934: 22+.

C9. **"San Diego Fair Meet."** (Mr. Spectator.) *The Sportsman Pilot,* Vol. 12, No. 3, September 15, 1934.

C10. **"West Indies Whys and Whithers."** *The Sportsman Pilot,* Vol. 12, No. 6, December, 1934: 14+.

C11. **"Won't You Sit Down?"** *The Sportsman Pilot,* Vol. 13, No. 1, January, 1935: 14+.

C12. **"Mahomet Comes to the Mountain."** *The Sportsman Pilot,* Vol. 13, No. 2, February, 1935: 22+.

C13. **"Story Vitality."** *Writer's Review,* Vol. 3, No. 10, July, 1935: 22+.

    b. *Writers of The Future, Volume IX,* Los Angeles: Bridge Publications, Inc., 1993: 75-80.

    c. *The Creative Writer's Handbook,* Los Angeles: Bridge Publications, Inc., to be published in 1995.

C14.   **"Circulate."**   *The Author & Journalist,* Vol. 20, No. 7, July, 1935: 11-12.

    b.   as "The Jungles of Craft." *To the Stars Magazine,* Issue No. 1, October-November, 1983.

    c.   *Ron the Writer, Issue 1, The Legend Begins,* Los Angeles: Bridge Publications, Inc., 1989: 62-65.

    d.   *Writers of The Future,* Vol V, Los Angeles: Bridge Publications, Inc., 1989: 69-75.

    e.   *The Creative Writer's Handbook,* Los Angeles: Bridge Publications, Inc., to be published in 1995.

C15.   **"Magic Out of a Hat."**   *Writer's Digest,* Vol. 16, No. 2, January, 1936: 17-20.

    b.   *The Creative Writer's Handbook,* Los Angeles: Bridge Publications, Inc., to be published in 1995.

C16.   **"The Campfire."**   (Letter to the Editor.) *Adventure Magazine,* Vol. 95, No. 5, September, 1936: 112-113.

    b.   *The Creative Writer's Handbook,* Los Angeles: Bridge Publications, Inc., to be published in 1995.

C17.   **"Argonotes."**   (Letter to the Editor.) *Argosy,* Vol. 268, No. 2, October 24, 1936: 141-142.

    b.   *Ron the Writer, Issue 1, The Legend Begins,* Los Angeles: Bridge Publications, Inc., 1989: 20-21

    c.   *The Creative Writer's Handbook,* Los Angeles: Bridge Publications, Inc., to be published in 1995.

C18.   **"Test Pilots, 1936."**   *The Sportsman Pilot,* Vol. 16, No. 2, August 15, 1936: 18+.

    b.   *Ron the Writer, Issue 1, The Legend Begins,* Los Angeles: Bridge Publications, Inc., 1989: 52-59.

C19.   **"Highly Hazardous—Pilots."**   *Five Novels Monthly,* Vol. 40, No. 3, December, 1937: 118+.

C20.   **"Suspense."**   *The Author & Journalist,* Vol. 22, No. 6, June, 1937: 3-5.

      b.   *Writers of The Future, Volume VI,* Los Angeles: Bridge Publications, Inc., 1990: 83-92.

      c.   *Ron the Writer, Issue 2, Changing a Genre,* Los Angeles: Bridge Publications, Inc., 1991: 53-61.

      d.   *The Creative Writer's Handbook,* Los Angeles: Bridge Publications, Inc., to be published in 1995.

C21.   **"Argonotes."**   (Letter to the Editor.) *Argosy,* Vol. 275, No. 3, August 21, 1937: 142+.

      b.   as "The Fast Production Writer," in *The Fabulous Faust Fanzine,* Vol. 2, No. 1, December, 1951.

      c.   *The Creative Writer's Handbook,* Los Angeles: Bridge Publications, Inc., to be published in 1995.

C22.   **"Salt."**   (Ken Martin) *Cowboy Stories,* Vol. 32, No. 2, August/Sept., 1937: 64+.

C23.   **"Highly Hazardous—Deep Sea Diver."** *Five Novels Monthly,* Vol. 42, No. 1, April, 1938: 143+.

C24.   **"It Bears Telling."** (Capt. L. Ron Hubbard) *Through Hell and High Water,* New York: Explorer's Club, May, 1941: 85-89.

      b.   *Ron Master Mariner, Issue II, Yachtsman,* Los Angeles: Bridge Publications, Inc., 1994: 28-35.

C25.   **"McKee Plants Fountain Fish."** *Catalina Islander,* November 21, 1946: 1.

C26.   **"Fortress in the Sky."** (Capt. B. A. Northrop) *Air Trails,* May, 1947: 22+.

C27.   **"Steps in the Right Direction."** An interview with L. Ron Hubbard by R. Walton Willems. *Writers' Markets & Methods,* Vol. 60, No. 1, January, 1949: 8-9.

      b.   *The Creative Writer's Handbook,* Los Angeles: Bridge Publications, Inc., to be published in 1995.

C28.   **"By L. Ron Hubbard."** *Deeper Than You Think—A Review on Fantasy,* Vol. 1, No. 3, March, 1969: 8+.

b. *Ron the Writer, Collectors' Edition,* Los Angeles: Bridge Publications, Inc., 1982: 4-8.

c. *The Creative Writer's Handbook,* Los Angeles: Bridge Publications, Inc., to be published in 1995.

C29. **"Tomorrow's Miracles."** *Ron The Writer Magazine, Collectors' Edition No. 1,* Hollywood: Dynasty, Master Designers, 1982.

b. *Writers of The Future, Volume IV,* Los Angeles: Bridge Publications, Inc., 1988: 7-19.

c. *Ron the Philosopher, Issue 1: The Quest for Truth,* Los Angeles: Bridge Publications, Inc., 1991: 27-34.

d. *The Creative Writer's Handbook,* Los Angeles: Bridge Publications, Inc., to be published in 1995.

C30. **"Search For Research."** *Ron The Writer Issue 1: The Legend Begins,* Los Angeles: Bridge Publications Inc., 1989: 42-49.

D. VERSE

This section lists both published and unpublished verse, providing an insightful, albeit brief, glimpse of another facet of Hubbard's creative range.

In addition to published poetry and verse related to his *Battlefield Earth* and *Mission Earth* novels, there exists a large body of verse by Hubbard which is relevant to his fiction works, but which he never submitted for publication. All works in this latter category are listed alphabetically in sub-section DD. Most are undated works of free verse. However, where the work is of a different classification, this is noted. Additionally, where dates and bylines are on the original work, this is also noted. Unnamed works are listed by the first line of the verse.

D. VERSE

(Listed chronologically by first publication date)

D1. **"The 'Edna Irene',"** ("The Beachcomber") in *The Catalina Islander*, Nov. 21, 1946.

VERSE IN FICTION WORKS

The following list of verse is from L. Ron Hubbard's fiction works—*Mission Earth, Battlefield Earth*, and the *Ole Doc Methuselah* series—in which verse is used as a literary device to augment the prose and dialogue of the story, especially the *Mission Earth* dekalogy with its classic elements of satire. The verse is listed in order of appearance in the work and cross-referenced to the corresponding entry.

BATTLEFIELD EARTH

D2. **"Galactic Bank!"** in *Battlefield Earth*, Bridge Publications, Inc. (See A27.)

MISSION EARTH

(The verses listed below are untitled, and listed here by first line.)

D3. **"And so faded my glow . . ."** in *The Invaders Plan*, Bridge Publications, Inc. (See A28.)

D4. **"If ever from life you need to fly . . ."** in *The Invaders Plan*, Bridge Publications, Inc. (See A28.)

D5. **"Money for my honey . . ."** in *The Invaders Plan*, Bridge Publications, Inc. (See A28.)

D6. **"Don't reimburse the purse . . ."** in *The Invaders Plan*, Bridge Publications, Inc. (See A28.)

D7. **"Dicies balm and calm . . ."** in *The Invaders Plan*, Bridge Publications, Inc. (See A28.)

D8. **"Conserve your nerve . . ."** in *The Invaders Plan*, Bridge Publications, Inc. (See A28.)

D9. **"Don't bust through the crust . . ."** in *The Invaders Plan*, Bridge Publications, Inc. (See A28.)

D10. **"Don't bruise with bad news . . ."** in *The Invaders Plan*, Bridge Publications, Inc. (See A28.)

D11. **"Down on a path in the forest today . . ."** in *The Invaders Plan*, Bridge Publications, Inc. (See A28.)

D12. **"Spaceward, ho!"** in *The Invaders Plan*, Bridge Publications, Inc. Song-chant. (See A28.)

D13. **"There once was a con who was awful, awful dry . . ."** in *Black Genesis*, Bridge Publications, Inc. (See A29.)

D14. **"She rose like the moon into heaven's embrace . . ."** in *The Enemy Within*, Bridge Publications, Inc. (See A30.)

D15. **"The nightingale lay trembling . . ."** in *The Enemy Within*, Bridge Publications, Inc. (See A30.)

D16. **"Unspent kisses clog my throat . . ."** in *The Enemy Within*, Bridge Publications, Inc. (See A30.)

D17. **"Let me drink of you . . ."** in *The Enemy Within*, Bridge Publications, Inc. (See A30.)

D18. **"You have no need of me . . ."** in *The Enemy Within*, Bridge Publications, Inc. (See A30.)

D19. **"Poor little baby . . ."** in *The Enemy Within*, Bridge Publications, Inc. (See A30.)

D20. **"Come wash my back, little Rudy . . ."** in *The Enemy Within*, Bridge Publications, Inc. (See A30.)

D21. **"One little kiss went to market . . ."** in *The Enemy Within*, Bridge Publications, Inc. (See A30.)

D22. **"Little, little feet on my tum, tum, tum . . ."** in *The Enemy Within*, Bridge Publications, Inc. (See A30.)

D23. **"Corn whiskey . . ."** in *An Alien Affair*, Bridge Publications, Inc. (See A31.)

D24. **"You are my monster . . ."** in *An Alien Affair*, Bridge Publications, Inc. (See A31.)

D25.   **"Little Bo Peep went do-da, do-da . . ."** in *An Alien Affair,* Bridge Publications, Inc. (See A31.)

D26.   **"You may be small . . ."** in *An Alien Affair,* Bridge Publications, Inc. (See A31.)

D27.   **"When I gaze into your eyes . . ."** in *Fortune of Fear,* Bridge Publications, Inc. (See A32.)

D28.   **"Sweet little woman . . ."** in *Fortune of Fear,* Bridge Publications, Inc. (See A32.)

D29.   **"Long and slow . . ."** in *Fortune of Fear,* Bridge Publications, Inc. (See A32.)

D30.   **"Fatal woman . . ."** in *Fortune of Fear,* Bridge Publications, (See A32.)

D31.   **"I'm dying . . ."** in *Death Quest,* Bridge Publications, Inc. (See A33.)

D32.   **"Here comes the bride . . ."** in *Death Quest,* Bridge Publications, Inc. (See A33.)

D33.   **"Freddie was a jumper . . ."** in *Death Quest,* Bridge Publications, Inc. (See A33.)

D34.   **"Subliminal, subliminal . . ."** in *Death Quest,* Bridge Publications, Inc. (See A33.)

D35.   **"Don't stop me . . ."** in *Death Quest,* Bridge Publications, Inc. (See A33.)

D36.   **"Do it in the morning . . ."** in *Death Quest,* Bridge Publications, Inc. (See A33.)

D37.   **"Shiver, shiver, shimmy . . ."** in *Voyage of Vengeance,* Bridge Publications, Inc. (See A34.)

D38.   **"Happy garbage to you . . ."** in *Voyage of Vengeance,* Bridge Publications, Inc. (See A34.)

D39.   **"I'm sneaking up on you . . ."** in *Voyage of Vengeance,* Bridge Publications, Inc. (See A34.)

D40. "Go on home . . ." in *Voyage of Vengeance*, Bridge Publications, Inc. (See A34.)

D41. "Get stoned with me . . ." in *Voyage of Vengeance*, Bridge Publications, Inc. (See A34.)

D42. "If ever from life you need to fly . . ." in *Voyage of Vengeance*, Bridge Publications, Inc. (See A34.)

D43. "An Ode to Spiteos . . ." in *Disaster*, Bridge Publications, Inc. (See A35.)

D44. "Oh, a soldier's life is the life for me . . ." in *Villainy Victorious*, Bridge Publications, Inc. (See A36.)

D45. "And here's a cheer . . ." in *Villainy Victorious*, Bridge Publications, Inc. (See A36.)

D46. "We hunt him here . . ." in *Villainy Victorious*, Bridge Publications, Inc. (See A36.)

D47. "Oh, welcome to us . . ." in *Villainy Victorious*, Bridge Publications, Inc. (See A36.)

D48. "The Devil's going to get you . . ." in *Villainy Victorious*, Bridge Publications, Inc. (See A36.)

D49. "Death to the Apparatus!" in *The Doomed Planet*, Bridge Publications, Inc. (See A37.)

D50. "The Fleet Marines . . ." in *The Doomed Planet*, Bridge Publications, Inc. (See A37.)

D51. "We'll end off our invasion . . ." in *The Doomed Planet*, Bridge Publications, Inc. (See A37.)

D52. "Psychedelic sunset!" in *The Doomed Planet*, Bridge Publications, Inc. (See A37.)

D53. "My mama never told me . . ." in *The Doomed Planet*, Bridge Publications, Inc. (See A37.)

D54. "Two on one is lots of fun . . ." in *The Doomed Planet*, Bridge Publications, Inc. (See A37.)

D55. "Ode to Earth," in *The Doomed Planet*, Bridge Publications, Inc. (See A37.)

D56. **"On Woman,"** in *Ole Doc Methuselah,* Bridge Publications, Inc. (See A16.) Originally published in *Astounding Science Fiction,* Jan. 1950, in the story "Ole Mother Methuselah." (See B203. Also, Q4.)

DD. UNPUBLISHED VERSE

(Listed alphabetically. Unnamed verse is listed by first line.)

DD1. **"The Alaska Chief."** Rhymed ballad with some chord notations. "To be played at midnight on a Spanish guitar or ukulele with two jugs of whiskey. And with proper sad emphasis."

DD2. **"The Atom."**

DD3. [Unnamed] **"The avenues . . ."**

DD4. **"Beggars."**

DD5. **"Bored."**

DD6. [Unnamed] **"A bridge . . ."**

DD7. [Unnamed] **"A Clever Man."**

DD8. [Unnamed] **"Cold, wet decks . . ."**

DD9. **"Communists Meeting."**

DD10. **"Condemned."**

DD11. **"The Curse of the Demon Rum."** Long rhymed ditty with chorus.

DD12. [Unnamed] **"Death . . ."**

DD13. [Unnamed] **"A demon caught me . . ."**

DD14. [Unnamed] **"Drum, Drummer, Drum!"**

DD15. **"Drummer."**

DD16. [Unnamed] **"Electric signs . . ."**

DD17. [Unnamed] **"The engineer's a hardy man . . ."** Rhymed sea ditty.

DD18. **"An Error in Scholastics."**

DD19. [Unnamed] **"The evil and sin . . ."**

DD20. **"Execution."**

DD21. **"The Fate of Smilin' Joe."** Rhymed ditty.

DD22. "Fifth Avenue."

DD23. "Five O'Clock."

DD24. [Unnamed] "From sea of dreams . . ."

DD25. "The Garden." A simple lyric poem.

DD26. [Unnamed] "A girl named Jane . . ." Limerick with a science fiction twist.

DD27. "Gratitude."

DD28. "The Hanged Man." Narrative poem about the cruel crimes of a hanged man with a concluding dramatic irony.

DD29. [Unnamed] "He had a rolling platform . . ."

DD30. [Unnamed] "He kissed . . ."

DD31. [Unnamed] "I cannot finish anything . . ."

DD32. [Unnamed] "I followed him . . ." Epic narrative about General Custer and his last battle.

DD33. [Unnamed] "I knew him when . . ."

DD34. [Unnamed] "I rolled along a littered dock . . ."

DD35. [Unnamed] "I smoke cigarettes . . ."

DD36. [Unnamed] "It's hard to tell when you see a kid . . ."

DD37. [Unnamed] "King Street."

DD38. [Unnamed] "Listen to the song."

DD39. [Unnamed] "Lost to the brightness of morning. . ."

DD40. "The Love of a Man." Lyric poem.

DD41. [Unnamed] "The men of reason . . ."

DD42. [Unnamed] "Men will come . . ."

DD43. [Unnamed] "My muse . . ."

DD44. [Unnamed] "O Vanderbilt is a hidden reef . . ." Rhymed ditty.

DD45. "Odd Mcintyre."

DD46.   [Unnamed] **"Of happiness I wonder . . ."**

DD47.   **"The Old Bold Mate of Henry Morgan."**
Rhymed ditty.

DD48.   **"Picketeer."**

DD49.   **"Poem II."**

DD50.   [Unnamed] **"Poor fool . . ."**

DD51.   **"Rebuttal."**

DD52.   **"The Retreat from Ft. McHenry."**

DD53.   [Unnamed] **"Rooms . . ."**

DD54.   **"Sable and Satin."**

DD55.   **"Sandwich Man."**

DD56.   [Unnamed] **"The ship of state . . ."**

DD57.   [Unnamed] **"Shining windows . . ."**

DD58.   [Unnamed] **"Steamshovels . . ."**

DD59.   **"Street Accident."**

DD60.   **"Street Walker."**

DD61.   **"Subway."**

DD62.   **"Suicide."**

DD63.   **"Sum of Man."**

DD64.   [Unnamed] **"Seven times seven veils . . ."**

DD65.   **"Tenement Summer."**

DD66.   [Unnamed] **"These are the Flowers . . ."**

DD67.   **"A Theory."**

DD68.   **"The Thirsty Knife."**

DD69.   [Unnamed] **"Today . . ."**

DD70.   [Unnamed] **"Tomorrow . . ."**

DD71.   **"To Youth."** Rhymed lyric poem.

E. AUDIO TAPES AND RECORDINGS

Listed chronologically in this section are audio recordings related to Hubbard's fiction works—including recently released fiction audio editions. Section EE lists the musical sound track recordings which the author wrote for *Battlefield Earth* and *Mission Earth*. All entries are cross-referenced to the book section.

E. AUDIO TAPES AND RECORDINGS

(Listed chronologically by release date.)

E1.   **"The Professor Was a Thief!"**   Story credit given by NBC Radio for the November 5, 1950 airing of a radio adaptation of the story (30 min.) originally published in 1940 (See B137). Arthur Maitland as "Pop," John Larkin as "Sweeney" and John Gibson as the "Professor." Announcer Fred Collins. Also distributed in the "Radio Yesterday" series, Sandy Hock, Connecticut: 1991.

E2.   **Mission Earth Volume 1, The Invaders Plan.**   New York: Random House Sound Editions, 1988. 2 cassettes (3 hours). Multi-cast dramatization with music and sound effects. (See A28.)

b. Los Angeles: Bridge Audio, 1993. 2 cassettes (3 hours).

c. Washington, DC: The Library of Congress, National Library Service for the Blind and Physically Handicapped, 1986.

E3.   **Mission Earth Volume 2, Black Genesis.**   New York: Random House Sound Editions, 1988. 2 cassettes (3 hours). Multi-cast dramatization with music and sound effects. (See A29.)

b. Los Angeles: Bridge Audio, 1994. 2 cassettes (3 hours).

c. Washington, DC: The Library of Congress, National Library Service for the Blind and Physically Handicapped, 1987.

E4.   **Mission Earth Volume 3, The Enemy Within.**   New York: Random House Sound Editions, 1988. 2 cassettes (3 hours). Multi-cast dramatization with music and sound effects. (See A30.)

b. Los Angeles: Bridge Audio, 1994. 2 cassettes (3 hours).

c. Washington, DC: The Library of Congress, National Library Service for the Blind and Physically Handicapped, 1987.

E5.   **Mission Earth Volume 4, An Alien Affair.**   New York: Random House Sound Editions, 1989. 2 cassettes (3 hours). Multi-cast dramatization with music and sound effects. (See A31.)

b. Los Angeles: Bridge Audio, 1994. 2 cassettes (3 hours).

c. Washington, DC: The Library of Congress, National Library Service for the Blind and Physically Handicapped, 1987.

E6.   **Mission Earth Volume 5, Fortune of Fear.**   New York: Random House Sound Editions, 1989. 2 cassettes (3 hours). Multi-cast dramatization with music and sound effects. (See A32.)

b. Los Angeles: Bridge Audio, 1994. 2 cassettes (3 hours).

c. Washington, DC: The Library of Congress, National Library Service for the Blind and Physically Handicapped, 1987.

E7.   **Mission Earth Volume 6, Death Quest.**   New York: Random House Sound Editions, 1989. 2 cassettes (3 hours). Multi-cast dramatization with music and sound effects. (See A33.)

b. Los Angeles: Bridge Audio, 1994. 2 cassettes (3 hours).

c. Washington, DC: The Library of Congress, National Library Service for the Blind and Physically Handicapped, 1987.

E8.   **Mission Earth Volume 7, Voyage of Vengeance.**   New York: Random House Sound Editions, 1990. 2 cassettes (3 hours). Multi-cast dramatization with music and sound effects. (See A34.)

b. Los Angeles: Bridge Audio, 1994. 2 cassettes (3 hours).

c. Washington, DC: The Library of Congress, National Library Service for the Blind and Physically Handicapped, 1988.

E9.   **Mission Earth Volume 8, Disaster.** New York: Random House Sound Editions, 1990. 2 cassettes (3 hours). Multi-cast dramatization with music and sound effects. (See A35.)

b. Los Angeles: Bridge Audio, 1994. 2 cassettes (3 hours).

c. Washington, DC: The Library of Congress, National Library Service for the Blind and Physically Handicapped, 1989.

E10.   **Mission Earth Volume 9, Villainy Victorious.**   New York: Random House Sound Editions, 1990. 2 cassettes (3 hours). Multi-cast dramatization with music and sound effects. (See A36.)

b. Los Angeles: Bridge Audio, 1994. 2 cassettes (3 hours).

c. Washington, DC: The Library of Congress, National Library Service for the Blind and Physically Handicapped, 1989.

E11.   **Mission Earth Volume 10, The Doomed Planet.**   New York: Random House Sound Editions, 1991. 2 cassettes (3 hours). Multi-cast dramatization with music and sound effects. (See A37.)

b. Los Angeles: Bridge Audio, 1994. 2 cassettes (3 hours).

c. Washington, DC: The Library of Congress, National Library Service for the Blind and Physically Handicapped, 1989.

Notes: The complete *Mission Earth* ten-volume audio series by Random House Sound Editions, was released in the United Kingdom in 1991 through New Era Publications, Ltd.

E12.   **Fear.**   Los Angeles: Bridge Audio, 1991. 2 cassettes (3 hours). Narrated by Roddy McDowall. (See A15.)

b. Tonbridge, Kent: New Era Publications, Ltd., 1991. [United Kingdom]

c. *Au bout du cauchmar.* Grenoble: La Voix De Son Livre, 1991. Unabridged, 8 cassettes (12 hours). Multi-cast dramatization with music and sound effects. [French]

d. Washington, DC: The Library of Congress, National Library Service for the Blind and Physically Handicapped, 1993.

E13.   **Final Blackout.**   Los Angeles: Bridge Audio, 1991. 2 cassettes (3 hours). Narrated by Roddy McDowall. (See A2.)

b. Washington, DC: The Library of Congress, National Library Service for the Blind and Physically Handicapped, 1992.

E14.   **Battlefield Earth, A Saga of the Year 3000.**   Los Angeles: Bridge Audio, 1991. 6 cassettes (8 hours). Narrated by Roddy McDowall. (See A27.)

b. Newport Beach: Books on Tape, 1994. Unabridged, 30 cassettes (45 hours). Narrated by Michael Russotto.

c. Washington, DC: The Library of Congress, National Library Service for the Blind and Physically Handicapped, 1993.

E15.   **Buckskin Brigades.** Los Angeles: Bridge Audio, 1992. 2 cassettes (3 hours). Narrated by Bruce Boxleitner. (See A1.)

E16.   **Ole Doc Methuselah.** Los Angeles: Bridge Audio, 1992. 4 cassettes (6 hours). Narrated by Roddy McDowall. (See A16.)

b. Thorndike: Thorndike Press, 1994. Unabridged, 8 cassettes (12 hours).

E17.   **The Guns of Mark Jardine.**   Los Angeles: Bridge Audio, 1993. 1 cassette (1 hour). Narrated by Geoffrey Lewis. (See A7.)

E18.   **Empty Saddles.**   Los Angeles: Bridge Audio, 1993. 1 cassette (1 hour). Narrated by Geoffrey Lewis. (See A40.)

E19.   **Slaves of Sleep & The Masters of Sleep.**   Los Angeles: Bridge Audio, 1993. 4 cassettes (6 hours). Narrated by Rene Auberjonois. (See B134 and B215.)

E20.   **Hot Lead Payoff.** Los Angeles: Bridge Audio, 1994. 1 cassette (1 hour). Narrated by Geoffrey Lewis (See B113.)

E21. **The Automagic Horse.** Los Angeles: Bridge Audio, 1994. 1 cassette (1 1/2 hours). Multicast dramatization with music and sound effects. (See B197)

E22. **Typewriter in the Sky.** Los Angeles: Bridge Audio, 1994. 2 cassettes (3 hours). Narrated by Jim Meskimen. (See A8.)

EE. MUSIC ALBUMS

EE1. **Space Jazz.** Los Angeles: Applause Records, 1982. Cassette and album formats. Music soundtrack for the novel *Battlefield Earth*. Words and music by L. Ron Hubbard. Performed by Chick Corea, Gayle Moran, Nicky Hopkins.

Track listings follow:

Side One	Side Two
Golden Era of SciFi	The Drone
Funeral for a Planet	Mankind Unites
March of the Psychlos	Alien Visitors Attack
Terl, the Security Director	The Banker
Jonnie	Declaration of Peace
Windsplitter	Earth, My Beautiful Home
The Mining Song	

EE2. **Battlefield Earth.** Los Angeles: BPI Records, 1984. Cassette and album formats. Music soundtrack for the novel *Battlefield Earth*.

EE3. **Mission Earth.** Santa Monica: Rhino Records, 1989. CD, cassette and album formats. Music soundtrack for the dekalogy *Mission Earth*. Words and music by L. Ron Hubbard. Performed by Edgar Winter.

Track listings follow:

Side One	Side Two
Mission Earth	Cry Out
Treacherous Love	Just a Kid
Bang-Bang	Spacer's Lot
Teach Me	Joy City

b. Frankfurt: CTE Records, 1989. CD and album formats.

c. Tokyo: JVC Victor, 1989. CD format.

F. Plays and Screenplays

This section lists both published and unpublished fiction plays and screenplays to show L. Ron Hubbard's early success as well as his later creativity in this form. Also listed, in addition to the Hollywood movies on which Hubbard received screen credits for his stories, are those screenplays he worked on as a studio screenwriter in the 1930s but for which—consistent with conventional studio practice of the time—he received no screen credits.

F. PLAYS & SCREENPLAYS

F1.   **The God Smiles.** L. Ron Hubbard, 1932. Prize-winning one-act play published in the May 24th edition of The George Washington University *University Hatchet Monthly Literary Review*, Vol. 28, No. 33, Section 2. Contest sponsored by the *University Hatchet Monthly Literary Review*. (See also B3.)

In a cafe in Tsingtau, China, a White Russian rebel and a cafe hostess are threatened with death by the appearance of the district's warlord. They resourcefully incapacitate him and escape to Manila.

F2.   **The Secret of Treasure Island.** Story by L. Ron Hubbard. Columbia Pictures, 1937. Full-length screenplay series based on his story *Murder at Pirate Castle*. Screen credit given to him for the story, and he also worked on the various script rewrites. One of Columbia Pictures' most enjoyable cliffhanger serials.

Newspaperman Don Terry is marooned on Treasure Island with a young woman who is searching for her father. There they find a wealthy oil magnate who owns a mysterious pirate's castle, and who is host to a motley collection of guests, including a gun-runner, a famous medium and even a murderous ghost. To complicate matters further, rumor has it that a million dollars in gold and jewels are hidden somewhere in the castle—and there are those who would stop at nothing to get their hands on the loot.

Episode titles:

1. "The Isle of Fear"

2. "The Ghost Talks"

3. "The Phantom Duel"

4. "Buried Alive"

5. "The Girl Who Vanished"

6. "Trapped by the Flood"

7. "The Cannon Roars"

8. "The Circle of Death"

9. "The Pirate's Revenge"

10. "The Crash"

11. "Dynamite"

12. "The Bridge of Doom"

13. "The Mad Flight"

14. "The Jaws of Destruction"

15. "Justice"

F3.   **The Adventures of the Mysterious Pilot** a.k.a. The Mysterious Pilot. Columbia Pictures, 1937. Hubbard worked on this as a Columbia screenwriter.

An agent of the border patrol is on the trail of criminals who are hiring pilots to steal mine dust and payrolls. The agent is framed, loses his job and pretends to become a criminal himself in order to stop the thieves.

F4.   **The Adventures of Wild Bill Hickock.** Columbia Pictures, 1937. Hubbard worked on this as a Columbia screenwriter.

F5.   **The Spider Returns.** Columbia Pictures, 1937. Hubbard worked on this movie series as a screenwriter with Norvell Page at Warner Bros.

F6.   **Riders of the Wind.** Complete synopsis of an air adventure screenplay. 1937.

When a pilot mistakenly lands his sailing plane on his boss' estate, causing havoc at a posh garden party, he is sacked on the spot and loses his girlfriend. Undaunted, he enters a dangerous plane race, flying just ahead of a storm. And he not only wins the race—but he gets his girl back as well.

F7.   **Aha, Toro!** Notes and title page for a play in three acts suggested by a tale by Giovanni Boccaccio. Circa 1938.

F8.   **Aida—With Swing!** Synopsis of a musical comedy. Circa 1938.

A famous torch singer and daughter of a millionaire learns from her father's will that all she has inherited is the opera house that he owned. She gathers some of her friends together to produce an opera, but their efforts are a miserable failure—until they decide to update Verdi's "Aida," adding "plenty of leg work," with "hot trumpet solos," and become a huge success.

F9.   **Judy.** Synopsis of a three-act play. Circa 1938.

A visiting nurse in the New York ghetto, who has aided those in misery and poverty her entire life, impulsively falls in love with a smooth and well-mannered newcomer, only to find that he is cheating the poor of their relief checks.

F10.   **The Printed Spot.** Synopsis of a mystery-detective screenplay with some camera directions.

A newspaper reporter is stopped from writing stories about crooked politicians, and is forced to run for his life. But he turns the tables on his opponents and ends up being hired as the new police chief by the police commissioner.

F11.   **Hoss Tamer.** Short story by L. Ron Hubbard adapted by Frank Gruber for the television series "The Tales of Wells Fargo." Directed by Earl Bellamy. Aired January 20, 1958, NBC. (See B204.)

F12.   **Revolt in the Stars.** Full-length science fiction screenplay written in 1977. Unpublished.

A fast action, science fiction epic that opens with the discovery of a time capsule containing the history of an ancient galactic civilization of which Earth was once a part. The story pits a ruthlessly ambitious galactic ruler against a courageous man and woman who lead the rebellion against him.

F13.   **Unnamed movie plot.** Synopsis of a mystery-detective movie written in June 1979.

Two boys watching a *Starsky and Hutch* crime drama on TV, decide to take the law into their own hands and set off eagerly on their bikes to answer a police call.

F14.   **Ai! Pedrito!** Full-length comedy screenplay written in 1981. Unpublished.

Two identical look-a-likes, one a straight-laced Navy

lieutenant and the other a devil-may-care South American, become embroiled in a dangerous game run by opposing intelligence agencies. Played out against the backdrop of South American mountains and plains, this sophisticated spy spoof is based on a true story.

F15. **A Very Strange Trip.** Full length time-travel comedy screenplay written in 1981. Unpublished.

A dim-witted but likable army private attempts to deliver a truck to an army base thousands of miles away. But unknown to him, the truck is actually a time machine—and the adventures that befall him when the machine is accidentally triggered are both unexpected and hilarious.

G. HONORS AND AWARDS FOR FICTION WORKS

Awards and recognitions that the author has received internationally for his fiction works are listed chronologically by category.

The categories are:

1. General author awards

2. Awards for specific titles

    a. *Battlefield Earth*

    b. *Mission Earth*

    c. *Writers of The Future*

G. HONORS AND AWARDS FOR FICTION WRITING

(Listed Chronologically)

1. General

"Guardian of the Gulch"—Official symbol from the City of Helena, Montana, to "Famed Author and Helena Man," from Mayor Russell J. Ritter. January 19, 1984.

"Palmas De Oro" (Golden Palm)—Presented by the National Association of Journalists in Mexico City to L. Ron Hubbard as "one of the most acclaimed and widely read authors of all time." 1989. Mexico.

"Golden Cross of Devotion and Merit"—Presented by the Commission Superieur Recompense for his outstanding contributions to the betterment of mankind. 1989. France.

"Golden Laurel Award"—Presented by the Comité France Promotion in the human sciences category for his literary contributions and the betterment of the French culture and its community. 1989. France.

European Literary Trophy—Presented by the European Committee of Prestige. May 1990.

"Palmas De Oro"—A second Golden Palm award presented by the National Association of Journalists as "A tribute to L. Ron Hubbard for the important legacy he left mankind through his technology and literary works during the past two decades." 1990. Mexico.

Golden Tie Award—Awarded posthumously by the French National Federation for Culture for outstanding achievements in the arts, sciences and literature. 1990. France.

"Gold Medal"—Awarded by the French Academy of Arts, Sciences & Letters for literary works and achievements. 1990. France.

Certificate of Doctor Honoris Causa—Presented by the European Academy of Arts. 1991.

Commemoration for Outstanding Achievement—"100 million books in print by L. Ron Hubbard." Presented by W & G Foyles, Ltd. February 1992. United Kingdom.

Acknowledgment as a Bestselling Author—for 32 national bestsellers and over 100 million works sold, Ingram Book Company. March 1992.

Acknowledgment as a Bestselling Author—for 32 national bestsellers and over 100 million copies of his works sold. Presented by *Magazine & Bookseller.* March 1992.

Honorary Degree, Doctor of Literature—Posthumous degree from Moscow State University for outstanding achievements in literature and philosophy. March 1992. See also Section H.

Author and Humanitarian of the Year—Nominated by the Editor and Test Panel of *Leamington Spa Journal*, United Kingdom. April 27, 1992.

2. Specific Titles

Battlefield Earth:

Golden Scroll Award—Presented by the Academy of Science Fiction, Fantasy and Horror Films. 1982.

Literary Selection—Selection by the Literary Guild of America. 1983.

Saturn Award—Presented by the Academy of Science Fiction, Fantasy and Horror Films. 1983.

Gutenberg Award—Presented to L. Ron Hubbard as a special tribute for *Battlefield Earth* and his exceptional contribution to science fiction literature. 1986.

Tetradrama D'Oro Award—Presented by *Il Corriere* newspaper for the message of peace contained in *Battlefield Earth*. 1987. Italy.

Mission Earth:

Literary Selection—All ten volumes selected by the Literary Guild of America. 1985-87.

Cosmos 2000 Award—From French science fiction readers who voted the *Mission Earth* series the most popular science fiction book. 1989. France.

Nova Science—Presented by the National Committee for Science Fiction and Fantasy for contributions to Italian science fiction. Hubbard was the first non-Italian to win this award. 1989. Italy.

Golden Headset Award. Best Audio Series, *Mission Earth*. 1989, 1991.

Ole Doc Methuselah:

Golden Scroll Award—Presented by the Academy of Science Fiction, Fantasy and Horror Films. 1992.

L. Ron Hubbard Presents
Writers of the Future:

L. Ron Hubbard Presents Writers of the Future Month—Proclaimed by Mayor Lawrence A. Santistevan in Taos, New Mexico, to honor The Writers of the Future workshop. May 1986.

Venture Award—Presented to L. Ron Hubbard's Writers of the Future by the science fiction and fantasy writers at the Life, the Universe and Everything Convention. 1988.

Award—Honoring L. Ron Hubbard's "invaluable contribution to science fiction and the arts through his Writers of The Future Contest" at the Brigham Young University Symposium of Science Fiction & Fantasy. February 7, 1988.

L. Ron Hubbard's Writers of the Future Month Proclaimed in Petaluma, California. September 1991.

L. Ron Hubbard's Illustrators of the Future Month
Proclaimed in Bend, Oregon. September 1991.

L. Ron Hubbard's Writers of the Future Day
Proclaimed in Houston, Texas. September 1993.

L. Ron Hubbard's Writers of the Future Week
Proclaimed in Huntington, Indiana. May 1994.

L. Ron Hubbard's Writers of the Future Week
Proclaimed in Portsmouth, New Hampshire. May 1994.

L. Ron Hubbard's Writers of the Future Week
Proclaimed in Fort Madison, Iowa. May 1994.

L. Ron Hubbard's Writers of the Future Week
Proclaimed in Lorain, Ohio. May 1994.

L. Ron Hubbard's Writers of the Future Week
Proclaimed in Denham Springs, Louisiana. May 1994.

L. Ron Hubbard's Writers of the Future Week
Proclaimed in Spartanburg, South Carolina. May 1994.

L. Ron Hubbard's Writers of the Future Week
Proclaimed in Kenner, Louisiana. May 1994.

L. Ron Hubbard's Writers of the Future Week
Proclaimed in Ponchatoula, Louisiana. May 1994.

L. Ron Hubbard's Writers of the Future Week
Proclaimed in Cape Girardeau, Missouri. May 1994.

L. Ron Hubbard's Writers of the Future Week
Proclaimed in Vineland, New Jersey. May 1994.

L. Ron Hubbard's Writers of The Future Week
Proclaimed in Schenectady, New York. May 1994.

L. Ron Hubbard's Writers of The Future Week
Proclaimed in Youngstown, Ohio. May 1994.

L. Ron Hubbard's Writers of the Future Week
Proclaimed in Thibodaux, Louisiana. May 1994.

H. Doctor of Literature Award Moscow State University

DEDICATION OF L. RON HUBBARD HALL

On February 23, 1992, officials of Moscow State University dedicated a hall, in the renowned Gorky Library, to American author L. Ron Hubbard. This occasion marked the first time in the history of the University that a foreign author was so highly recognized.

The following is a transcription of the speech made by Dean Yassen Zassoursky of the School of Journalism and Foreign Literature:

> *On behalf of Moscow University and the Faculty of Journalism, I am happy to inaugurate this day, this hall as L. Ron Hubbard's Hall—of our library, of our school.*
>
> *It is in recognition of the great achievements of the great man, great author, great adventurer, that we do this.*
>
> *We hope that the library will be helpful in the publishing of L. Ron Hubbard's books in our country, in Russian and in many other languages of the Commonwealth of Independent States which now form the former Soviet Union.*
>
> *It is promoting his ideas, his thoughts—especially his views on curing drug addicts and alcoholics, and his views on permanent education—which are very close to my heart, and certainly his ideas of man. These are the greatest achievements of this world, and we are very grateful to you for bringing us these books.*
>
> *I am very happy to give you this proclamation in recognition of L. Ron Hubbard's achievements.*

Dean Yassen Zassoursky
Moscow State University

RIBBON CUTTING CEREMONY

On March 10, 1992, just three days before the birth date of L. Ron Hubbard, a ribbon-cutting ceremony to open the hall, attended by 200 VIPs, television, radio and press, was officiated by Vladimir Komchatov, Moscow aide to President Boris Yeltsin. Komchatov was assisted by Dean Zassoursky, Fred Harris from Author Services, Inc. (L. Ron Hubbard's literary agency) and the ribbon was cut by Larisa Shikhmuradova, Deputy Chief of the Gorky Library.

CONFERRAL OF DOCTORATE DEGREE

At the ceremony, L. Ron Hubbard was awarded an Honorary Degree of Doctor of Literature, Moscow University, "For outstanding achievements in literature and philosophy and for his great humanitarian activities." In an official letter following the ceremony, Shikhmuradova expressed her hopes that the new hall would help "readers and workers of our library to get acquainted with the life and works of L. Ron Hubbard and will help bring further connection and mutual understanding of our peoples."

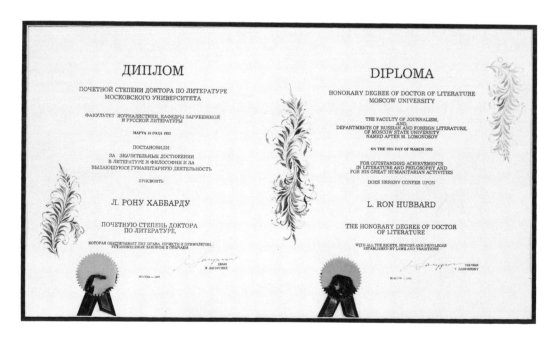

I. Critical Appreciation

This section provides a selection of critical appreciation for L. Ron Hubbard and his major works from publications, reviewers and other authors. Included are statements ranging from enthusiastic 1930's critiques by science fiction editor John W. Campbell, Jr. to Stephen King's acclamation for the republication of *Fear*. Selections have been made on the basis of 1) relevance, 2) insight, and 3) influence of the sources. The selected quotes are categorized as follows:

(An index to this section by author or periodical quoted is in Section R.)

1.   L. RON HUBBARD THE WRITER

"... back in the 1930s and '40s Hubbard was a leader among the crew of fast, versatile wordsmiths who produced the reams of copy needed to fill the pages of the pulps. In SF, he gained a reputation as a superlative storyteller with total mastery of plot and pacing."

Publishers Weekly

"L. Ron Hubbard was one of the most colorful writers of science fiction's golden age."

Atlanta Journal and Constitution

"... probably ranks as one of the brightest luminaries in the *Astounding Science Fiction* galaxy. He's good."

George Ebey
Fantasy Commentator

"We do not collect trendy authors, nor do we collect minor authors. In the field of American literature, for instance, we select with care only those American or Californian authors who we determine are important contributors to the state, to the country and to the world.

"L. Ron Hubbard is perhaps <u>the</u> quintessential western author, and his works fit perfectly in our collection."

Thomas V. Lange
The Huntington Library

"Ron Hubbard exploded onto the science fiction scene nearly half a century ago, and the reverberations haven't died yet . . . a powerfully charismatic and fascinating human being."

Frederik Pohl

2.   BUCKSKIN BRIGADES

"... Mr. Hubbard has reversed a time-honored formula and has given a thriller to which, at the end of every chapter or so, another paleface bites the dust . . . an enthusiasm, even a freshness and sparkle, decidedly rare in this type of romance."

New York Times Book Review

"Reading *Buckskin Brigades* is like watching a Saturday afternoon serial at the downtown Bijou. Each chapter leaves you hanging, but the master storyteller often began the next chapter by keeping that ball in the air while picking up another situation.

". . . Hubbard's most important contribution is a story told through the mind and body of an American Indian. That alone makes it worthwhile."

The Forum-Fargo

"We admire greatly the work of words expressed in *Buckskin Brigades*.

"Like 'Yellow Hair' you have walked the Blackfeet path with honor and have showed our people in a true light. Never has our morals and ethics been presented with such clarity."

Council Members of the Blackfeet Nation

3.   BATTLEFIELD EARTH

"This has everything: suspense, pathos, politics, war, humor, diplomacy and intergalactic finance . . . Hubbard keeps things moving so irresistibly . . . and the 800 pages go by quickly . . .

"SF's new, larger audience is about to discover an old master."

Publishers Weekly

"*Battlefield Earth* is a voluminous work. Well-written. Hubbard really brings characters to life. His action leads to more action and keeps you reading."

Yoji Kondo

"*Battlefield Earth* is like a 12-hour 'Indiana Jones' marathon. Non-stop and fast-paced. Every chapter has a big bang-up adventure."

Kevin J. Anderson

"... one of the great formula and pulp writers of the golden age of science fiction ... huge, rollicking saga ... The pace starts fast and never lets up."

Atlanta Journal and Constitution

"If you like ... fast, unrelenting 'Raiders of the Lost Ark' action, then this is the book for you. It's a real page turner."

Rocky Mountain News

"Think of the 'Star Wars' sagas, and 'Raiders of the Lost Ark,' mix in the triumph of 'Rocky I,' 'Rocky II,' and 'Rocky III' and you have captured the exuberance, style and glory of *Battlefield Earth*."

Baltimore Evening Sun

"I read *Battlefield Earth* straight through in one sitting although it's immense ... I was fascinated by it."

Frederik Pohl

"Pure science fiction ... 430,000 words written by a super-writer of the Golden Age of Science Fiction ... the great pulp music in every line ... will be talked about for a decade ... wonderful adventure ... great characters ... a masterpiece."

A.E. van Vogt

"A legendary master of the Golden Age of Science Fiction returns after thirty years with a monumental new work, a gigantic achievement."

Forrest J. Ackerman

"Hubbard celebrates 50 years as a pro writer with this huge (800+ pages) ... gripping slugfest ... tight plotting, furious action ... have at 'em entertainment."

Kirkus Reviews

"Good old fashioned space opera (Buck Rogers stuff) makes a solid comeback in L. Ron Hubbard's *Battlefield Earth* ... If you think they don't write 'em anymore like they used to, take heart—here's 800 pages from one of the originals."

New York Newsday

". . . it is simply a corking good adventure-love-war story that sweeps the reader along in its classic themes and roaring pace. *Battlefield Earth* is the culmination of a writing lifetime, its author's masterpiece, and is superb entertainment."

Deland Sun News

4.   DEATH'S DEPUTY

"Nostalgia buffs will love this. *Death's Deputy* brings back the glory of World War I."

Robert Bloch

"The smooth flowing narrative we have come to associate with this prolific but conscientious author is such that we become thoroughly bemused with the idea . . ."

Thomas Sheridan
Fantasy Review

5.   FINAL BLACKOUT

"The hero of *Final Blackout* has glowed in my mind ever since I read the initial magazine version in 1939. This final version shows that the story, like all timeless works of fiction, is also timely."

Philip Jose Farmer

". . . Hubbard's best science fiction novel . . . compelling . . . riveting . . . a superior piece of pulp adventure writing . . ."

Publishers Weekly

"A chilling and lucid picture of the effects of incessant warfare."

Kirkus Reviews

"The work of a master at the peak of his powers. The style is flowing and lean; the prose crackles with energy and bite . . . a gritty, imaginative tale of survival and heroic leadership that is a chilling prophesy for our time. A work of stunning vision that is right on the mark."

Greg Dinallo

"L. Ron Hubbard's *Final Blackout* presents a gripping portrait of the Lieutenant, a soldier left to prosecute the conflict created by the incompetence of politicians. Rigid military code, denial of nerves and callous distribution of death guided his life, and inevitably, ended it. Whether he spills the blood of others or sheds his own, the Lieutenant screams out a message even more relevant today than when L. Ron Hubbard created him.

"Dynamic and vivid, L. Ron Hubbard's *Final Blackout* fills us with the legacy of war—duty, honor and death."

Edward G. Gibson

"*Final Blackout* is as perfect a piece of science fiction as has ever been written."

Robert A. Heinlein

"This is a good story in a kind of universal sense. A classic . . . a survivor of the test of time. The story strikes deep."

Larry Niven

". . . well written and powerful . . . Ron Hubbard has perfectly captured the archetypal man of the eighties."

Ray Faraday Nelson

"*Final Blackout* is an apocalyptic view of the end of civilization as it still may happen. Years before Hiroshima, L. Ron Hubbard looked past the stories of atomic holocaust that now seem unlikely. He created a currently believable paradigm of future conflicts where bankrupt, desperate countries turn to uncontrollable but cheap nerve gases and man-made plagues. If this book is prophecy, only a magnificently protected America can avoid a world-wide Dark Age."

Jay Kay Klein

"A landmark classic! It has been remembered through the decades as one of the all-time memorable classics of the science fiction field."

Robert Bloch

"*Final Blackout* was the best anti-war story that I've read. A classic of its kind and really a kind of pre-vision of what would later come to be called meta fiction and be brought to greater heights by contemporary stars of the literary field like John Varth and others."

James Gunn

6.   FEAR

"L. Ron Hubbard's *Fear* is one of the few books in the chiller genre which actually merits employment of the overworked adjective 'classic', as in 'This is a classic tale of creeping, surreal menace and horror.' If you're not averse to a case of the cold chills—a rather bad one—and you've never read *Fear*, I urge you to do so. Don't even wait for a dark and stormy night. This is one of the really, really good ones."

Stephen King

". . . a true scare."

Ray Bradbury

"*Fear* is L. Ron Hubbard's finest work!"

Robert Bloch

"*Fear* is one of the most compelling fantasies ever written, with all the scary logic and authority of genuine nightmare. Hubbard didn't need werewolves and bloody axes—he could scare the daylights out of you with a hat, or a stairway, or a little boy sitting on a rock and scratching his initials in the dirt with a stick. *Fear* is a terribly powerful story."

Tim Powers

"A classic masterpiece of psychological horror."

Robert Silverberg

"*Fear* is the best piece of fiction L. Ron Hubbard ever wrote. It is one of the foundations of the contemporary horror genre, widely influential, and powerfully effective. *Fear* is a work of deep psychological insight and moral complexity that helped to transform horror literature from an antiquarian or metaphysical form into a contemporary and urban form with the gritty details of everyday realism. From Ray Bradbury to Stephen King, a literary debt is owed to L. Ron Hubbard for *Fear*."

David Hartwell

"I recall how shaken I was by L. Ron Hubbard's classic story, *Fear*, one of the most vividly imagined inner landscapes in horror fiction."

Ramsey Campbell

"One of the most brilliant psychological thrillers of all time, one of the finest horror stories ever written."

Karl Edward Wagner

"The triumphant pioneer of psychological thrillers."

Jack Williamson

"L. Ron Hubbard has been, since the 40's, one of the five writers in the SF field who have served me as models and teachers. His stories, *Fear* in particular, directly influenced all my work . . ."

Ray Faraday Nelson

"When I was a kid it was the first psychological horror fiction I ever read and it had a tremendous effect on me. It scared the very devil out of me. It made me leery of ever going down to the basement again."

Edward Bryant

"Hubbard effectively develops the situation and characters and deftly builds suspense, all in about half of the wordage that many modern authors would require. A first-class work—heartily endorsed by no less than Ray Bradbury and Stephen King—a must purchase for horror collections."

Booklist

". . . a story of fantasy and terror that helped pave the way for today's style in horror fiction. *Fear* does something very rare—it lives up to its title. Hubbard defines the essence of what it means to be afraid."

Atlanta Journal and Constitution

7.   THE GHOUL

"I nominate as [one of] the ten best stories . . . for the year 1939 . . . *The Ghoul* . . . five-star yarns."

Isaac Asimov

8.   THE INDIGESTIBLE TRITON

". . . an uproarious adventure-fantasy of a specially entrancing sort . . . fast and funny and altogether entertaining . . . enthusiastically recommended."

Frederik Pohl

". . . a free fantasia on mermen and other unlikely sea denizens which reaches delightful heights of absurdity."

New York Herald Tribune

9.   OLE DOC METHUSELAH

"Delightful, amazing and filled with wonder!"

Robert Silverberg

". . . a crackling sense of wonder . . . super science and more exotic planets than you could stuff into an atlas."

Kevin J. Anderson

"*Ole Doc Methuselah* resonates with the hum of high energy, captivating characters and great adventure. Ole Doc and his sidekick Hippocrates will grab your imagination, and your heart strings, and take you on adventures that you will never forget. A cornucopia of fabulous adventure, wonderful characters and great fun."

Roddy McDowall

"Some slam-bang glories of youth don't age, and the grand space opera of Doc Methuselah is one of them."

Gregory Benford

"*Ole Doc Methuselah* is perfect Golden Age Science Fiction."

Edward Bryant

"L. Ron Hubbard remains one of science fiction's most romantic writers and Ole Doc Methuselah is one of his larger-than-life characters."

Brad Linaweaver

"Classic adventures by a classic writer."

Roger Zelazny

10.   SLAVES OF SLEEP

"I stayed up all night finishing it. The yarn scintillated."

Ray Bradbury

"This is an excellent, highly imaginative book . . . it has everything: boats, romance, violence, beautiful women, drama, suspense, love and an excellent set of characters."

The Tempest

"*Slaves of Sleep* became a sort of buzz word. There are bits and pieces from Ron's work that became part of the language in ways that very few other writers imagined."

Frederik Pohl

"A lusty and satisfying adventure . . . Perhaps its superiority lies in the authenticity of the maritime flavour (derived no doubt from the author's own seafaring experience) . . . Altogether a delightful fireside adventure for a winter's night."

Kemp McDonald
Fantasy Review

11. TO THE STARS

"*To The Stars*, by L. Ron Hubbard, I thought was the greatest novel that has ever been written in the history of mankind."

Jerry Pournelle

"He wrote a story called *To The Stars* which was one of the first, if not the first, stories ever written about time dilation effect."

Sam Moskowitz

". . . an unusual yarn in that the true plot is entirely developed in the last three paragraphs."

John W. Campbell, Jr.
Astounding Science Fiction

12. TYPEWRITER IN THE SKY

"I particularly like *Typewriter in the Sky* because it was such a skillful parody of adventure fiction and was written with a great deal of lightness and touch which you didn't get much in those days."

James Gunn

13. MISSION EARTH

"You will lose sleep. You will miss appointments. If you don't force yourself to set it down and talk to your family from time to time, you may be looking for a new place to live. Reading *The Invaders Plan* is simply the most fun you can have by yourself . . . Ironic, exciting, romantic and hilarious. It delighted me from the beginning. Remember how you felt the first time you saw *Star Wars*? This book will do it to you again."

Orson Scott Card

"For readers who enjoy action, adventure, and just flat-out good entertainment, the *Mission Earth* series is a most enjoyable experience . . . Hubbard, long considered one of the most influential writers of the world, was at his best with a wit and energy which only he, and he alone, could write."

Cleveland Advocate

"L. Ron Hubbard's latest book, *The Invaders Plan*, confirms the notion that he is one of the finest writers of this particular genre.

To call Hubbard a master storyteller would be a gross understatement."

The Collegian
University of Massachusetts

"Marvelous satire by a master of adventure."

Anne McCaffrey

". . . a big humorous tale of interstellar intrigue in the classical mold. I fully enjoyed it."

Roger Zelazny

"Wry humor abounds—but never lets you relax for very long.
You think you know Earth? L. Ron Hubbard shows it from some different angles . . . An unparalleled saga of satire."

F.M. Busby

"I loved *Mission Earth*. The CIA will hate it. Hubbard has produced a real knee-slapper . . . he's laughing at the Sacred Cow of the Eighties, the so-called intelligence community . . . Few writers have had the knack of making a serious philosophical point without ever stopping to preach, without ever slowing the action for an instant."

Ray Faraday Nelson

"A wicked satire . . . more addictive than salt and peanuts."

Gene Wolfe

". . . a remarkable publishing success story . . . I don't know anything in publishing history to compare with it."

James Gunn

"The *Mission Earth* books by L. Ron Hubbard bring back the pleasures of the Golden Age when storytelling was at its finest. The reader is swept up in Hubbard's universe-wide plot and not let go until the very end."

Ed Gorman

"One of the most impressive literary achievements in the science fiction genre is Hubbard's 10-volume satire series. It's easy to see why these have gained bestseller status: as a unit they are remarkable."

The Bookwatch

"While much of the book is social satire, worthy of Mark Twain or H.G. Wells, the book clearly has its roots in the science fiction of the past. It contains plenty of fast-paced action scenes, sexual antics, mutant freaks and futuristic space machines."

Bloomington Herald

". . . the book delivers all the entertainment anybody could ask for, with satiric zingers at several deserving targets. On its own terms, clearly a success."

New York Newsday

"*The Invaders Plan*, the first book in L. Ron Hubbard's enormously successful *Mission Earth* dekalogy, is stupendous . . . The book is often exciting, inventive, and always interesting. The characters are superb. The result is an L. Ron Hubbard masterpiece destined to become a classic."

Mark Tompkins
Starship Express

". . . action-packed, intricately plotted . . . The 10-volume series, which has been setting sales records, is a cross between Flash Gordon and 007, as told by the evil Emperor Ming and Ernst Blofeld, head of SMERSH."

Buffalo News

". . . L. Ron Hubbard is assured a place in the pantheon of Science Fiction Masters. These novels contain all the elements that lead people to read science fiction in the first place: imaginative speculation, adventure, satire, interesting characters, exotic locales, and a vivid sense of wonder."

Partners in Peril

"L. Ron Hubbard is one of the most influential and best selling authors in the world today. Millions of readers around the world have relished his distinctive pace, artistry and humor for over 50 years . . . his unprecedented 10-volume *Mission Earth* series—a brilliantly conceived fusion of action, romance, satire and drama—written with that unique Hubbard hallmark, confirms his position as one of the most versatile and talented writers of the twentieth century."

Childress Index

"The key to this novel's success is Hubbard's eye to detail, augmented by his keen sense of characters. Strange as it may seem, the detail brings the reader into the story through its involvement with the characters . . . Hubbard doesn't allow the reader to get off the 'edge of his seat' for a moment."

Iowa State Daily

"Each book is a significant explosion of wonder, and far superior to the previous book. I figure that by . . . volume 10, we'll have a story beyond perfection. Read them!"

Voyage

"What we have in *Mission Earth* is an extended satire which [is] taking on most governmental institutions, psychiatry, public relations, and higher education, to name a few of his targets. In this volume he even spoofs the pornography trade. If you haven't sampled this series, you should. While satire is not for everyone, Hubbard may be read as straight adventure."

Memphis Commercial Appeal

". . . fast-paced and thoroughly enjoyable . . . The novel's offbeat characters and their endless adventures serve as the means for Hubbard to unleash a stream of wicked satire and social commentary. It's Jonathan Swift with a laser gun."

Seattle Post-Intelligencer

"The first book was a surprise, a wildly wicked and deliciously cynical work that mocked virtue, skewered hypocrisy and gave a hilariously satirical view of society through the Voltar Confederacy. Yes, and it was funny."

Kansas City Star

". . . a delicious read . . . as one would expect of an experienced pro . . ."

Washington Post

"Each chapter of Hubbard's narrative is fast-paced . . . espionage and intrigue prevail . . . Hubbard's laser-like wit and tongue-in-cheek assessment of contemporary living make it easy to read while at the same time lending literary value to the genre of science fiction."

Atlanta Journal and Constitution

"This ambitious novel, the first of a 10-volume series by SF veteran Hubbard . . . is space opera in the grand tradition . . ."

Library Journal

"L. Ron Hubbard's *The Invaders Plan* reflects a splendid talent combined with careful workmanship that is the very definition of conceptual quality—sought by so many and achieved by so few."

The Midwest Book Review

"The old master has created a new genre and a veritable blockbuster . . . He breaks all the rules and moves the art of science fiction into a new realm of entertainment as well as education."

Everett Herald

J. ABOUT THE AUTHOR: SELECTED LETTERS AND ARTICLES

This section includes excerpts from selected published and personal letters, and editorial comments regarding or from the period 1932—1948.

STUDENTS TO VISIT OLD SPANISH MAIN

50 College Boys to Cruise Waters Once Infested by Pirate Ships.

The waters of the Spanish Main, once infested by pirates, will be invaded this Summer by a group of 50 American college boys sailing on a four-masted schooner.

L. R. Hubbard of George Washington University is handling all local arrangements for the expedition, which will set sail June 20 from Baltimore aboard the Doris Hamlin.

Two other George Washington students, H. A. Glidden and Ray Heimburger, will make the trip.

At various historical spots along the several thousands of miles of the tour the students will make motion pictures based on facts and legends concerning the lives of famous pirates. The trip is expected to last about four months.

Among the members of the expedition, it was said, will be several biologists and botanists, who will make scientific studies with apparatus furnished by the University of Michigan.

The Doris Hamlin, 200 feet in length, will be manned by a crew of eight men, under Capt. Fred E. Garfield, a master with 30 years' experience.

Plans Cruise
G. W. U. STUDENT TO VISIT SPANISH MAIN.

L. R. HUBBARD.
—Star Staff Photo.

THE PILOT

The Magazine for Aviation's Personnel

Vol. 7   JULY, 1934   No. 6

« « Who's Who » »

By H. LATANE LEWIS II

RON HUBBARD

Whenever two or three pilots are gathered together around the Nation's Capital, whether it be a Congressional hearing or just in the back of some hangar, you'll probably hear the name of Ron Hubbard mentioned, accompanied by such adjectives as "crazy," "wild," and "dizzy." For the flaming-haired pilot hit the city like a tornado a few years ago and made women scream and strong men weep by his aerial antics. He just dared the ground to come up and hit him.

In the beginning, Ron (also known as "Flash") hailed from out west, but only stayed long enough to be born. Since then he has been a dweller of the world at large, and there are few nooks and corners of the earth that he hasn't poked into. Before he fell from grace and became an aviator, he was, at various times, top sergeant in the Marines, radio crooner, newspaper reporter, gold miner in the West Indies, and movie director-explorer, having led a motion picture expedition into the south seas aboard an ancient windjammer.

❖

RON HUBBARD

❖

Then he turned to glider flying. And that is what gave Washsington its biggest thrill, for Ron could do more stunts in a sailplane than most pilots can in a pursuit job, He would come out of spins at an altitude of thirty inches and thumb his nose at the undertakers who used to come out to the field and titter.

Once he took a glider up at a Chicago airport which was surrounded by a concrete road. It was a hot day and waves of heat were rising off the road as if it had been a stove. Ron sat on that up current of air and stayed there. Round and round the airport he went like a merry-go-round, until everybody got dizzy from watching him. Finally, he got tired of chasing his tail and came down, after establishing something of a record for sustained flight over the same field.

Then, one day he got fed up with gliders and decided to try something with power. So he climbed into a fast ship and, without any dual time at all, gave the engine the soup and hopped off. Well, he got back on the ground with the plane still all in one piece and, going on the theory that its a good landing if you can walk away from it, he realized that he was now a pilot.

Fired by his new prowess, he immediately started barnstorming and ensnared many an unsuspecting passenger. He flew under every telephone wire in the Middle West and cows and horses in that section still shy at the sound of an airplane motor.

After being one of aviation's most distinguished hell-raisers, he finally settled down with great dignity and became director of the flying club at George Washington University. And to make his taming complete, he took unto himself a co-pilot, a very wise and charming little aviatrix, whom Ron refers to as "the skipper."

At present, our young hero is buzzing around on the West Coast, where he writes magazine stories between flights. His playboy days over, he is now recognized as one of the outstanding glider pilots in the country.

Five Novels Monthly

F. A. McCHESNEY, Editor

VOLUME XXX   MAY, 1935   NUMBER 2

"I've been through a hurricane in the Caribbean, and I know my Venezuela coast, and it so happens that Hubbard's descriptions are accurate to the hair. Stories like 'Sea Fangs' keep me from being bored with life."

False Cargo ....

"What I liked about Hubbard's 'Hurtling Wings' is that it is not one of these cut and dried stories, but full of action. It makes one wish he was going up in the air, riding adventure and thrills, instead of reading it."

Raking Guns   28

"I'd like to see another story like 'Hurtling Wings' or 'Twenty Fathoms Down.' They were exceptionally good."

Th   160

What Do You Think? .... $2.40 a Year

"'The Lieutenant Takes the Air' suited me right down to the ground. More power to Hubbard—and more Hubbard novels, please. I get a great kick out of his stories, and look forward to seeing more. F.N. is tops. It's alive, every word of it."

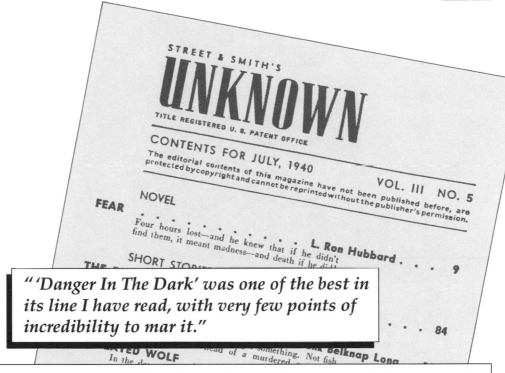

Street & Smith's

UNKNOWN

TITLE REGISTERED U. S. PATENT OFFICE

CONTENTS FOR JULY, 1940

The editorial contents of this magazine have not been published before, are protected by copyright and cannot be reprinted without the publisher's permission.

VOL. III   NO. 5

NOVEL

FEAR . . . . L. Ron Hubbard 9
Four hours lost—and he knew that if he didn't find them, it meant madness—and death if he did.

SHORT STORIES

" 'Danger In The Dark' was one of the best in its line I have read, with very few points of incredibility to mar it."

"It was just top-flight entertainment in any man's language. I liked it. And that's against my principles. The same goes for Hubbard's 'Danger in the Dark,' another demon tale. Before I finished the story, I found myself half believing in the island monster, and thoroughly enjoying the yarn. 'This has got to stop,' I told myself. 'I don't like weird fiction!' "

" 'The Ultimate Adventure' was pretty good. Gad! A horrible thought just came to me. What if they had made Stevie read one of Lovecraft's stories! If 'Ultimate Adventure' is ever made into a movie I can just picture the three Ritz brothers as the three ghouls."

"The April issue was a knockout. 'The Ultimate Adventure' is the best fantasy I have read in years. It surpasses everything Hubbard has done. Let's have more like it from him."

STORIES
79–89 SEVENTH AVENUE
NEW YORK, N.Y.

EDITORIAL
DEPARTMENT

STREET & SMITH
PUBLISHERS

January 23, 1939

Mr. L. Ron Hubbard,
Rt. 1, Box 452,
Port Orchard, Wash.

Dear Ron:

I'm damn glad you'll be with us on the Arabian
Nights stuff---and you needn't worry about having it yours. I've been telling a few of the
boys to read Washington Irving as an example of
pure fantasy and complete acceptance of matic,
enchantment, et cetera, and adding that they
aren't to do Arabian Nights because the field
is preempted by you. It's been held open for
you.

As soon as I can get hol

The Sportsman Pilot
INC.
515 MADISON AVENUE
TELEPHONE PLAZA 3-6969
NEW YORK, N.Y.

November 25, 1936

Mr. L. Ron Hubbard
1212 Gregory Way
Bremerton, Washington

Dear Mr. Hubbard:

In reply to your letter to Mr. Lay I can only say that as
usual I should be very glad to receive any material which
you think would fit into the magazine.

I expect that your trip to Alaska may produce some material
which would be of interest to the private flier and I hope
you will keep us in mind throughout your trip.

Very truly yours,

Charles H. Gale
Managing Editor

CHG:MD

Thrilling Adventures
Thrilling Detective
Thrilling Love
Thrilling Ranch Stories
Thrilling Western
Sky Fighters
The Lone Eagle
The Phantom Detective
Popular Western
Popular Detective

STANDARD MAGAZINES, Inc.
22 WEST 48th STREET
NEW YORK

Cable Address
"MAGSTAND"

February 26
1 9 3 5

Mr. L. Ron Hubbard
222 Riverside Drive
New York City.

Dear Ron:

There's a gaping hole in the inven-
tory of THRILLING ADVENTURES – that just must
be filled.

The requirements are simple – a fast
moving action story, locale, any spot on earth.
Nothing barred – from westerns, pseudo-scientific,
detective, costume to the good old-fashioned he-man
American soldier-of-fortune running amuck around
the world.

And all lengths – from two thousand
word short-shorts to twenty thousand word novelettes.
And we have no taboos because of an odd length.

We'll pay one cent a word – with a
quick decision and prompt payment on acceptance.

Have you anything on hand to shoot
along?

Sincerely yours,

LEO MARGULIES
Editorial Director

lm;cl

J-5 • Letters to L. Ron Hubbard from Editors • 1935, 1936, 1939

This letter came to Hubbard with a request for one of his photos of the Great Wall of China:

Dear Mr. Hubbard:

I've listened with my mouth open to tales of China, told by many of my friends who have been there. One, a red-headed devil, made many trips up the Yangtse; another had a humdinger of an orchestra in Singapore; another made several trips up through Peiping to Manchuria; and yet another, a blond Russian, came here from Harbin.

I've been planning to go back to Harbin with him some day, to visit his folks. We intend to make the trip across in a small ketch, when finances permit. If we ever see our way clear to make it, I'd like to corner you and get the low-down on some of those Chinese enigmas.

Ever been in Mexico? The old itching foot is again bothering yours truly considerably, so I intend to pile the camp gear in either a motorcycle side-car or an Austin roadster and highball it down over that new highway from Laredo, Texas, to Mexico City next winter. Stay a few months, doing a bit of jungle trekking in Yucatan, and then maybe trade the outfit for a small boat and hit across to the West Indies or down to Central and South America.

> — Elwood W. Cooper
> Chico, California

Answer by Mr. Hubbard:

That itching foot is a very bothersome thing, but I can't figure a man wanting to go places when he lives in the vicinity of Chico. That Feather River country is great stuff. I was flying there a few months ago—flew from the coast to Tahoe in nothing more airworthy than an Aeronca.

But about Mexico: there's a peach of a road from Tijuana down to Mexico City. It isn't as far as you'd think, either. And the country isn't so settled. Nothing can beat a motorcycle in country like that. I'll bet you have a swell time of it!

About China: It's a great country, a dirty country, and an expensive country for a white man. The worst thing I can imagine is getting stuck along the Yellow Sea without a pocket full of jack. Believe me when I say that nobody is your pal in Yellow Peril Land when you're broke.

I've always wanted to cruise along that way in a small boat, but lately I've been obsessed with another idea. Why not take a tramp out to Shanghai, buy a sea-going junk and sail that thing back home? These junks are quite seaworthy, and they're like fish in the water in spite of their looks. Under the waterline they're built with real streamline design. All that overhang stern is just so much show. With a hold full of rice and dried fish you could pick your crew from dozens and dozens of applicants—and Chinese sailors know the score, I'll tell you.

From Shanghai, I'd sail down into the waters of Australia and thereabouts, taking in the South Pacific.

The idea may sound nutty, but all adventure comes from loco thoughts. A sane man isn't apt to stumble into excitement, because, consciously or unconsciously, he is plotting twenty-four hours a day how to save himself the trouble of being annoyed!

> — L. Ron Hubbard

Vol. 93. No. 5   October 1, 1935   Twice A Month

THE
CAMP-FIRE

where readers, writers
and adventurers
meet

L. RON HUBBARD joins our Writers' Brigade with his Leatherneck yarn, "He Walked to War." Hubbard is a tall red-haired chap with a service background, his father being an officer. He introduces himself at the Camp-Fire:

I was born in Nebraska and three weeks later went to Oklahoma. From there to Missouri, then to Montana. When I was a year old, they say I showed some signs of settling down, but I think this is merely rumor. Changing locales from the Pacific Coast to the Atlantic Coast every few months, it was not until I was almost twelve that I first left the United States. And it was not until I was sixteen that I headed for the China Coast.

In spite of changing schools, I received an education. I have some very poor grade sheets which show that I studied to be a civil engineer in college.

Civil engineering seemed very handsome at the time. I met the lads in their Stetsons from Crabtown to Timbuctu and they seemed to lead a very colorful existence squinting into their transits. However, too late, I was sent up to Maine by the Geological Survey to find the lost Canadian Border. Much bitten by seven kinds of insects, gummed by the muck of swamps, fed on johnny cake and tarheel, I saw instantly that a civil engineer had to stay far too long in far too few places and so I rapidly forgot my calculus and slip stick and began to plot ways and means to avoid the continuance of my education. I decided on an expedition into the Caribbean.

It was a crazy idea at best and I knew it, but I went ahead anyway, chartered a four-masted schooner and embarked with some fifty luckless souls who haven't ceased their cursings yet. Our present generation just doesn't take to salt horse, dried peas, and a couple quarts of water a day.

But the expedition did the trick. I did not have to return to college. Instead I returned to the West Indies.

I might remark upon a coincidence which has always amazed me. While in the West Indies I discovered signs of gold on an island and, harboring the thought that the *Conquistadores* might have left some gold behind, I determined to find it.

But just before my return to the island, I met a very lovely young lady who happened to own a farm up in Maryland. She did not particularly want me to go away, but I said that gold was calling and so I went. After half a year or more of intensive search, after wearing my palms thin wielding a sample pick, after assaying a few hundred sacks of ore, I came back, a failure.

But a month after my return to Maryland, I discovered a vein of honey-comb quartz in the back pasture of my lady's farm. The body of ore was tremendous, the visible vein several yards wide at the narrowest. Under the $20.67 an ounce, it assayed $82.34 a ton, and it is now worth about $145 a ton. However, to mine it takes money and I would have to stay close to Maryland. It's still there.

Chronological narration, in this short sketch, is impossible. Therefore, permit me to jump about a bit.

I was once convinced that the future of aviation lies in motorless flight. Accordingly I started gliding and soaring with the rest of the buzzards, and finally succeeded in establishing a record which has no official existence whatever and no reason, indeed, for existing. I traveled better than eighty miles an hour for twelve minutes in a soaring plane, maintaining the same altitude about an airport which is set on a flat plain. Answer: Heat lift from the circling concrete road.

From there I went into power flight, the high spot of which came on a barnstorming trip through the Mid-West in a five-lunged crate which staggered rather than flew. All one summer, I tried very hard to meet St. Pete, but evidently that gentleman either lost my name from the roll or my luck is far better than I think it is.

Unfortunately, in my Asiatic wanderings, no one, not even Hindu fortune tellers, thought to inform me that I would some day make my living with a typewriter and so I completely forgot to conduct myself informatively and devoted my time to enjoying life.

In Peiping, for instance, I did not avail myself of photographic impressions I might well have gained. I completely missed the atmosphere of the city, devoting most of my time to a British major who happened to be head of the Intelligence out there.

In Shanghai, I am ashamed to admit that I did not tour the city or surrounding country as I should have. I know more about 131 Bubbling Wells Road and its wheels than I do about the history of the town.

In Hong Kong . . . well, why take up space?

Time after time, people accuse me of having been in the Marines. Pushed right up against the wall, I am forced to admit a connection with that very cosmopolitan outfit, however short lived and vague. I was once a top-kicker in the 20th

because as they sing in Shin-ho,

> I walked down the street
> Without a cent in my jeans,
> And that is the reason
> I joined the Marines.

I am not sure that calling squads east and west fits a man for writing, but it does give him a vocabulary.

One thing I might mention in connection with the leathernecks, most of the fiction written about them is of an intensely dramatic type, all do and die and *Semper Fidelis* and the dear old flag.

To me the Marine Corps is a more go-to-hell outfit than the much lauded French Foreign Legion ever could be. The two are comparable in many ways. God knows what you'll find in either, from college professors to bellhops. Just why the disappointed lover has to sneak off for North Africa all the time is a riddle. More men have taken refuge in the Corps than in the Legion and, judging from association, leathernecks certainly lead a sufficiently exciting existence.

I've known the Corps from Quantico to Peiping, from the South Pacific to the West Indies, and I've never seen any flag-waving. The most refreshing part of the U.S.M.C. is that they get their orders and start out and do the job and that's that. Whether that job was to storm the heights of Chapultepec so that the United States Army could proceed, or to dislodge a crazy gentleman named John Brown from an arsenal at Harper's Ferry, or to knock off a few Boxers for the glory of England, your marine went and did the job and then retired to bind up his wounds while every one else went on parade.

Let it suffice. This is more than a thumbnail sketch, but I hope it's a passport to your interest. I know a lot of you out there, and I haven't heard from you in years. I know I haven't had any address, but I'm certain the editor will forward my mail.

When I get back from Central America, where I'm going soon, I'll have another yarn to tell.

170 King Street,
North Bay,Ontario,
29th. May 1936.

Mr. L. Ron Hubbard,
40 King Street,
New York City,N.Y..

Dear Mr. Hubbard,

Received your very generous letter in answer to my query.
I feel I cannot let it pass without letting you know how much I appreciate
the trouble you took to inform me about things I couldn't have known
otherwise,or without wasting a good deal of time,effort and perhaps money.
A three page letter packed full of meat of the kind I've been wanting is
what I got. Thanks to you,I'm going at the writing game much less blindly
with regard to trying to hit markets,and with a good deal more confidence.
To show you there IS a great disadvantage in being away from the hub of
things,it's taken me nearly four years of blind groping to get the sort of
stuff you've handed me from your experience as a writer that has arrived.
I'm not likely to forget you took the trouble to grind out three pages of
that experience,when honestly I expected a terse reply,if any at all. And
that cynical attitude is largely the result of accumulated rejection
slips,which ih turn,in many case were the result of not knowing the ropes.

Yours sincerely.

Gordon Walsh.

ARGOSY

Action Stories of Every Variety.

Volume 268   **OCTOBER 24, 1936**   Number 2

Argonotes
The Readers' Viewpoint

IN the Argonotes for last week we were discussing the matter of authenticity in story backgrounds. This week, fortunately, we can take a back seat and turn the rest of the argument over to our writers. Quite unasked, several of them have dropped us letters lately telling us what they are up to. A couple of these fit right in with our discussion.

One of ARGOSY's authors who has been doing a series based on hazardous occupations has been having the time of his life living his stories before he writes them. "Deep-Sea Diver," in this issue, is one of them. There are more to come. Listen to what is promised, and how it is lived, by

L. RON HUBBARD

These series will either be the making or the ruination of me. Lately I've been following your Argonotes, in which several gentlemen have taken several of us poor writers for a ride. I anticipate a lot of copy for that section with these hazardous occupation stories judging from the diversity of opinions I have received in collecting the material. For instance, two loggers I was talking to last month almost came to blows over the right name for the lad who strings cables in the lumber camps. One claimed it was "high-rigger," the other, "high faller." According to location, I suppose.

Mining is another thing that varies to beat the devil. All depends upon district, whether coal or metal mining, whether you are a miner or a mining engineer.

Oil wells are the most variable thing in the lot. Every section of the world has a different nomenclature, different methods. I took Texas because I'm familiar with their methods there, but ten to one some roughneck in California is going to pop up with vast objections.

So, I anticipate lots of fun. All along I've realized the score on this and so I have checked and rechecked the data contained in the stories, and I think I've got an airtight answer for every possible squawk.

Something else has amused me considerably. Writers, treating the same subject time after time in fiction, gradually evolve a terminology and a pattern for certain types of stories as you well know. This creates an erroneous belief in readers that they are familiar with a certain subject through reading so much fiction dealing with it. I've had to shed a lot of that for the sake of accuracy and I'm very, very anxious to have my hand called on some of it. Oil well stories, for instance, always seem to have a villain who, in the height of hate, drops a wrench or something down a well to ruin it. Dropping things into the hole is common. In cable tool drilling, so many hours or days are regularly estimated in with the rest of the work for fishing. The tools fall in, wrenches drop, bits stick, cables break, and wells are never, never abandoned because of it, or is it considered at all serious.

In the oil well story Mike McGraw gnaws upon a lighted cigar while he mixes nitroglycerin. He shoots fulminate caps with a slingshot to explode them. He is, in short, doing everything a man shouldn't do—accordingly to popular opinion. There'll be fireworks in that quarter. Plenty of fireworks. But I've nailed the answers down. Soup, unless confined, will burn slowly when ignited. Smoking while making it is no more dangerous than smoking in a gasoline station—and everybody does that. As for caps, they explode only when they are scratched with steel or when they have been hammered hard. I almost

went crazy in Puerto Rico while surveying a metal mine. The native in charge of dynamite was very, very careless, so I thought. One day, after he had blown a series along a drift, I told him what I thought about it. He was smoking and carrying 60% dynamite at the same time. To my horror he shoved the lighted end of his cigar against a stick. It burned no faster than a pitchy piece of kindling. He used to shoot dogs with fulminate triple-force caps.

The process of digging up data is interesting when I can get these gentlemen to give me a hand. The navy diver here is responsible for the data and authenticity of this story. Going down off the end of a dock didn't give me such a good idea of what it was all about after all. Never got so scared before in all my life. Something ghastly about it. And the helmet is enough to deafen you and the cuffs were so tight my hands got blue.

But it was lots of fun!

When these stories start to come out and when the letters start to come in calling me seven different kinds of a liar (which they will), sit easy and grin and shoot them this way. There isn't anything reasonable in the way of criticism I can't answer about this collected data.

It was either bow to popular fallacy and avoid all technical descriptions, or ride roughshod, make sure I was right and damn the torpedoes. Making the latter choice, I've laid myself wide open several times to crank letters. So be it.

THE NATIONAL AERONAUTIC

ASSOCIATION

DUPONT CIRCLE • WASHINGTON • DC

February 14, 1938

Brig. Gen. Walter C. Kilner
Assistant Chief of Air Corps
War Department
Washington, D.C.

Dear General Kilner;

When you asked me last week to procure advice on the problem of bringing a more agreeable and adventurous type of young man into the Air Corps, I did not know I would be fortunate enough to receive a call today from Captain L. Ron Hubbard, the bearer.

Captain Hubbard, whom you know as a writer and lecturer, is probably the best man to consult on this subject due to his many connections. He has offered to deliver his views in person.

As a member of the Explorer's Club he has occasion to address thousands of young men in various institutions concerning his sea adventures and his various expeditions. Though he only pursued soaring and power flight long enough to emass story information, he is still much respected in soaring societies for the skill and daring which brought him to hold two records. He often speaks at Harvard, George Washington University and other schools and should know the reactions of the young men on whom you wish information.

You may have had in mind some one who might act as public relations on this problem but I seriously doubt if Captain Hubbard would take the job. However he might be able to suggest some one and his advice on this is, of course, valuable.

My kindest personal regards and best wishes,

Respectfully,

H. Latane Lewis

H. Latane Lewis II
Assistant Editor
NATIONAL AERONAUTICS

J-10 • Letter about L. Ron Hubbard • 1938

"Isn't It Great To Be An American"

The Stars and Stripes Is Your Flag

Alaska Fishing News

Member United Press

Everything in News

VOL. VII NO. 681   KETCHIKAN, ALASKA, FRIDAY, OCTOBER 18, 1940   PRICE FIVE CENTS

EXPLORER AND WRITERS IN KETCHIKAN

(By RICHARD A. RAMME)

By the end of the week Mr. and Mrs. Ron L. Hubbard will be saying goodbye to their many friends in Ketchikan and return to Seattle on their 34 foot sloop Magician, and from Seattle by more modern means of transportation to New York, their home town.

Mr. Hubbard is a writer by profession and has had more than four million words published. Among the magazines his stories have appeared are the Saturday Evening Post, the Liberty magazine and many other leading American periodicals.

Writing is Mr. Hubbard's business and navigation his hobby. During the last summer Mr. and Mrs. Hubbard have spent several months surveying the coast of British Columbia and furnishing the data to both the U. S. and the Canadian Hydrographic office. In Granville channel the Hubbards discovered a large sand bar which only was one foot below the low tide level, but there was no change in the color of the water because the sand was white. The marking of the bar on charts will prove a definite aid to navigation.

Mr. Hubbard is especially interested in radio direction finders as an aid to navigation and during the last winter he had asked a professor of the New York city College to work a position computer. The scientist has worked out a formula and Hubbard tried out the theories by practical experience and believes that the position computer will be used on all radio direction finders in the very near future.

In Mr. Hubbard's opinion Alaska is a great country with many of the natural resources now unproductive due to high rates and that all what is possible should be done by the federal government to encourage business and enterprise in the territory.

Mrs. Hubbard shares her husband's interest in navigation. She is an expert navigator. Hubbard is a member of the New York Explorers Club and had traveled 250 thousand miles before he was nineteen years old.

While the boat was in Ketchikan a new motor was installed in the Magician and the Hubbard's are well prepared for any weather they might encounter on their trip to Seattle this late in the season.

Ketchikan Alaska Chronicle, Saturday, August 31, 1940.

Author Comes Here In Small Boat

Captain L. Ron Hubbard And Wife Are After Adventure, Writing Data

Captain L. Ron Hubbard, author and world traveler, arrived in Ketchikan yesterday in company with his wife aboard the vest pocket yacht, Magician.

His purpose in coming to Alaska was two-fold, one to win a bet and another to gather material for a novel of Alaskan salmon fishing.

According to Captain Hubbard, several associates maintained it would be impossible for him to sail a vessel as small as the Magician, which is a 27 foot auxiliary sloop to Alaska. Knowing the smallness of the boats which take this route, Captain Hubbard covered their bets and, now that he has arrived, will have the satisfaction of collecting.

"The trip" said Hubbard, "was not so difficult even though we ran into heavy weather in Queen Charlotte sound, Straits of Georgia and Dixon entrance.

GLAD TO BE HERE

"I never much suspect myself of patriotism when I am within the limits of the states but right now I am waving the flag. We came into Revillagigedo channel in the dark and rain with the wind screaming in our rigging and, if we had still been in British Columbia, nothing would have kept us from going ashore. But there were the lights, certain and well planned and by golly, it was just like walking up Broadway. Good charts, good lights, good channels. Uncle Sam's got them all whipped down to a frazzle wherever I go."

His wife, besides being cook and boatswain, also is his navigator and, according to the captain, "a darned good one."

The Magician, lying in the Thomas basin, will be here for several days.

A CHAT WITH THE RANGE BOSS

Here's the low-down on L. Ron Hubbard, whose "Shadows From Boothill" appears in this issue. His literary and other achievements make him blush modestly not only to the roots of his hair but clear out to the end of it.

Dear Range Boss:

Two towns argue about my birth. Tilden, Nebr., says I was born in Lincoln, Nebr.—and Lincoln says I was born in Tilden. I left those parts at the age of three weeks because grandpappy sold out in Nebraska (it was getting too tame) and got himself a spread in Oklahoma. Then it got too tame there and when I was two, I was hauled off to Kalispell, Montana. Because my folks disapproved of the way I walked they glued me to a McClellan saddle and there I stuck unto the age of seven.

My dad, however, being an officer in the navy, didn't like the idea of a bowlegged sailor. So he took me to sea; they say I'd traveled a quarter of a million miles at the age of nineteen.

Got tired of life when very young and took up flying. An old article about me in *The Pilot* says: ". . . The undertakers used to come down to the field and titter." Barnstormed the West and then left wings in favor of sails.

This spring's issue of the *Explorer's Journal* says: "Mr. Hubbard is essentially a writer, but as a trained engineer has done important field work. In 1932-33 he conducted a West Indies Minerals Survey, making a complete mineralogical survey of Puerto Rico. He also directed a motion-picture expedition to the West Indies for submarine movies—at the same time obtaining important data for the Government Hydrographic Office. More recently he has been interested in adding to the knowledge of unfrequented passages and islands of the Northwest coast, U.S.A."

Somehow I got started in the writing business. Leaned on my experiences in the West, Asia, the Caribbean, as a pilot, sailor and—*calf-roper*! By some fluke, when I started I fanned out a story a day for six weeks and have since sold all but two. This, of course, spoiled me. Since then I haven't done a tap of *work*—I just *write* which, as everybody knows (har-har!) isn't really work. Four million of my words have been published in fifty-five different magazines. Various moom pitchers have been filmed from my fiction, too. Just now I'm larruping fantasy fiction more than anything else, though I've been writing Westerns for some time too.

Hope your readers like "Shadows From Boothill." Truth is that the old West was superstitious in the extreme and Injun lore reeks with more fantasy than the Arabian Nights.

Tell the readers to yelp loud and long if they like my Western fantasy—and to keep kinda quiet ifn they don't.

The Old Word Wrangler,

L. Ron Hubbard.

If they like it, Mr. Hubbard, we'll send you to yore cupboard to dish us up some more.

The Explorers Journal

VOL. XVIII   SPRING, 1940

HUBBARD, LAFAYETTE RONALD—*Active Non-Resident*. Route One, Box 449, Port Orchard, Washington.

   Mr. Hubbard is essentially a writer but as a trained engineer has done important field work. In 1932-33 he conducted a West Indies minerals survey, making a complete mineralogical survey of Puerto Rico. He also directed a Motion Picture Expedition to the West Indies for Submarine movies at the same time obtaining important data for the Government Hydrographic Office. More recently he has been interested in adding to the knowledge of unfrequented passages and islands of the North West Coast.

The Moving Finger Writes,

···AND HAVING WRIT···

Letter to the Editor:

Dear Sir:

Back in 1940, July, to be exact, I read a story by L. Ron Hubbard called "Fear." As a fantasy, it was the finest, most heart-pounding thing I've ever finished in one reading. It opened up a field of writing that I didn't know existed. "Fear" had been a story that will not let go of my mind. I'm not much of a pulp reader. Not too high-brow understand, but just so damned busy scribbling my own stuff that I never get to them.

That story persisted in hanging on with a bull dog grip. I saved the magazine and have it with my most valued books. Such a story in hard binding would set a few of our best sellers on the back shelves.

With the thing in mind, I picked up October Unknown Worlds last week and read every story in the book. That's a new high for pulp reading on my part. My password has always been, "read one and you've read 'em all." No good now. I have tossed the line into the wastebasket and decided to try your escape fiction as a steady diet.

Tell the boys who produced "Land Of Unreason" that they have an imagination that I hope to have with practice. A really fine story for a cold, rainy night.

For bed-light reading, your mag has something they can't take away from you with the best Western or adventure yarns on the stands.

If I can escape Podrang—the Gnome King, Georgie—the Smoke Ghost, and Kobolds, I'll be coming along one of these days with a nice wild mixture of fairy magic myself.

— LeRoy Yerxa,
  946 Windsor Avenue, Chicago.

TO THE STARS

L. Ron Hubbard and I were not unlike most of the writers and artists whose work was published in the science fiction pulp magazines of the late Thirties and early Forties. Those days have been called "The

Golden Age of Science Fiction," but we did not think them golden at the time. We all lived from issue to issue, story to story, and check to check. There was some fame; there was no fortune. That Ron and I made our livelihoods through dreams of space travel, alien life, and unknown worlds was as astounding as the science fiction and fantasy stories themselves.

Hubbard and I first met in editor John W. Campbell's office at the Street and Smith building in Manhattan. Except for an occasional meeting in that office, at a lunch, and at a few science fiction conventions, my contact with Ron was through his manuscripts. With the advent of the fantasy pulp *Unknown* it did not take long before

Campbell was publishing a lot of Ron's work and I was given the opportunity to depict much of it. I illustrated more stories by Hubbard than for any other author during my years of work for both *Unknown* and *Astounding Science Fiction.*

Illustrating Ron's tales was a welcome assignment because they always contained scenes or incidents I found easy to picture. With some writer's work I puzzled for hours on what to draw and I sometimes had to contact Campbell for an idea. That never happened with a Hubbard story. His plots allowed my imagination to run wild and the ideas for my illustrations would quickly come to mind.

Hubbard's work for *Unknown* was well suited to the magazine and to my style. Campbell made a special point of letting me illustrate Ron's stories. They offered fantastic opportunities to draw blustering, swaggering heroes and wickedly depraved villains. In the novels "Slaves of Sleep" and "Typewriter in the Sky" Ron gave free rein to the swashbuckling, historically costumed characters I loved to sketch. I was able to fill my illustrations with humorously grotesque faces and to add atmosphere with old guns, burning candles, rope and swords. Ron's other novels in *Unknown* allowed me to depict my visions of his ghouls, devils, demons, and old hags. Those type of ghastly characters in "Death's Deputy," "Fear," and "The Case of the Friendly Corpse" were among my specialties. I relished the chance to draw them and often enjoyed adding a smile or hint of humor to their gruesomeness.

Though I painted only a handful of covers for the pulps, two of them happened to be for Hubbard's novels, "Death's Deputy" and

"The Indigestible Triton," when they appeared in *Unknown*. Both paintings were done in oils. The devil on the cover for "Death's Deputy" seemed to be a favorite with many readers. The strong orange and red colors of the illustration stood out quite well at the newsstands, but caused some people to describe *Unknown*'s covers as lurid. Their complaints about it and other paintings of a similar sort soon led to the end of the magazine's full-colored cover illustrations. They were replaced by a very conservative listing of contents described as "dignified" by Campbell. Unfortunately, the change took place just before Ron's novel "Fear" was published. What a cover I could have done for that tale; lurid, yes, but in a dark and menacing way that would have only hinted at the violence revealed in the story's climax. Indeed, much of Ron's work for *Unknown* was of the fearsome, haunting vein that I delighted in illustrating.

Of course, neither Hubbard nor any other author could write a story as lurid as the real world war that caused me to lose contact with the pulps for about five years. When I returned from combat in Europe *Unknown* was dead, a victim of wartime paper shortages. However, *Astounding Science Fiction* still lived and soon Ron and I were teamed up once again.

Campbell had me illustrate Hubbard's "Ole Doc Methuselah" for a 1947 issue of *Astounding*. That short story was the beginning of the famous series about Ole Doc, Hippocrates, and their stellar travels on behalf of the Universal Medical Society. I worked on quite a few of Ron's stories for *Astounding*, but it was Ole Doc's adventures that many people, including myself, recall most fondly. Readers liked my depiction of Hippocrates and I always enjoyed drawing the little, antennaed, four-armed creature. Oddly enough, in 1952 my wife, Gina, found a large five-legged frog in our yard. The extraordinary coincidence of the frog's arrival and my illustration of Hippocrates still astounds me. Needless to say, the mutant frog was instantly dubbed Hippocrates or Pocrates, for short. He resided with honor in a garden pool and

was featured in many local newspaper articles. The frog's existence was as if Ron's writings and my illustrations had come to life to prove that science fiction's imaginative ideas are quite within the realm of possibility.

In a letter to me, L. Ron Hubbard once wrote "Thanks for Ole Doc, my talented cohort. Your Hippocrates is just plain wonderful." To me, it was wonderful that our work together complemented each other's abilities, enhanced our reputations, and brought a large measure of enjoyment to the readers of fantasy and science fiction. Ron and I could not have hoped for much more than that.

—*Edd Cartier*
May 1982

K. Biographical Entries

A list of the biographical reference books and awards listing L. Ron Hubbard and the entry awards.

Who's Who. 1943.

Two Thousand Notable Americans. First edition.

Biographical Roll of Honor. Second edition.

5,000 Personalities of the World.

Community Leaders of America. 1970.

Community Leaders of America. 1972.

International Who's Who in Community Service. 1973.

Men of Achievement. 1974.

Intercontinental Register of Biographies Registered in the United Kingdom. 1975.

Community Leaders of America. 1975.

Men of Achievement. 1976.

Who's Who in America. Thirty-fourth edition. 1976.

Men of Achievement. 1977.

Who's Who in the South and Southeast. Sixteenth edition. 1978.

Dictionary of International Biography. England. 1979.

International Who's Who of Intellectuals. England. 1979.

Marquis Who's Who in the East. Eighteenth edition. England. 1981.

International Who's Who of Intellectuals. Sixth edition. England. 1983.

Who's Who in Europe. 1984.

Who's Who in the East. Nineteenth edition. England. 1983.

Biographical Roll of Honor. Plaque of recognition. 1984.

International Register of Biographies. First edition. 1984.

Who's Who in the World. Seventh edition. 1984.

International Register of Biographies.
Second edition. 1985.

Who's Who of Intellectuals Honors List. 1986.

Who's Who of Contemporary Foreigners. Japan. 1992.

L. ABOUT THE AUTHOR: MONOGRAPHS, INTERVIEWS, REFERENCES & REVIEWS

This is a chronological list of reference works and materials which deal with the author or his works in depth or in passing.

L1.　**"I was Buried Alive."** *Personal Adventure Stories*, Oct. 14, 1936. (Issued by *Argosy* to promote the "Hell-Job" series. See Q2.)

L2.　**"Pseudonym Sidelights."** By Mort Weisinger, in *The Author and Journalist*, Aug. 1935: 7-9.

L3.　**"Mr. Hubbard Points the Way."** By George Ebey, in *Fantasy Commentator*, Winter 1948-1949: 21-23.

L4.　**"The Swashbuckling Schizophrenic."** By Kemp McDonald, in *Fantasy Review*, Feb.-Mar. 1949: 24-25.

L5.　**"Immortal Lieutenant."** By Thomas Sheridan, in *Fantasy Review*, Feb.-Mar. 1949: 27p.

L6.　**"A List of Pen Names."** As compiled by Mr. Richard Elsberry, in *The X-Ray*, Vol. 1, No. 2, Jan. 1950: 14p.

L7.　**"The Science Fiction Novel—A Lost Art Form?"** By Lemuel Craig, in *Cosmag: Science Fiction Digest*, Nov. 1951: 117p.

L8.　**"Science Fiction Bookcase."** By Sam Merwin, in *Amazing Stories*, Nov. 1951: 158-59.

L9.　**"Science Fiction."** By H. H. Holmes, in the *Herald Tribune*, New York City, Mar. 2, 1952.

L10.　**"Readin' and Writhin'."** By Damon Knight, in *Science Fiction Quarterly*, Feb. 1953: 77-78.

L11.　**A Handbook of Science Fiction and Fantasy 2nd Edition.** Compiled by Donald H. Tuck. Hobart, Tasmania: Donald H. Tuck, 1959: 153p. In two volumes.

L12.　**A Requiem for Astounding**. By Alva Rogers, with editorial comments by Harry Bates, F. Orlin Tremaine and John W. Campbell, Jr. Chicago: Advent Publishers, Inc., 1964: 77-84, 148-49.

L13.　**The Creation of Tomorrow: Fifty Years of Magazine Science Fiction.** By Paul A. Carter. New York: Columbia University Press, 1977. Indexed.

L14.　**Science Fiction Criticism: An Annotated Checklist.** By Thomas Clareson. Kent, OH: The Kent State University Press, 1972. Indexed.

L15. **Billion Year Spree: The True History of Science Fiction.** By Brian W. Aldiss. New York: Schocken Books, 1974. Indexed.

L16. **The Encyclopedia of Science Fiction and Fantasy: Through 1968.** Compiled by Donald H. Tuck. Chicago: Advent Publishers, Inc., 1974: 232-33. In two volumes.

L17. **"El-Ron of the City of Brass."** By L. Sprague de Camp, in *Fantastic Sword & Sorcery and Fantasy Stories*, Aug. 1975: 57-68.

L18. **Science Fiction and Fantasy Pseudonyms (Revised and Expanded).** Compiled by Barry McGhan. Dearborn, MI: Howard DeVore, 1976: 32,37.

L19. **Index to Stories in Thematic Anthologies of Science Fiction.** Edited by Marshall B. Tymn, Martin H. Greenberg, L. W. Currey and Joseph D. Olander with an introduction by James Gunn. Boston: G. K. Hall & Co., 1978.

L20. **Author Biographies Master Index.** Edited by Dennis La Beau. Volume 1: A-K. Gale Biographical Index Series No. 3, Detroit, MI: Gale Research Co., 1978.

L21. **Literary Criticism and Author's Biographies: An Annotated Index.** Compiled by Alison P. Seidel. Metuchen, NJ and London: The Scarecrow Press, Inc., 1978.

L22. **The Science Fiction Encyclopedia.** Edited by Peter Nicholls. Garden City, NY: Dolphin Books-Doubleday & Co., Inc., 1979.

L23. **A Reader's Guide to Science Fiction.** Edited by Baird Searles, Martin Last, Beth Meacham and Michael Franklin. New York: Avon Books, 1979: 87.

L24. **The World of Science Fiction: 1926-1976.** By Lester Del Rey. New York: Ballantine Books, 1979. (Hubbard is mentioned in the section on The Golden Age and in the Appendices.)

L25. **Survey of Science Fiction Literature.** Edited by Frank N. Magill. Vol. 2, Englewood Cliffs: Salem Press, 1979: 761-65.

L26.   **Science Fiction and Fantasy Authors: A Bibliography of First Printings of Their Fiction and Selected Nonfiction.** By L. W. Currey with the editorial assistance of David G. Hartwell. Boston: G. K. Hall & Co., 1979: 256-57.

L27.   **Index to British Science Fiction Magazines 1934-1953.** Vol. 2, Author Index compiled by Graham Stone. Sydney: Australian Science Fiction Assoc., 1980.

L28.   **The Complete Index to Astounding/Analog.** Compiled by Mike Ashley, with the assistance of Terry Jeeves. Oak Forest, IL: Robert Weinberg Publications, 1981.

L29.   **The Pendex.** By Susannah Bates. New York & London: Garland Publishing, Inc., 1981.

L30.   **Twentieth-Century Science-Fiction Writer.** Edited by Curtis C. Smith. New York: St. Martin's Press, 1981.

L31.   **General Studies (Twentieth Century).** By Joseph Weixlmann, Athens, OH: Swallow Press Books, 1982. (A reference to a review of "Fear" in *In Search of Wonder: Essays on Modern Science Fiction,* by Damon Knight. 2nd Ed. Chicago: Advent, 1967.)

L32.   **Science Fiction Writers.** By E. F. Bleiler. New York: Charles Scribner's Sons, 1982. Indexed.

L33.   **"'Battlefield' offers 'pure' science fiction."** By Sam White in *San Jose State University Spartan Daily,* Dec. 8, 1983. (Review on "Battlefield Earth".)

L34.   **The Complete Book of Science Fiction and Fantasy Lists.** By Maxim Jakubowski and Malcolm Edwards. London, Toronto, Sydney, New York: Granada Publishing, Ltd., 1983. (Hubbard appears in the following lists: "Twelve Ways of Travelling in Time Without a Time Machine," "Four Instances of Migrating Characters," "1940: Best SF Novels of the Year," "1947: Best SF Novels of the Year," "Authors' Pets: Their Favorite Stories," "SF and Fantasy Writers Who Gave It Up and Did Better Doing Something Else," and "The Launch Pad: A List of Authors' First SF/Fantasy Appearance in Print.")

L35. **Dream Makers Volume II: The Uncommon Men and Women Who Write Science Fiction.** By Charles Platt. New York: A Berkley Book-Berkley Publishing Company, 1983: 177-90.

L36. **"Illustrating the Stories of L. Ron Hubbard."** By Edd Cartier, in *To the Stars*, Aug. 1983: 10-11. Premiere Issue number 0.

L37. **Index to Literary Biography.** By Patricia Pate Havlice, 1975. First supplement, 1983.

L38. **Literary Criticism Index.** By Alan R. Weiner and Spencer Means, 1984. A reference to *American Short-Fiction Criticism & Scholarship, 1959-1977*, by Joe Weixlmann. Chicago: Swallow Press, 1982.

L39. **Age of Wonders.** By David G. Hartwell. McGraw-Hill Book Company, 1984. Hubbard is mentioned in the chapters: "The Golden Age of Science Fiction Is Twelve," "Worshipping at the Church of Wonder," "When It Comes True, It's No Fun Anymore," and "Science Fiction Writers Can't Write for Sour Apples."

L40. **Wonder's Child: My Life in Science Fiction.** By Jack Williamson. New York: Bluejay Books, Inc., 1984. Indexed.

L41. **The John W. Campbell Letters, Vol. I.** Edited by Perry A. Chapdelaine, Sr., Tony Chapdelaine and George Hay. Franklin, TN: AC Projects, 1985. Indexed.

L42. **Inside Outer Space.** Edited by Sharon Jarvis. Science fiction professionals look at their craft. New York: Frederick Ungar Pub. Co., 1985: 43p.

L43. **Trillion Year Spree: The History of Science Fiction.** By Brian W. Aldiss with Dave Wingrove. London: Gollancz, 1986: 463p.

L44. **Godbody.** By Theodore Sturgeon. New York: Donald I. Fine, Inc., 1986. There is a Hubbard anecdote in the introduction by Robert A. Heinlein, "Agape and Eros: The Art of Theodore Sturgeon."

L45. **Nuclear Holocausts: Atomic War in Fiction, 1895-1984.** By Paul Brians. Kent, OH and London: The Kent State University Press, 1987. Indexed.

L46.   **The New Encyclopedia of Science Fiction.** Edited by James Gunn. New York, London: Viking-Penguin, 1988, Indexed. Hubbard is mentioned in the sections on *Analog Science Fiction/Science Fact*, Awards, Algis Budrys, Edd Cartier, Cosmology, Editors, L. Ron Hubbard, Illustration, Pseudoscience, Publishers, Time Travel, A.E. van Vogt, and War.

L47.   **Bookman's Price Index.** Edited by Daniel F. McGrath. Vol. 35. Detroit, MI: Gale Research Co., 1988.

L48.   **The Old Book Value Guide.** By the editors of Collector Books, Paducah, KY. Collector Books-Schroeder Publishing Co., 1988.

L49.   **"Sci-Fi Offers Solution to 'Greenhouse Effect."** By Neil Erickson in Concordia College *Spectator*, Oct. 5, 1988. Opinion on Hubbard's theory in *Mission Earth* to use spores to handle pollution and ozone layer depletion.

L50.   **Bloomsbury Good Reading Guide to Science Fiction and Fantasy.** By M.H. Zool. London: Bloomsbury Reference, 1989.

L51.   **Mandeville's Used Book Price Guide.** Edited by Richard Collins. Kenmore, WA. Price Guide Publishers, 1989.

L52.   **Olderr's Fiction Index, 1989.** Edited by Steven Olderr, M.A.L.S. and Kay Sodowsky, M.S. Chicago and London: St. James Press, 1989.

L53.   **An Annotated Bibliography of Recursive Science Fiction.** Compiled by Anthony R. Lewis. Cambridge, MA. New England Science Fiction Association, Inc., 1990.

L54.   **Reader's Guide to Twentieth-Century Science Fiction.** Compiled and edited by Marilyn Fletcher, James L. Thorson, consulting editor. Chicago: American Library Association, 1989.

L55.   **"A Metaphysical Unease."** By Gail Regier, in *The World & I*, Washington, D.C., June 1991. (A perceptive and scholarly comparison of "Fear" to other works of classic literature. See notes to "Fear," B147.)

L56. **The Dark Descent.** Edited by David G. Hartwell. New York: A Tor Book by Tom Doherty Associates, Inc., 1991. (Lengthy introduction delineates the evolution of horror with mention of Hubbard and the genrification of psychological fiction.)

L57. **Reginald's Science Fiction & Fantasy Awards.** By Daryl F. Mallett and Robert Reginald. San Bernardino, CA. The Borgo Press, 1991.

L58. **Biography Index.** Edited by Charles R. Cornell. New York: The H.W. Wilson Co., 1992.

L59. **Danger Is My Business: An Illustrated History of the Fabulous Pulp Magazines, 1896-1953.** By Lee Server. Chronicle Books, 1993. Indexed.

L60. **The Encyclopedia of Science Fiction.** Edited by John Clute and Peter Nicholls. New York: St. Martin's Press, 1993.

L61. **Senior Science Book 2.** By Bob McCallister, Peter Stannard and Ken Williamson, South Melbourne: 1994. (Chapter 8 explores the relationship between "science" and "science fiction," gives five main science fiction themes and provides an extract from "Mission Earth" and discussion of the scientific possibilities in the passage.)

M. Miscellanea

This section includes the following lists:

1. Pen Names

2. Memberships

3. Colleges and Universities using L. Ron Hubbard's Fiction Works

4. Exhibitions, Displays and Collections

5. Aviation, Marine Navigation & Exploration Certificates and Awards

6. Early Recognitions

1. PEN NAMES

An alphabetical listing of verified pen names in both the fiction and nonfiction categories.

A. FICTION PEN NAMES

Winchester Remington Colt
Lt. Jonathan Daly
Capt. Charles Gordon
Capt. L. Ron Hubbard
Bernard Hubbel
Michael Keith
Rene Lafayette
Legionnaire 148
Legionnaire 14830
Ken Martin
Scott Morgan
Lt. Scott Morgan
Kurt von Rachen
Barry Randolph
Capt. Humbert Reynolds
John Seabrook

B. NONFICTION PEN NAMES

Tom Esterbrook
George Kellogg
Capt. B. A. Northrop
Mr. Spectator

2. MEMBERSHIPS

The following is a list, in alphabetical order, of memberships held by L. Ron Hubbard.

American Artists Professional League

American Biographical Institute, Inc.

American Biographical Institute Research Association

American Defense Preparedness Association

American Fiction Guild

American Film Institute

American Forestry Association

American Geographical Society

American Guild of Authors & Composers

American Humane Association

American Institute for Economic Research

American Management Association

American Museum of Natural History

American Ordinance Association

American Polar Society

American Rocketry Association

American Security Council, National Advisory Board

American Society of Composers, Authors and Publishers

Arctic Institute of North America

The Army & Navy Club, United Kingdom

The Arts Guild, United Kingdom

Audio Club of Great Britain

Authors Guild

Authors League of America

Bilingual Foundation of the Arts

Capital Yacht Club

Clubman's Club

Cousteau Society, Inc.

The Collectors Guild, Ltd.

The Cruising Association, United Kingdom

Danish-Japanese Association

Danish World Wildlife Foundation

Disabled American Veterans

The Dramatists Guild, United Kingdom

The East Grinstead Operatic Society, United Kingdom

El Teatro Campesino

The Explorers Club

Friends of Buckminster Fuller

The Friends of Photography

H. G. Wells Society, United Kingdom

The Historic Preservations of America, Inc.

The Hollywood Arts Council

The Hollywood Chamber of Commerce

Hollywood Heritage, Inc.

The Humane Society of the United States

International Biographical Association

International Photography Society

International Oceanographic Association

International Platform Association

Knights of Malta

The Los Angeles Conservancy

The Museum of Modern Art

The Musical Heritage Society

National Eagle Scout Association

National Geographic Society

National Historical Society

National Parks & Conservation Association

National Police Reserve Officers Association

National Rifle Association of America

National Trust for Historic Preservation

National Wildlife Federation

New York Institute of Photography

The Nature Conservancy

Port Orchard Yacht Club

The Publishers Association, United Kingdom

The Royal Automobile Club, United Kingdom

Royal National Lifeboat Institute, United Kingdom

Royal Naval Sailing Association, United Kingdom

Royal Photographic Society of Great Britain

Royal Society for the Prevention of Cruelty to Animals

The Science Fiction Writers of America

Smithsonian Institute

Statue of Liberty Ellis Island Foundation

Television and Screen Writers Guild, United Kingdom

U.S. Naval Institute

Venturers Search & Rescue, United Kingdom

World Wildlife Fund

Writers Guild of Great Britain

3. COLLEGES & UNIVERSITIES USING L. RON HUBBARD'S FICTION WORKS

A listing of colleges and universities where L. Ron Hubbard's fiction works have been used, or the L. Ron Hubbard Writers of the Future Contest and anthology have been recommended or required. (See Section O for more on the contest and anthology.) Entries in this section are alphabetical by state.

1. Troy State University, Troy, Alabama.
2. Glendale Community College, Glendale, Arizona.
3. Northern Arizona University, Flagstaff, Arizona.
4. Henderson State University, Arkadelphia, Arkansas.
5. University of Arkansas, Little Rock, Arkansas.
6. Arkansas Tech University, Russellville, Arkansas.
7. University of Victoria, Victoria, British Columbia, Canada.
8. California State Polytechnic University, Pomona, California.
9. California State Polytechnic University, San Luis Obispo, California.
10. California State University, Fullerton, California.
11. California State University, Long Beach, California.
12. California State University, Northridge, California.
13. California State University, San Bernardino, California.
14. El Camino College, Torrance, California.
15. Occidental College, Los Angeles, California.
16. Pepperdine University, Malibu, California.
17. San Diego State University, San Diego, California.
18. Southern California College, Costa Mesa, California.
19. University of California, Riverside, California.
20. University of California, San Diego, California.

21. University of California, Santa Cruz, California.
22. University of the Pacific, Stockton, California.
23. Colorado State University, Ft. Collins, Colorado.
24. University of Northern Colorado, Greeley, Colorado.
25. Fairfield University, Fairfield, Connecticut.
26. The George Washington University, Washington, D.C.
27. University of Florida, Gainesville, Florida.
28. Florida State University, Tallahassee, Florida.
29. DePaul University, Chicago, Illinois.
30. Rose-Hulman Institute of Technology, Terra Haute, Indiana.
31. University of Kansas, Lawrence, Kansas.
32. Harvard University, Cambridge, Massachusetts.
33. Michigan State University, East Lansing, Michigan.
34. Eastern Montana College, Billings, Montana.
35. University of Nebraska, Lincoln, Nebraska.
36. Union County College, Cranford, New Jersey.
37. Rutgers University, New Brunswick, New Jersey.
38. New Mexico State University, Las Cruces, New Mexico.
39. Cornell University, Ithaca, New York.
40. Duke University, Durham, North Carolina.
41. North Carolina State University, Raleigh, North Carolina.
42. Johnson & Wales College, Providence, Rhode Island.
43. Providence College, Providence, Rhode Island.
44. Memphis State University, Memphis, Tennessee.
45. Texas A & M University, College Station, Texas.
46. University of Houston, Houston, Texas.
47. Brigham Young University, Provo, Utah.

4. EXHIBITIONS, DISPLAYS & COLLECTIONS

The L. Ron Hubbard Life Exhibition

6331 Hollywood Blvd., Los Angeles, California
(213) 960–3511.

Hosted tours of more than 30 high-tech displays provide an informative and comprehensive "walk through the life" of L. Ron Hubbard, featuring some of his major fiction works and his remarkable achievements. The $5 admission also includes a 48-page brochure of Hubbard's life and works. The bookstore offers a large range of books, magazines, tapes and videos by the author. Open to the public from 9:30 am until 10:00 pm, seven days a week. Advance bookings recommended.

The L. Ron Hubbard Gallery

7051 Hollywood Blvd., Los Angeles, California
(213) 466-3310.

Author Services, Inc., international representative for the literary, theatrical and musical works of L. Ron Hubbard, maintains a display of limited edition art prints which depict the cover art, characters and scenes from the author's bestselling fiction books. A complete collection of early fiction works is on display in the Board Room. There is also a full range of L. Ron Hubbard's fiction books in the bookstore where translations for all of his fiction books and audio recordings can be purchased. Copies of the "L. Ron Hubbard Classic Fiction Series," leatherbound editions and signed books are also available. Monthly readings of the current "L. Ron Hubbard Classic Fiction Series" release feature celebrity actors and entertainers. Advance bookings recommended.

Saint Hill Manor

Saint Hill, East Grinstead, West Sussex, England.

This historical mansion and 55-acre estate which L. Ron Hubbard acquired as his home in 1959 from the

Maharajah of Jaipur has been beautifully restored to its original historical English style and beauty from Hubbard's extensive research of its history back to 1567.

*Saint Hill Manor
East Grinstead,
Sussex, England*

One of the best examples of Sussex sandstone structures in existence, the estate mansion contains the original Georgian plasterwork, woodwork and architectural features; Italian marble columns, floors and fireplaces; and a unique and delightful mural of 145 monkeys from 20 species painted in 1946 by Sir Winston Churchill's nephew, John Spencer Churchill. From this location, in the 1960s, L. Ron Hubbard delivered more than 400 lectures during the most intense period of his Scientology research. He also planned the Saint Hill Castle in detail, modeling his designs after a Norman castle in the nearby medieval town of Tonbridge. It was officially opened on October 5, 1990.

The L. Ron Hubbard library, located in the Saint Hill Manor, has one of the most complete and unique collections of his published works on Dianetics and Scientology, as well as selected fiction works. These are overseen by his personal librarian who has kept it up-to-date since the early 1960s. Daily tours available, 2:00 P.M.–5:00 P.M.

L. Ron Hubbard Hall

School of Journalism, Department of Russian & Foreign Literature, Moscow State University.

Located in the historic Russian university as part of the Gorky Library and School of Journalism, Department of Russian & Foreign Literature, a full library of L. Ron Hubbard's works is available for student and faculty use in all languages. See also Section H for more information on the hall dedication and the honorary doctorate degree conferred upon L. Ron Hubbard in 1992 at the hall opening.

LIBRARY COLLECTIONS

L. Ron Hubbard's fiction works can be found through any library in the United States and Canada, and many throughout the world, given that they have been published in a dozen languages in more than 100 countries.

Following is a list of the more significant collections and sources of early works.

Yale University's Beinecke Rare Book and Manuscript Library

contains a large collection of L. Ron Hubbard's works, including the 1948 editions of *Final Blackout* and *Slaves of Sleep*, in the western authors collection.

Harvard University's Widener Library

contains a large collection of current publications of Hubbard's works, including republished works in the Classic Fiction Series.

Huntington Library

in Pasadena, California. Holdings contain a collection of current publications of Hubbard's fiction works, including republished works in the Classic Fiction Series and a signed edition of *Battlefield Earth*.

University of California at Riverside

which has the largest science fiction collection in the world, contains a large collection of the early pulp magazines.

Smithsonian Institution Libraries

in Washington, D.C. has in its possession one of the rare signed editions of *Battlefield Earth* in its science fiction collection.

Center for the Study of Science Fiction, University of Kansas

contains a wide selection of L. Ron Hubbard's science fiction and fantasy works from the Golden Age to the present.

5. AVIATION, MARINE NAVIGATION & EXPLORATION CERTIFICATES & AWARDS

This is a categorized, chronological list of certificates and awards presented to L. Ron Hubbard in the areas of aviation, marine navigation and exploration. The list includes issuer and date.

AVIATION

U.S. Volunteer Air Service

Academy of Civilian and Military Aeronautics
(May 1931)

Glider Pilot's License

U.S. Department of Commerce Aeronautics Branch
(September 1, 1931)

Student Pilot's Permit

U.S. Department of Commerce Aeronautics Branch
(September 22, 1932)

Pilot's License

U.S. Department of Commerce Aeronautics Branch
(February 25, 1935)

MARINE NAVIGATION

License to Master of Steam and Motor Vessels

U.S. Department of Commerce Bureau of Marine Inspection and Navigation
(December 17, 1940)

License to Master of Sail Vessels (Any Ocean)

U.S. Department of Commerce Bureau of Navigation and Steamboat Inspection
(March 29, 1941)

Certificate of Recognition of Fellow Status with International Oceanographic Foundation

International Oceanographic Foundation.
(November 17, 1959)

EXPLORATION

Lifetime Member Certificate	Explorers Club (February 19, 1940)
Explorers Club Flag #105 for the Alaskan Radio Experimental Expedition	Explorers Club (May 1940)
Explorers Club Flag #163 for the Ocean Archaeological Expedition	Explorers Club (June 1961)
Explorers Club Flag #163 (2nd award) for the Hubbard Geological Survey Expedition	Explorers Club (December 1966)

6. EARLY RECOGNITIONS

A chronological list of awards received by L. Ron Hubbard between the ages of twelve and twenty-one. The list includes issuer and date of award.

Second Class Boy Scout

Boy Scouts of America
(May 8, 1923)

First Class Boy Scout

Boy Scouts of America
(July 5, 1923)

Life Scout Medal, Star
Scout Medal

Boy Scouts of America
(February 26, 1924)

Eagle Scout

Boy Scouts of America
(March 25, 1924)

Most Original Cast Award
Vigilante Day Parade

The Helena Independent
Helena, Montana
(May 5, 1928)

National Oratorical Contest
Winner for his speech on
"The Constitution: A Guarantee
of the Liberty of the Individual."

Woodward School for Boys
Washington, D.C.
(March 25, 1930)

First prize in the One-Act Play
Contest for "The God Smiles."
(See F1 & B3.)

The George Washington University
University Hatchet Monthly
Literary Review
May 14, 1932

N. INTRODUCTION TO BATTLEFIELD EARTH

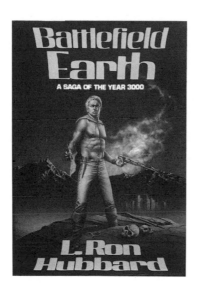

Written by Hubbard as the introduction to his science fiction masterpiece *Battlefield Earth*, this essay offers a retrospective view of his rewarding career, a brief history of science fiction and a delineating statement on the genres of science fiction and fantasy.

INTRODUCTION TO BATTLEFIELD EARTH
BY L. RON HUBBARD

Recently there came a period when I had little to do. This was novel in a life so crammed with busy years, and I decided to amuse myself by writing a novel that was *pure* science fiction.

In the hard-driven times between 1930 and 1950, I was a professional writer not simply because it was my job, but because I wanted to finance more serious researches. In those days there were few agencies pouring out large grants to independent workers. Despite what you might hear about Roosevelt "relief," those were depression years. One succeeded or one starved. One became a top-liner or a gutter bum. One had to work very hard at his craft or have no craft at all. It was a very challenging time for anyone who lived through it.

I have heard it said, as an intended slur, "He was a science fiction writer," and have heard it said of many. It brought me to realize that few people understand the role science fiction has played in the lives of Earth's whole population.

I have just read several standard books that attempt to define "science fiction" and to trace its history. There are many experts in this field, many controversial opinions. Science fiction is favored with the most closely knit reading public that may exist, possibly the most dedicated of any genre. Devotees are called "fans," and the word has a special prestigious meaning in science fiction.

Few professional writers, even those in science fiction, have written very much on the character of "sf." They are usually too busy turning out the work itself to expound on what they have written. But there are many experts on this subject among both critics and fans, and they have a lot of worthwhile things to say.

However, many false impressions exist, both of the genre and of its writers. So when one states that he set out to write a work of *pure* science fiction, he had better state what definition he is using.

It will probably be best to return to the day in 1938 when I first entered this field, the day I met John W. Campbell, Jr., a day in the very dawn of what has come to be known as The Golden Age of science fiction. I was quite ignorant of the field and regarded it, in fact, a bit diffidently. I was not there of my own choice. I had been summoned to the vast old building on Seventh Avenue in dusty, dirty, old New York by the very top brass of Street and Smith publishing company—an executive named Black and another, F. Orlin Tremaine. Ordered there with me was another writer, Arthur J. Burks. In those days when the top brass of a publishing company—particularly one as old and prestigious as Street and Smith—"invited" a writer to visit, it was like being commanded to appear before the king or receiving a court summons. You arrived, you sat there obediently, and you spoke when you were spoken to.

We were both, Arthur J. Burks and I, top-line professionals in other writing fields. By the actual tabulation of A. B. Dick, which set advertising rates for publishing firms, either of our names appearing on a magazine cover would send the circulation rate skyrocketing, something like modern TV ratings.

The top brass came quickly to the point. They had recently started or acquired a magazine called *Astounding Science Fiction*. Other magazines were published by other houses, but Street and Smith was unhappy because its magazine was mainly publishing stories about machines and machinery. As publishers, its executives knew you had to have *people* in stories. They had called us in because, aside from our A. B. Dick rating as writers, we could write about *real people*. They knew we were busy and had other commitments. But would we be so kind as to write science fiction? We indicated we would.

They called in John W. Campbell, Jr., the editor of the magazine. He found himself looking at two adventure-story writers, and though adventure writers might be the aristocrats of the whole field and might have vast followings of their own, they were *not* science fiction writers. He resisted. In the first place, calling in top-liners would ruin his story budget due to their word rates. And in the second place, he had his own ideas of what science fiction was.

Campbell, who dominated the whole field of sf as its virtual czar until his death in 1971, was a huge man who had majored in physics at Massachusetts Institute of Technology and graduated from Duke University with a Bachelor of Sciences degree. His idea of getting a story was to have some professor or scientist write it and then doctor it up and publish it. Perhaps that is a bit unkind, but it really was what he was doing. To fill his pages even he, who had considerable skill as a writer, was writing stories for the magazine.

The top brass had to directly order Campbell to buy and to publish what we wrote for him. He was going to get *people* into his stories and get something going besides *machines*.

I cannot tell you how many other writers were called in. I do not know. In all justice, it may have been Campbell himself who found them later on. But do not get the impression that Campbell was anything less than a master and a genius in his own right. Any of the stable of writers he collected during this Golden Age will tell you that. Campbell could listen. He could improve things.

He could dream up little plot twists that were masterpieces. He well deserved the title that he gained and kept as the top editor and the dominant force that made science fiction as respectable as it became. *Star Wars,* the all-time box office record movie to date (exceeded only by its sequel), would never have happened if science fiction had not become as respectable as Campbell made it. More than that—Campbell played no small part in driving this society into the space age.

You had to actually work with Campbell to know where he was trying to go, what his idea was of this thing called "science fiction." I cannot give you any quotations from him; I can just tell you what I felt he was trying to do. In time we became friends. Over lunches and in his office and at his home on weekends—where his wife Doña kept things smooth—talk was always of stories but also of science. To say that Campbell considered science fiction as "prophecy" is an oversimplification. He had very exact ideas about it.

Only about a tenth of my stories were written for the fields of science fiction and fantasy. I was what they called a high-production writer, and these fields were just not big enough to take everything I could write. I gained my original reputation in other writing fields during the eight years before the Street and Smith interview.

Campbell, without saying too much about it, considered the bulk of the stories I gave him to be not science fiction but fantasy, an altogether different thing. Some of my stories he eagerly published as science fiction—among them *Final Blackout.* Many more, actually. I had, myself, somewhat of a science background, had done some pioneer work in rockets and liquid gases, but I was studying the branches of man's past knowledge at that time to see whether he had ever come up with anything valid. This, and a love of the ancient tales now called *The Arabian Nights,* led me to write quite a bit of fantasy. To handle this fantasy material, Campbell introduced another magazine, *Unknown.* As long as I was writing novels for it, it continued. But the war came and I and others went, and I think *Unknown* only lasted about forty months. Such novels were a bit hard to come by. And they were not really Campbell's strength.

So anyone seeking to say that science fiction is a branch of fantasy or an extension of it is unfortunately colliding with a time-honored professional usage of terms. This is an age of mixed genres. I hear different forms of music mixed together like soup. I see so many different styles of dance tangled together into one "dance" that I wonder whether the choreographers really know the different genres of dance anymore. There is abroad today the concept that only *conflict* produces new things. Perhaps the philosopher Hegel introduced that, but he also said that war was necessary for the mental health of the people and a lot of other nonsense. If all new ideas have to spring from the conflict between old ones, one must deny that virgin ideas can be conceived.

So what would *pure* science fiction be?

It has been surmised that science fiction must come from an age where science exists. At the risk of raising dispute and outcry—which I have risked all my life and received but not been bothered by, and have gone on and done my job anyway—I wish to point out some things:

Science fiction does *not* come after the fact of a scientific discovery or development. It is the herald of possibility. It is the plea that someone should work on the future. Yet it is not prophecy. It is the dream that precedes the dawn when the inventor or scientist awakens and goes to his books or his lab saying, "I wonder whether I could make that dream come true in the world of real science."

You can go back to Lucian, second century A.D., or to Johannes Kepler (1571–1630)—who founded modern dynamical astronomy and who also wrote *Somnium*, an imaginary space flight to the moon—or to Mary Shelley and her Frankenstein, or to Poe or Verne or Wells and ponder whether this was really science fiction. Let us take an example: a man invents an eggbeater. A writer later writes a story about an eggbeater. He has *not*, thereby, written science fiction. Let us continue the example: a man writes a story about some metal that, when twiddled, beats an egg, but no such tool has ever before existed in fact. He has now written science fiction. Somebody else, a week or a hundred years later, reads the story and says, "Well, well. Maybe it could be done." And makes an eggbeater. But whether or not it was possible that twiddling two pieces of metal would beat eggs, or whether or not anybody ever did it afterward, the man still has written science fiction.

How do you look at this word "fiction?" It is a sort of homograph. In this case it means two different things. A professor of literature knows it means "a literary work whose content is produced by the imagination and is not necessarily based on fact; the category of literature comprising works of this kind, including novels, short stories, and plays." It is derived from the Latin *fictio*, a making, a fashioning, from *fictus*, past participle of *fingere*, to touch, form, mold.

But when we join the word to "science" and get "science fiction," the word "fiction" acquires two meanings in the same use: 1) the science used in the story is at least partly fictional; and 2) any *story* is fiction. The *American Heritage Dictionary of the English Language* defines science fiction as "fiction in which scientific developments and discoveries form an element of plot or background; especially a work of fiction based on prediction of future scientific possibilities."

So, by dictionary definition and a lot of discussions with Campbell and fellow writers of that time, science fiction has to do with the material universe and sciences; these can include economics, sociology, medicine, and suchlike, all of which have a material base.

Then what is fantasy?

Well, believe me, if it were simply the application of vivid imagination, then a lot of economists and government people and such would be fully qualified authors! Applying the word "imaginative" to fantasy would be like calling an entire library "some words." Too simplistic, too general a term.

In these modern times many of the ingredients that make up "fantasy" as a type of fiction have vanished from the stage. You hardly even find them in encyclopedias anymore. These subjects were spiritualism, mythology, magic, divination, the supernatural, and many other fields of that type. None of them had anything really to do with the real universe. This does not necessarily mean that they never had any validity or that they will not again arise; it merely means that man, currently, has sunk into a materialistic binge.

The bulk of these subjects consists of false data, but there probably never will come a time when *all* such phenomena are explained. The primary reason such a vast body of knowledge dropped from view is that material science has been undergoing a long series of successes. But I do notice that every time modern science thinks it is down to the nitty-gritty of it all, it runs into (and sometimes adopts) such things as the Egyptian myths that man came from mud, or something like that. But the only point I am trying to make here is that there is a whole body of phenomena that we cannot classify as "material." They are the nonmaterial, nonuniverse subjects. And no matter how false many of the old ideas were, they still existed; who knows but what there might not be some validity in some bits of them. One would have to study these subjects to have a complete comprehension of all the knowledge and beliefs possible. I am not opening the door to someone's saying I believe in all these things: I am only saying that there is another realm besides dedicated—and even simple-minded—materialism.

"Fantasy," so far as literature is concerned, is defined in the dictionary as "literary or dramatic fiction characterized by highly fanciful or supernatural elements." Even that is a bit limited as a definition.

So fantasy could be called any fiction that takes up elements such as spiritualism, mythology, magic, divination, the supernatural, and so on. *The Arabian Nights* was a gathering together of the tales of many, many countries and civilizations—not just of Arabia as many believe. Its actual title was *A Thousand and One Nights of Entertainment.* It abounds with examples of fantasy fiction.

When you mix science fiction with fantasy you do not have a pure genre. The two are, to a professional, separate genres. I notice today there is a tendency to mingle them and then excuse the result by calling it "imaginative fiction." Actually they don't mix well: science fiction, to be credible, has to be based on some degree of plausibility; fantasy gives you no limits at all. Writing science fiction demands care on the part of the author; writing fantasy is as easy as strolling in the park. (In fantasy, a guy has no sword in his hand; bang, there's a magic sword in his hand.) This doesn't say one is better than the other. They are simply very different genres from a professional viewpoint.

But there is more to this: science fiction, particularly in its Golden Age, had a mission. I cannot, of course, speak for my friends of that period. But from Campbell and from "shooting the breeze" with other writers of the time, one got the very solid impression that they were doing a heavy job of beating the drum to get man to the stars.

At the beginning of that time, science fiction was regarded as a sort of awful stepchild in the world of literature. But worse than that, science itself was not getting the attention or the grants or the government expenditures it should have received. There has to be a *lot* of public interest and demand before politicians shell out the financing necessary to get a subject whizzing.

Campbell's crew of writers were pretty stellar. They included very top-liner names. They improved the literary quality of the genre. And they began the boom of its broader popularity.

A year or so after The Golden Age began, I recall going into a major university's science department. I wanted some data on cytology for my own serious researches. I was given a courteous reception and was being given the references when I noticed that the room had been gradually filling up. And not with students but with professors and deans. It had been whispered around the offices who was in the biology department, and the next thing I knew, I was shaking a lot of hands held out below beaming faces. And what did they want to know: What did I think of this story or that? And had I seen this or that writer lately? And how was Campbell?

They had a literature! *Science fiction!*

And they were proud of it!

For a while, before and after World War II, I was in rather steady association with the new era of scientists, the boys who built the bomb, who were beginning to get the feel of rockets. They were all science fiction buffs. And many of the hottest scientists around were also writing science fiction on the side.

In 1945 I attended a meeting of old scientist and science fiction friends. The meeting was at the home of my dear friend, the incomparable Bob Heinlein. And do you know what was their agenda? How to get man into space fast enough so that he would be distracted from further wars on Earth. And they were the lads who had the government ear and authority to do it! We are coming close to doing it. The scientists got man into space and they even had the Russians cooperating for a while.

One can't go on living a naive life believing that everything happens by accident, that events simply follow events, that there is a natural order of things and that everything will come out right somehow. That isn't science. That's fate, kismet, and we're back in the world of fantasy. No, things do get planned. The Golden Age of science fiction that began with Campbell and *Astounding Science Fiction* gathered enough public interest and readership to help push man into space. Today, you hear top scientists talking the way we used to talk in bull sessions so long ago.

Campbell did what he set out to do. So long as he had his first wife and others around him to remind him that science was for *people,* that it was no use to just send machines out for the sake of machines, that there was no point into going into space unless the mission had something to do with people, too, he kept winning. For he was a very brilliant man and a great and very patient editor. After he lost his first wife, Doña, in 1949—she married George O. Smith—and after he no longer had a sounding-board who made him keep people in stories, and when he no longer had his old original writing crew around, he let his magazine slip back, and when it finally became named *Analog,* his reign was over. But The Golden Age had kicked it all into high gear. So Campbell won after all.

When I started out to write this novel, I wanted to write *pure* science fiction. And not in the old tradition. Writing forms and styles have changed, so I had to bring myself up to date and modernize the styles and patterns. To show that science fiction is not science fiction because of a particular kind of plot, this novel contains practically every type of story there is—detective, spy, adventure, western, love, air war, you name it. All except fantasy; there is none of that. The term "science" also includes economics and sociology and medicine where these are related to material things. So they're in here, too.

In writing for magazines, the editors (because of magazine format) force one to write to exact lengths. I was always able to do that—it is a kind of knack. But this time I decided not to cut everything out and to just roll her as she rolled, so long as the pace kept up. So I may have wound up writing the biggest sf novel ever in terms of length. The experts—and there are lots of them to do so—can verify whether this is so.

Some of my readers may wonder that I did not include my own serious subjects in this book. It was with no thought of dismissal of them. It was just that I put on my professional writer's hat. I also did not want to give anybody the idea I was doing a press relations job for my other serious works.

There are those who will look at this book and say, "See? We told you he is just a science fiction writer!" Well, as one of the crew of writers that helped start man to the stars, I'm very proud of also being known as a science fiction writer. You have satellites out there, man has walked on the moon, you have probes going to the planets, don't you? Somebody had to dream the dream, and a lot of somebodies like those great writers of The Golden Age and later had to get an awful lot of people interested in it to make it true.

I hope you enjoy this novel. It is the only one I ever wrote just to amuse myself. It also celebrates my golden wedding with the muse. Fifty years a professional—1930–1980.

And as an old pro I assure you that it is *pure* science fiction. No fantasy. Right on the rails of the genre. Science is for people. And so is science fiction.

Ready?

Stand by.

Blast off!

L. Ron Hubbard
October 1980

O. CELEBRATING A DECADE OF HELPING NEW WRITERS

L. RON HUBBARD'S WRITERS OF THE FUTURE

L. Ron Hubbard established and sponsored the *Writers of The Future Contest* in late 1983 to discover and encourage new writers of speculative fiction, a genre whose place in mainstream literature he had helped, instrumentally, to define and enlarge. The contest represented a culminating step in his lifelong commitment to helping other writers, particularly the beginner, become more skilled and productive in their craft.

The *Writers of The Future* program—with its companion competition for illustrators—continues to be administered by L. Ron Hubbard's literary agency, Author Services, Inc., and has become the largest, most successful and demonstrably the most influential discovery vehicle for budding creative talent in the world of contemporary fiction.

A special brochure, marking the tenth anniversary of the *Writers of The Future* program and celebrating its theme of "a decade of helping new writers" was published in May 1994. Offering a strikingly detailed text-and-illustration description of the history, scope and impact of this remarkable program, the brochure has been adapted for this bibliography as a primary reference in the pages that follow.

L. RON HUBBARD'S
WRITERS
OF THE
FUTURE

*Celebrating
a decade of helping
new writers*

"A culture is as rich and as capable of surviving as it has imaginative artists.

The artist is looked upon to start things. The artist injects the spirit of life into a culture.

And through his creative endeavors, the writer works continually to give tomorrow a new form. ...

It is with this in mind that I initiated a means for new and budding writers to have a chance for their creative efforts to be seen and acknowledged."

— L. Ron Hubbard

"With the prestige of having major figures in SF as judges, and substantial prizes handed out, the Hubbard Awards have to be considered together with the Hugos and Nebulas as forming a triad of major science fiction awards."
— SCIENCE FICTION WRITERS OF AMERICA BULLETIN, FALL 1988

THE L. RON HUBBARD GOLD AWARD
PRESENTED ANNUALLY TO THE
WINNER OF THE WRITERS OF THE FUTURE
STORY OF THE YEAR

THE L. RON HUBBARD
WRITERS OF THE FUTURE® CONTEST

A Decade Strong

Established and sponsored by L. Ron Hubbard in 1983, the "Writers' Award Contest" was a budding competition aimed at discovering, and eventually publishing, deserving amateur and aspiring writers. The field of speculative fiction, an embracing term for science fiction and fantasy, was chosen not only for Mr. Hubbard's love of and success within the genre—but for the freedom of imagination and expression which it allowed as "a herald of possibility."

At the time of its inception, the very idea of a contest of this scope and of a book filled with first-time fiction by amateur writers was seen in many literary venues as "untried" and "challenging," but at the same time as something both "desirable" and "long-needed." Expert opinions said it couldn't be done.

Algis Budrys was the first Coordi-

L. Ron Hubbard

> *"A very generous legacy from L. Ron Hubbard—a fine, fine fiction writer—for the writers of the future."*
> — ANNE McCAFFREY
> *Award-winning author*

nating Judge of the Contest and Editor of the *L. Ron Hubbard Presents Writers of The Future* anthology, two

positions—among others—he would go on to hold for seven more years. To garner their professional expertise in the judging of the entries, he brought together such stellar genre names as Gregory Benford, C.L. Moore, Robert Silverberg, Theodore Sturgeon, Jack Williamson and Roger Zelazny. Other

notable names have contributed to the judging since that time: Ben Bova, Ramsey Campbell, Orson Scott Card, Frank Herbert, Anne McCaffrey, Larry Niven, Andre Norton, Frederik Pohl, Jerry Pournelle, Tim Powers, Marta Randall, John Varley, Gene Wolfe, and Dave Wolverton.

Contest entries are received from all over the world.

Illustrator Sergey V. Poyarkov (above), from the Ukraine, proudly hoists his trophy upon being named the Grand Prize Winner at the 1991 L. Ron Hubbard Awards Event. At the 1993 event, an elated Karawynn Long (right) embraces her trophy and $4000 check, becoming the youngest person, at 23, to win the Grand Prize.

The eligible entrant was any amateur writer who had not professionally published more than three short stories or more than one novelette, or who had not yet professionally published a novel. The rules were simple. The quarterly prizes were handsome: 1st Place-$1000, 2nd Place-$750, 3rd Place-$500. There was no entry fee and the entrant retained all rights to his story.

The guiding principles and high standards of competition, defined by Mr. Hubbard at the Contest's inception, have been stringently observed since the first quarter began January 1, 1984. The very nature of the competition established both the Contest and the resultant anthology as the premiere showcase for beginning writers in the speculative fiction genre. No less important is the encouragement and acknowledgement of aspiring writers everywhere.

▲

"Thank you L. Ron Hubbard! Thank you America!"
— **SERGEY V. POYARKOV**
1990 Hubbard Gold Award Winner

▼

Significant ideas never remain static. And so it is with the L. Ron Hubbard Writers of The Future Contest. Word of the Contest spread from writer to writer, instructor to student, father to son, reporter to reader, friend to friend, professional to amateur. Based upon the success of the first year—which ended on September 30, 1984—the Contest was renewed for another year and

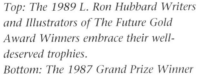

Top: The 1989 L. Ron Hubbard Writers and Illustrators of The Future Gold Award Winners embrace their well-deserved trophies.
Bottom: The 1987 Grand Prize Winner with $4000 award check in hand.

From the top: Senior Contest Advisor, Fred Harris, announces a Grand Prize winner. • John Varley (left) congratu-ates a first place quarterly winner.
• Another winner is announced.
• Dr. Yoji Kondo (left), Nancy (the voice of Bart Simpson) Cartwright, and Frederik Pohl seal predictions in the Time Capsule.

From the top: Algis Budrys with yet another happy winner. • Len Forman, Executive Director of Bridge Publica-tions, presents Volume IX of the anthology in Hollywood. • Algis Budrys with the 1988 Contest year winners at the United Nations.

became the "Writers of The Future Contest."

The first L. Ron Hubbard Awards ceremony, honoring the winners of the 1984 Contest year, was held at Chasens famous restaurant in Bever-ly Hills in February 1985. Algis Budrys recalls, "We invited all of our writers from all over the country. ... It was our SF family party for the writers. It was a delight to meet them; to find that behind the good work were good people...as various and striking as their stories, and promising exciting new work in the future."

All of the first place quarterly winners were presented with the L. Ron Hubbard Award, a sterling silver quill and star set in blue-based lucite—significant recogni-tion of accomplishment. Stunning

---

"The L. Ron Hubbard Writers of The Future Contest has carried out the noble mission of nurtur-ing new science fiction and fan-tasy writers for a decade now with resounding success."
— **DR. YOJI KONDO**
NASA/Goddard Space Lab

---

certificates were also created for the award-winning writers.

Hans Janitschek, President of the Society of Writers at the United Nations, welcomes the winners, judges and guests to the 1989 L. Ron Hubbard Awards Event, held in the Trusteeship Council Chamber at the United Nations.

The Diplomatic World Bulletin, the official newspaper of the United Nations, carried five full pages of coverage of the L. Ron Hubbard Awards.

the DIPLOMATIC WORLD
BULLETIN
DEDICATED TO SERVING THE UNITED NATIONS AND THE INTERNATIONAL COMMUNITY
and DELEGATES WORLD BULLETIN

| VOLUME 20 NUMBER 5 | NEW YORK CITY | $5.00 per copy | April 17 - 24, 1989 |

Page 8   DIPLOMATIC WORLD BULLETIN   April 17 - 24, 1989   April 17 - 24, 1989   DIPLOMATIC WORLD BULLETIN   Page

L. Ron Hubbard Writers of The Future Awards to be Presented at a Meeting at United Nations

Society of Writers at UN Hosts Awards Symposium

Janitschek Heads Active Society of Writers at UN

Hans W. Janitschek, assistant to the Executive Director of the Population Fund at the United Nations, and took a position as advisor to the chairman of the Austrian Socialist Party. Three

SCHEDULE OF EVENTS
TRUSTEESHIP COUNCIL CHAMBER
FRED HARRIS-MASTER OF CEREMONIES

April 29
12:30 Reception

1:00 **Panel: EARTH, MY BEAUTIFUL HOME**
The role of the Artist in shaping the
Environmental Future of Our Planet

Dr. Charles Sheffield   Frederik Pohl
(Moderating)   Jack Williamson
Tim Powers   John Varley
Robert Welch   Frank Kelly-Freas

2:00 **Panel: WHICH TOMORROW?**
The role of The Scientist in
Choosing the Future

Algis Budrys (moderating)   Dr. Yoji Kondo
Dr. Sheldon Glashow   Dr. Ed Gibson
Dr. Gerald Feinberg   Dr. Jerry Pournelle

3:00 Intermission - Refreshments

3:30 The Fifth Annual Writers of the
Future Awards and Special Presentations

5:00 End of Symposium and
Special Awards Presentations

SYMPOSIUM PANEL 1:
1:00 P.M. Saturday, April 29, 1989
EARTH, MY BEAUTIFUL HOME: The Role of the Artist in Shaping the Environmental Future of our Planet.

Discussants should consider the following:

While the facts of environmental pollution have been gathered and studied by scientists, the reality has been conveyed to the public through communications channels used by artists. Books, such as Rachel Carson's SILENT SPRING, photographs of oil-polluted wildlife, evocations of the effects of pollution by concerned makers of film and television documentaries, and the like, are the means by which the situation is translated into public awareness. It is notable that individual artists create this reality first, to be followed by the news media only after the media realize that an audience has been prepared for them.

In speculative literature, typically produced by artists well-versed in the disciplines of science, there is a vast body of profession-ally convincing dramas depicting life in a devastated environment. For an audience of over 6 million for the English-language texts alone, there is a body of informed literature in which many conceivable futures has been explored or at least pointed toward. Many other language-groups, large and small,

(Continued on page 14)

SYMPOSIUM PANEL 2:

The Best NEW SF of the Year

L. RON HUBBARD
Presents
WRITERS OF
THE FUTURE
VOLUME V

Unique Event Merges Arts, Sciences at UN

A unique event, merging the arts and sciences to create answers to timely concerns, will be held at the United Nations Headquarters April 29, 1989. Called The Writers of The Future symposium, it will bring together internationally known figures in the arts and sciences. They will present expert scenarios for dealing with our environment and our future.

The symposium has been arranged with the cooperation of the Society of Writers at The United Nations. Hans Janitschek, President of the Society, declared: "The world today is awakening to the urgent need to solve massive environmental problems in the face of a rapidly increasing population. It must also prepare for the expanding technological future. The nature of that future will be determined by actions taken over the next few years. We must synergize all our creative resources to help the world choose the best possible actions."

The Writers of The Future program was designed and founded in 1983 by author-philosopher L. Ron Hubbard to being forward significant new talent in speculative literature. So doing, he declared his determination to sustain what he considered a vital cultural interaction. Earlier, he had written: "A culture is as rich as it has imaginative artists, skilled men of science, a high elite level, workable government, land and natural resources."

Capping the symposium will be a series of awards to the best new speculative-fiction authors found

L. Ron Hubbard (1911-1986), planner and founder of the L. Ron Hubbard Writers of The Future international literary contest launched in 1983. Author-philosopher Hubbard wrote: "A culture is only as great as its dreams, and its dreams are dreamed by artists." Since its inception, the Contest has brought forward over 75 new writers of science fiction and fantasy, many of whom have gone on to extensive publication, and recognition as significant new talents in the genre. In addition to the U.S. and Canada,

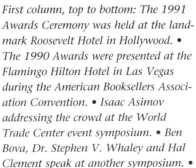

First column, top to bottom: The 1991 Awards Ceremony was held at the landmark Roosevelt Hotel in Hollywood. • The 1990 Awards were presented at the Flamingo Hilton Hotel in Las Vegas during the American Booksellers Association Convention. • Isaac Asimov addressing the crowd at the World Trade Center event symposium. • Ben Bova, Dr. Stephen V. Whaley and Hal Clement speak at another symposium. •

Publishers Weekly Editor, John F. Baker, with two L. Ron Hubbard Gold Award winners. Middle column, top to bottom: Julius Schwartz (left) with other guests at the L. Ron Hubbard Gallery during the 1993 event. • The symposium panel addresses the audience in the National Archives theater. • Contest Judges surround the 1992 L. Ron Hubbard Gold Award Winner. • Legendary SF illustrator, Frank Frazetta, with characters from his anthology cover, brought to life. Right column, top to bottom: Dr. Jerry Pournelle, Dr. Gerald Feinberg and Nobel Laureate, Dr. Sheldon Glashow, at the United Nations event. • Dr. Charles Sheffield says a few words at the 1988 event in Hollywood. • A toast to the new winners and Volume V of the anthology at the United Nations Plaza Hotel.

Top: The first L. Ron Hubbard Gold Award was presented by Jack Williamson and Anne McCaffrey. Bottom: Kristine Kathryn Rusch and Dean Wesley Smith presenting an Award in 1991.

Culminating the event was the release of the initial *L. Ron Hubbard Presents Writers of The Future* anthology representing, in most cases, the winning writers' first publishing experience. Also included were helpful, talent-nurturing commentaries for new writers by the professionals. According to Algis Budrys, "Prepublication orders throughout the U.S. set records, and a succession of print order increases occurred at a gratifying and startling pace." Nine more anthologies have been published since that time with another, Volume XI, now in the formative stages. These anthologies have also been used as an instructional text in creative writing

Above: Proud winners at the United Nations. Right: Another L. Ron Hubbard Gold Award winner.

and literature classes in scores of colleges and universities, including such distinguished schools as Rutgers University, Pepperdine University, University of Kansas, University of Houston, Brigham Young University, as well as the University of Victoria, British Columbia, among others.

The 1985 year saw the formation of satellite offices of the Contest in the United Kingdom and Australia/New Zealand, to facilitate English-language entries from those two continents. Since that time, entries have been received from a multitude of countries in Europe,

Asia, Africa, South America, North America, and Australia.

Though the ever-increasing popularity of the Contest and its anthology kept everyone busy, yet another avenue was undertaken, by Mr. Hubbard's original design, to help launch the newly-discovered writers in their chosen profession, the L. Ron Hubbard Writing Workshop. First held in May, 1986, in Taos,

---

"I'm delighted to see how many of the winners have gone on to bigger and better careers."
— **RAMSEY CAMPBELL**
Award-winning author

Left column, top to bottom: Contest and United Nations representatives seal a Time Capsule.
• Dr. Jerry Newman, Chairman Emeritus National Commission of Libraries and Information Sciences holds the Gold Award trophy in anticipation of the winner being named. • Kevin J. Anderson addresses attendees of the 1993 event. Right column, top to bottom: A. E. van Vogt and Jack Williamson enjoying themselves at the L. Ron Hubbard Awards ceremony. • Julius Schwartz, Kelly Freas and Ray Bradbury at the launching of the Illustrators of The Future Contest, Thanksgiving 1988. • Symposium panelist Dr. Doug Beason in the National Archives Theater.

New Mexico, the Workshop has since been held annually in conjunction with the Awards Ceremonies.

The L. Ron Hubbard Gold Award, a magnificent trophy with a gold quill pen and star set in red-based lucite, was created to present to the annual Grand Prize winner, selected from among the four first-place quarterly winners. The Gold Award carries with it a $4000 prize amount for the Author of the Story of the Year. The first Grand Prize recipient was Robert Reed, author of "Mud-puppies," named on March 21, 1986, at the Second Annual L. Ron Hubbard Awards ceremony held during Norwescon—an annual regional convention attended by SF celebrities from all over North America. Succeeding Gold Award winners include Dave Wolverton, Nancy Farmer, Gary Shockley, James Gardner, James C. Glass, Brian Burt and Karawynn Long.

As science fiction typically deals with the future, 1987 saw the beginning of a new tradition—that of eliciting predictions and sealing them in a time capsule, to be opened from 25 to 50 years hence. Hundreds of people—ranging across the professions, government, and the arts and sciences—have participated with the winners and judges of the Contest in this annual activity, including Costa Rica President Oscar Arias, John Travolta, baseball manager Tommy Lasorda, astronaut and space station planner Dr. Ed Gibson, among others.

In 1988, under L. Ron Hubbard's inspiration, a companion Contest for new illustrators was founded to encourage the speculative fiction artist, in much the same way the Writers' Contest has done for authors. Winning illustrators—three each quarter—take the winning stories and illustrate them for the annual anthology. There is also an L. Ron Hubbard Gold Award Trophy—and $4000 prize money—awarded in this competition.

To give the Contest winners the broadest possible showcase, other outstanding venues for the L. Ron Hubbard Awards ceremony have included the top of the World Trade Center in New York City, the American Booksellers Association Convention in Las Vegas, the theater of the National Archives in Washington, D.C., and the Trusteeship Council Chamber of the United Nations, under the auspices of the Society of Writers at the U.N.

The L. Ron Hubbard Writers of The Future Program, established in the finest tradition of the professional giving a helping hand to the novice, has become the largest, the most well-known and the best established discovery vehicle in the field. □

THE JUDGES

Masters from the "Golden Age" to the Present

From the outset, the L. Ron Hubbard Writers of The Future Contest panel of judges has represented an extraordinary gathering of many of the greatest names in speculative and contemporary fiction—authors whose distinguished careers collectively span virtually the entire history of modern science fiction and fantasy, from the masters of the "Golden Age"—the immense flourishing of the genre in the 1930's and 1940's—to the present.

The professional authors have brought to the Writers of The Future Contest, the annual anthology and the writing workshops—

Judges pictured on this page, top, left to right: Kelly Freas, Ramsey Campbell, Larry Niven and Frederik Pohl. Right: Orson Scott Card. Far right: Algis Budrys.

L. Ron Hubbard's
Writers of The Future

individually and collaboratively— their superb creative talents and energies, their deep professionalism, and their wholehearted commitment to discovering novice writers

---

"The Contest has opened the way for scores of writers and has set them out on the fine careers they deserve."

— JACK WILLIAMSON
Grand Master of Science Fiction Award recipient

---

of ability and promise, then assisting them in their quest for publication and professional recognition.

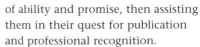

The support from the world of speculative fiction for the Writers of The Future Program has been enthusiastically evident from the beginning, and nowhere more clearly than in the remarkable make-up of the panel itself.

Luminaries all, the judges have sought with zeal and great distinction to help fulfill L. Ron Hubbard's defining goal for the program: to nurture the beginning writer, without whom there exists no literary future. □

Upper row: Jack Williamson. • Kelly Freas and Roger Zelazny. Middle row: Anne McCaffrey. • Robert Silverberg, Roger Zelazny and Dr. Gregory Benford. • Tim Powers. • The late Theodore Sturgeon. Bottom row: Dave Wolverton. • Dr. Jerry Pournelle. Not pictured: Andre Norton.

THE L.RON HUBBARD
WRITING WORKSHOP
Polishing New Talent

It is a matter of record that from his earliest years as a professional writer, L. Ron Hubbard helped other writers develop their talents. It is not surprising that the magazine articles he authored in those early years for *Writer's Digest*, *Writer's Review*, *The Author & Journalist* and *Writers' Markets & Methods*, are still used today in workshops to teach the basic skills of

Preceding page: Algis Budrys, Coordinating Judge of the L. Ron Hubbard Writers of The Future Contest 1984 – 1991, instructs the L. Ron Hubbard Writing Workshop at The George Washington University.

L. Ron Hubbard Writing Workshop.

Instructed from the outset by author/editor Algis Budrys, the first of these workshops was held in May, 1986 in Taos, New Mexico, open to the 1985 Contest-awarded writers only. The assistant instructors included Jack Williamson, Gene Wolfe and Frederik Pohl. Succeeding invitational writing workshops have been held at Sag Harbor, New York; Pepperdine University, Malibu, California; Boulder

Hubbard Gallery, Hollywood, California. Other assistant instructors have included Orson Scott Card, Tim Powers and Dave Wolverton. In 1991, Dave Wolverton assumed the duties of the L. Ron Hubbard Writing Workshop Instructor with his

Clockwise from upper left: Charles N. Brown addresses the L. Ron Hubbard Writing Workshop. • Attendees receiving Certificates of Completion. • Students studying materials. • Tim Powers instructing a workshop session.

story writing because they are both encouraging and understanding of the aspiring writer's plight, as well as accurate in their statement of techniques. They are the basis of the

City, Nevada; California State Polytechnic University, Pomona, California; The George Washington University, and the Library of Congress, Washington, D. C.; and the L. Ron

other positions of Coordinating Judge of the Contest and Editor of the anthology.

"What astonished me was how much more was accomplished in only a few days than most workshops accomplish in weeks or months or even years."
— ORSON SCOTT CARD
Award-winning author

As acclaim for the L. Ron Hubbard Writing Workshop spread through the Contest award-winning participants, novice writers and instructors around the world clamored for these same writing materials to be made widely available. This has resulted in public workshops held in such prestigious venues as Harvard, DePaul, Duke and Brigham Young Universities, and even The Charles Dickens House in London, England. No less important are the workshops which have been held in conjunction with science fiction conventions throughout the continental United States.

hensively include L. Ron Hubbard's articles, essays, letters and personal reflections on the art, technique and practice of successful story writing. □

Clockwise from top: Attendees enjoying the National Air and Space Museum exhibits, watching the finale at the L. Ron Hubbard Life Exhibition, at the Library of Congress, the class at The George Washington University, the National Archives and Harvard University.

L. Ron Hubbard's lifetime legacy to new writers would not be complete without publication of his insights to creative writing. To make these valuable writing materials even more widely and readily available, planning has begun on the publication of a book that would compre-

IN THE NEWS

The L. Ron Hubbard Writers of The Future Program and its growing impact on the world of speculative fiction and other literary genres has attracted widespread media attention, and won enthusiastic recogniton from government officials, civic leaders and other community figures throughout the United States and in other parts of the world.

Demand by newspapers and magazines, television and radio for news about the program in all its aspects has mounted steadily over the years. In meeting this demand with individual stories and background material, the Program has focused a further spotlight on the Contest winners, giving their aspirations and careers a special, added boost.

"Prior to L. Ron Hubbard's Writers of The Future Contest starting there was no field which enabled the new writer to compete with his peers— other new writers."

— KEVIN J. ANDERSON
New York Times bestselling author

Hubbard sponsors contest for beginning writers

Austinite wins Hubbard award

Science fiction giant leaves big legacy to Writers of the Future

Pasadena writer wins L. Ron Hubbard award

Hubbard Contests Award $4,000 Prizes

Star's theater editor is named fantasy writers contest finalist

Freireich vies for Hubbard award in August

Houdek attends Hubbard awards in Hollywood

Larchmont Artist Wins Ron Hubbard Competition

The writers who succeed persist in search of goal

Local author gets published

American, Soviet Share Hubbard Prizes

Contest Winners Received Hubbard Award in Washington, D.C.

PUBLISHERS WEEKLY / MAY 22, 1987

Kansas Contest Winner Receive Hubbard Award in Washington, D.C. Ceremonies

WINNING WRITERS, ILLUSTRATORS TO ATTEND HUBBARD AWARDS IN HOLLYWOOD

A Contest Prize With a Touch of Class

Hubbard Awards, Three Years Old, Find Sanction

Arts and Entertainment

Young writer wins out-of-this-world award

Writers of the Future at the United Nations

Hubbard sci-fi compilation scores

L. RON HUBBARD WRITERS OF THE FUTURE

LOCUS

Hubbard New Writers' Bash

Proclamation

PROCLAMATION OF RECOGNITION

Writers of the Future Workshop

Sci-fi writer gets recognition

By PAUL DELLINGER
Staff Writer

L. Ron Hubbard
Writers of the Future Day

City of Petaluma
PROCLAMATION

Presented With Appreciation to AUTHOR SERVICES INC In Honor of L. RON HUBBARD'S Invaluable Contributions To Science Fiction and the Arts Through his Writers and Illustrators of the Future Programs

BRIGHAM YOUNG UNIVERSITY SYMPOSIUM of SCIENCE FICTION and FANTASY

February 7, 1992

Publishers Weekly
THE WEST WATCH
Onward & Upward with L. Ron Hubbard

Writers, Illustrators Of Speculative Fiction Given Showcase In Ninth Hubbard Series

VENTURE AWARD 1988
L. RON HUBBARD'S
WRITERS OF THE FUTURE - FOR INCREASING SERVICE

FULFILLING THE L. RON HUBBARD LEGACY:

Launching New Careers

As L. Ron Hubbard intended, the Writers of The Future Program has given aspiring writers an unparalleled opportunity to have their creative efforts seen and acknowledged.

The success of this program, however, cannot be defined simply by the number of deserving writers dis-

> *"Over the years I managed to become a Grand Prize winner, a contest judge, a contributor to the anthologies, and eventually the Coordinating Judge. I have seen the contest from all sides. It has been my privilege to grow with it and to watch dozens of other authors and artists grow with it."*
> — **DAVE WOLVERTON**
> *Coordinating Judge 1991 to present*

covered through the merit competition, or the number of students who have completed the writing workshop, or even by the number of writers who have been published in the annual anthology, many for the first time. The only definitive, long-lasting measurement of its

success—fulfilling L. Ron Hubbard's expressed goal for the Writers of The Future Program and carrying out his legacy—is the writer's continuing contributions to the literature and creative standards of today and tomorrow.

Here then—pictured on the following page—is a sampling of the work being produced by Writers of The Future award-winners who have gone on to publication and outstanding professional success in the field of the novel as well as the short story, in both speculative fiction and other literary genres. □

After winning the L. Ron Hubbard Writers of The Future Contest, winners have gone on to sell nearly 100 novels and almost 1,000 short stories.

> *"This Contest is the best legacy, except for the body of work a writer leaves behind, that any science fiction writer has given the field."*
> — **VALERIE J. FREIREICH**
> *1990 L. Ron Hubbard Award-winner*

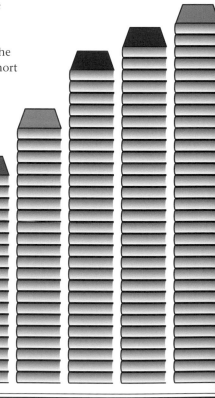

L. RON HUBBARD

The Writer's Writer

L. Ron Hubbard was the writer's writer; the quintessential professional who, throughout a career that embraced more than half a century of prodigious work, gave freely and generously of his time and energies to help other writers, especially the beginner, become better and more productive at his trade.

His creativity is legendary—for the speed with which he could deliver a manuscript and meet deadlines, for the vast array of story ideas that flowed from his typewriter, for his huge productivity, and for the

intense individuality of each of his works.

Born in Tilden, Nebraska and raised in Montana, young L. Ron Hubbard was acquainted with a rugged outdoor life during which he became a blood brother of the Blackfeet Indian and America's youngest Eagle Scout. As a teenager, thirsting for adventure, he undertook voyages to the Far East, filling a series of diaries with narrative ideas that crowded his novels and short stories when he burst onto the landscape of American popular fiction in the early 1930's.

Returning to the U.S. in 1929 from his travels and adventures in the Orient, he took his insatiable curiosity and demand for excitement to the sky as a daring glider pilot and barnstormer. It was during this time that a national aviation magazine reported that Ron set a national soaring record for sustained flight over the same field.

While studying engineering and the physical sciences at The George Washington University in Washington, D.C., he was a correspondent for *The Sportsman Pilot*, a national magazine, and a reporter for his college newspaper, the University Hatchet. He also began drawing on his experiences to

Top: Ron riding at age three. Middle, left to right: Age 19 at the typewriter. • Ron, the barnstormer. • In the Far East with his parents. Bottom, left to right: During the Mineralogical Expedition in Puerto Rico. • The youngest Eagle Scout.

write short stories and an award-winning play for the university's literary review.

In 1932, he led a photographic expedition of 54 college students aboard a four-masted schooner in the Caribbean, and shortly afterward, conducted a mineralogical expedition to Puerto Rico, where his adventures generated further story ideas that would later nurture his storytelling art. Upon his return to the mainland, he continued in what became a fabled career as a professional fiction writer. His first adventure story about a U.S. Naval

> *"Just to show you how good an author I consider Hubbard… especially after 'Ultimate Adventure,' I consider anything below perfect a letdown. I eagerly await 'The Ghoul' and as many more yarns as Hubbard can write."*
>
> — ISAAC ASIMOV
> *As published in* Unknown *magazine, September 1939*

Intelligence Officer in China, "The Green God," appeared in the February issue of *Thrilling Adventures* magazine.

The scope of his subsequent productivity was phenomenal: air, land and sea adventures, then mysteries, detective fiction and westerns—a richly diverse catalogue of entertainment. Yet, he was always willing to share his hard-earned experience with the novice. At universities such as Harvard and George Washington, he addressed aspiring writers on how they could get their careers started, and in 1935, at the age of 24, his "how to" articles about writing began appearing in profes-

sional writers' magazines of the day. To further encourage budding writers, then as now, he initiated a contest by radio, in Ketchikan, Alaska, in 1940.

L. Ron Hubbard also had a philosophy about a writer being in debt to life:

"That means living and learning. It means doing all you can, studying all you can, learning all you can. It means borrowing from the Bank of the World in ideas and knowledge

L. Ron Hubbard, Hollywood, circa 1937.

and experience. Recognize this as a debt to the people around you, a debt the writer must pay back with his writings. It isn't a hard debt to pay, for the repayment will be made easy by borrowing; the greater the borrowing, the greater the ease with which the payments can be made. The writer who has drawn much from the world will find that his mind is filled with material that can be used to make the

payments. The more the writer throws himself into debt, the more he will have with which to repay."

In 1936, Ron was elected the president of the New York Chapter of the American Fiction Guild which included Raymond Chandler, Dashiell Hammett and Edgar Rice Burroughs among its membership.

As with the other leading writers of the era, Mr. Hubbard was invited to Hollywood in 1937, where he wrote the original story and scripts for fifteen chapters of Columbia's box office hit serial, "The Secret of Treasure Island." He also worked on story lines and wrote for a number of films, including "The Mysterious Pilot," "The Great Adventures of Wild Bill Hickok" and "The Spider Returns."

Returning to New York in 1938, he was approached by Street & Smith, the publishers of *Astounding Science-Fiction* magazine, who wanted to give the magazine a needed circulation boost. He was introduced to the new editor, John W. Campbell, Jr., who was instructed to buy everything Hubbard wrote—a testimony to the appeal of the L. Ron Hubbard byline on a magazine cover. He was reluctant at first and protested that he did not write about machines and machinery but that he wrote about people. Street & Smith executives told him that was exactly what they wanted.

He discovered he loved the field of science fiction, which he was able to enrich and change by injecting strong characters and human interest into his stories. He also began to turn out remarkably inventive fantasy stories which Campbell relished and even launched a separate magazine, *Unknown*, to feature them.

The result was a wealth of celebrated science fiction and fantasy stories—including such acknowledged literary landmarks as *Fear, Final Blackout, Slaves of Sleep,* and *Typewriter in the Sky*—which not only expanded the scope of these genres but established him as one of the founders and creative wellsprings of the Golden Age of Science Fiction.

Awarded membership in the prestigious Explorers Club in New York in February 1940, he shortly thereafter carried their flag on an expedition to chart the coastal

> *"There are three main plots for the human interest story: boy-meets-girl, The Little Tailor, and the man-who-learned-better. Credit the last to L. Ron Hubbard; I had thought for years that there were but two plots—he pointed out to me the third type."*
> — **ROBERT A. HEINLEIN**
> *Grand Master of Science Fiction Award recipient*

waters of British Columbia and Alaska and study native Indian tribes. His mastery of the ocean earned him a Master Mariners license, granting him the authority to sail any vessel, any ocean.

With the advent of World War II, he was called to active duty as an intelligence officer in the U.S. Navy. The course of this global war interrupted his writing career as he served his country and it was not until 1947 that he once again began producing exciting stories for his

legions of readers. Among these were the popular "Ole Doc Methuselah" series, *To The Stars,* and *The End Is Not Yet.* No less significant is the assistance he gave to amateur writers—along with other noted professionals—in organized

science fiction groups.

He also continued his high-production writing—for which he was celebrated—in the adventure, western, mystery and detective genres providing his millions of fans with endless hours of entertainment. By the age of 39, he had already written and published more than 260 novels, novelettes and short stories, totalling over sixteen million words.

L. Ron Hubbard's ability to sit down and not only plot and write a particular story on request but to create it to a prescribed word length was a rare talent indeed.

He could excercise the same talent verbally.

There were evenings when friends would gather and sometimes he would entertain them with a tale or two. Some of the gatherings included other writers such as L. Sprague de Camp and Robert A. Heinlein. Isaac Asimov was there and remembered: "I and Bob Heinlein and Sprague de Camp were three prima donnas who had no objection to holding the

Top: L. Ron Hubbard, in center, at the Fiction Writers Guild in New York. Center: A selection of magazines which had published L. Ron Hubbard's stories and a poster from the screenplay he wrote for "The Secret of Treasure Island." Bottom: A few of his classic fiction works, including his first published novel, Buckskin Brigades.

floor. Anyway, Hubbard took over. Absolutely charismatic. I remember noticing at the time, I was perfectly content to be silent, so was Heinlein, so was Sprague. We all sat around and listened and Hubbard entertained us for the entire party. He told us stories in perfect paragraphs, he reminisced, he sang and played guitar. … I can't imagine anyone else ever keeping we three completely tamed while we listened. … It seems to me that his stories were funny rather than tragic, that we were amused because we laughed. I of course sat there admiring the way the stories required no editing. If you had printed them as he said them they would make perfect sense. There were no unfinished sentences, no hesitation sounds, no radical changes of subject as he started saying

Within a span of five years, L. Ron Hubbard produced thirteen consecutive New York Times fiction bestsellers, a publishing phenomenon. Among these, Battlefield Earth *and each of the* Mission Earth *volumes were Literary Guild Alternate Selections.*

something in the middle of something else. If you were to transcribe my interview like that you'd find all these things. You didn't find them in what he said. And somehow they didn't give me the impression of having been memorized. It just seemed he had this ability."

"A brilliant science fiction author."
— NEW YORK DAILY NEWS

In 1950, with the culmination of years of research on the subject of the mind resulting in the publication of *Dianetics: The Modern Science of Mental Health,* L. Ron Hubbard left the field of fiction and for the next three decades dedicated his life to

writing and publishing millions of words of non-fiction concerning the nature of man and the betterment of the human condition.

However, in 1980, in celebration of his 50th anniversary as a professional writer, Ron returned to the science fiction genre with the internationally acclaimed *Battlefield Earth, A Saga of the Year 3000.*

Always a writer's writer, L. Ron Hubbard then continued his own phenomenal literary production with his 1.2 million word, comic-satire masterpiece, the unprecedented 10-volume *Mission Earth* dekalogy.

In 1983, viewing the difficult business conditions at that time, he established and sponsored the Writers of The Future Contest in the continuing tradition he began many years before of the professional assisting the novice.

Current New York Times bestselling author Kevin J. Anderson states: "The Writers of The Future Contest gave me a goal to shoot for—prize money, trophy, participation in the writing workshop which I had heard so much about and publication in the *L. Ron Hubbard Presents Writers of The Future* volumes. Though I never won the Contest, through its quarterly deadlines, I improved so much that I started making sales.

"When looking over past volumes of Writers of The Future, it becomes apparent how great an impact L. Ron Hubbard and this Contest has had on the entire field

of science fiction."

During a "Decade of Helping New Writers," the L. Ron Hubbard Writers of The Future Program has: • Actively discovered and launched the professional careers of over 150 writers • Provided encouragement and impetus to tens of thousands of aspiring writers internationally • Awarded quarterly prizes totalling $87,750 • Awarded Grand Prizes in the amount of $36,000 • Conferred nearly 900 certificates of merit • Bestowed forty L. Ron Hubbard Awards • Bestowed nine L. Ron Hubbard Gold Awards •

"I know of no one who has done more for new writers of fantastic literature in the last decade than the WOTF Contest. It is a credit to American literature and a singular, generous event."
— **DR. GREGORY BENFORD**
Award-winning author

Presented a significant publishing platform for Contest winners and selected finalists in ten editions of *L. Ron Hubbard Presents Writers of The Future* • Received tens of thousands of manuscripts from aspiring writers all over the world • Delivered eight invitational L. Ron Hubbard Writing Workshops as well as innumerable public workshops to hundreds of writers.

Though we celebrate between these pages a Decade of Helping New Writers, one can not go very far, in speaking of the Writers of The Future Program, without bringing proper notice to the companion Contest established for illustrators.

In the Golden Age of Science

Fiction Mr. Hubbard so fondly remembered, the illustrators of the stories written then were as important to the readers as were the writers. The characters and their drama came alive as much pictorially as they did in prose. Particular writers and illustrators often formed strong relationships, exchanging ideas and working, in effect, as partners. As this creative synergy was in danger of becoming a lost thing, the

L. Ron Hubbard— one of the most acclaimed and widely read authors of all time.

Illustrators' Contest was founded to ensure that the relationships between the written word and the illustrator's art would not die.

This Contest has run concurrently with the Writers' Contest and gives their work a showcase between the pages of the *L. Ron Hubbard Presents Writers of The Future* volumes— accompanying the stories, as was

"I met L. Ron Hubbard on January 4, 1940, in John W. Campbell's office and was extremely impressed because I had been reading his early stories in Unknown *and loved them."*
— **ISAAC ASIMOV**
Grand Master of Science Fiction Award recipient

done during the Golden Age of Science Fiction.

L. Ron Hubbard's lifelong commitment to the profession and craft of writing and the arts ended when he passed from this life in January, 1986; however, his extraordinary legacy—through the immense body of his own work and the L. Ron Hubbard Writers and Illustrators of The Future Contests—continues to this day and will endure into the future. □

"What Hugo Gernsback did in the 1920's and 1930's and John W. Campbell, Jr., did through the 1940's and 1950's, the L. Ron Hubbard Writers of The Future Contest is doing in the 1980's and 1990's: identifying the writers who will shape the field into the next millenium."
— **DAVID PHALEN**
1992 Writers of The Future Award-winner

... and never stop dreaming

They're dreamers, but they're tired. They work hard, year after year, getting better at their dreams, better at communicating them, but they sometimes get discouraged. Recognition seldom comes quickly in the dreaming business. Sometimes, they wonder if it will come at all.

Who are they? They're unpublished authors of speculative fiction—horror, fantasy and science fiction—and if it sounds like I know how they feel, that's because I *was* one of them. I know the effort it takes to reach deep inside for dreams no one else has dreamed. I know the hope that comes from mailing dreams to editors. And I know the heartbreak when those dreams are tarnished by rejection. I'm all too familiar with doubt and the idea of publication seeming farfetched.

That's in the past, though. Now, I haven't those doubts, I believe in my dreams.

What brought on this change? I can tell you in an acronym: WOTF. It stands for L. Ron Hubbard's Writers of The Future Contest, and in the ten years since its creation by SF legend L. Ron Hubbard, it has helped launch a number of careers and given over 150 writers their first publication.

It's a simple concept, but a powerful one. The publishing business is driven by the cold equations of name value and track record—not promising for the novice. What if there were a place where none of that mattered? What if someone would judge a new writer's work on merit alone?

What if...WOTF?

When I first entered, my confidence was not high. I hardly suspected the opportunity that was to come

my way. A finalist award in 1989 got my story, "Mothers of Chaos," into Volume VI of the anthology of winners and from that moment forward, good things began to happen. I found that attitudes changed, that my work was now taken seriously. More and more often editors responded favorably to my stories. And now and then, when I mailed a story out, it would never come back. Instead, I'd receive a check and the story would be published.

For that alone, I would have been eternally grateful to WOTF. But there's more. In 1993, I *returned* to the WOTF anthology as a bona fide winner. This afforded me the unique opportunity to relive the events that so changed my life: another Writing Workshop, another Awards Event, more book signings and radio interviews, and, once again, publication in one of the hottest SF anthologies of all time.

As I stood on the stage receiving my award from none other than Jack Williamson, whose work inspired me at age 15, I knew that I had truly come home. I saw how far I had traveled toward my goals—a dozen short story sales, two novels on the market—and how much of that I owed to the boost given me in 1989 when WOTF took an unknown writer and published him. I don't think I realized until then how close I had come to giving up. WOTF was a lifesaver for me—literally. For with-

out its timely intervention, I might have turned my back on my dreams, lived some *other* life, a life without writing, a life I could never be happy living. But now I believe in a bright future, and I've been given a gift more precious than any other: faith in that future.

It was hard letting go, that second time, and there were tears in

Pete D. Manison receives his award from Contest Judge Jack Williamson at the 1993 L. Ron Hubbard Awards Event in Hollywood.

my eyes as the plane took off to deliver me back home. I knew that it was over and this time I could never go back.

But now I can say this: Don't give up. There is hope, and if you try hard enough you *will* succeed. Believe in yourself. And never stop dreaming.

— Pete D. Manison

For more information, write to:
L. Ron Hubbard's
Writers of The Future Contest
P.O. Box 1630
Los Angeles, California 90078

L. RON HUBBARD
WRITERS OF THE FUTURE AWARD WINNERS
HONOR ROLL

Ray Aldridge	Karen Joy Fowler	Mary Catherine McDaniel	Richard Urdiales
Mark Anthony	Valerie J. Freireich	Bridget McKenna	James Verran
Virginia Baker	R. García y Robertson	Michael Paul Meltzer	Sharon Wahl
Alan R. Barclay	Mark Andrew Garland	Jerry Meredith	Elizabeth E. Wein
Don Baumgart	Carolyn Ives Gilman	Michael D. Miller	K. D. Wentworth
Stephen M. Baxter	Ron Ginzler	Stephen Milligan	Ross Westergaard
Christine Beckert	Dan Gollub	Dennis E. Minor	Alan Wexelblat
M. Shayne Bell	Michael Green	John Moore	Lori Ann White
Michael C. Berch	Jon Gustafson	Jamil Nasir	Sean Williams
Öjvind Bernander	Bruce Hallock	Marianne O. Nielsen	Matthew Wills
Jo Beverley	Sheila Hartney	Scot Noel	Sam Wilson
Flonet Biltgen	David Hast	Michael H. Payne	Stephen Woodworth
James Gleason Bishop	Mark D. Haw	David Phalen	J. Steven York
Gene Bostwick	Eric M. Heideman	Dennis J. Pimple	Mary Frances Zambreno
R. V. Branham	Howard V. Hendrix	C. Maria Plieger	David Zindell
Mark Budz	Vaughn Heppner	John W. Randal	
Laura E. Campbell	Nina Kiriki Hoffman	Wendy Rathbone	
Leonard Carpenter	D. A. Houdek	Jean Reitz	**L. RON HUBBARD**
David Carr	Norma Hutman	Barry H. Reynolds	**GOLD AWARD**
L. E. Carroll	Parris ja Young	Bruce Holland Rogers	**WINNERS**
David Ira Cleary	Jor Jennings	Victor L. Rosemund	
Stoney Compton	C. W. Johnson	Charles M. Saplak	**1985**
Randell Crump	Douglas Jole	Don Satterlee	Robert Reed
Kathleen Dalton-Woodbury	James Gladue Jordan	Michael L. Scanlon	
Dan'l Danehy-Oakes	Astrid Julian	Mark Schimming	**1986**
Camilla Decarnin	Sansoucy Kathenor	W. Eric Schult	Dave Wolverton
John Richard DeRose	Kevin Kirk	Kenneth Schulze	
Nicholas A. DiChario	Susan Kroupa	Merritt Severson	**1987**
James S. Dorr	Michael I. Landweber	Jason Shankel	Nancy Farmer
Tom Drennan	Audrey Lawson	Annis Shepherd	
Steve Duff	Jo Etta Ledgerwood	Lisa Smedman	**1988**
J.R. Dunn	Michelle L. Levigne	D. E. Smirl	Gary Shockley
Charles D. Eckert	Diana Lofgran-Hoffman	Allen J. M. Smith	**1989**
Paul Edwards	Rayson Lorrey	Dean Wesley Smith	James Gardner
Bronwynn Elko	P. H. MacEwen	Martha Soukup	**1990**
Larry England	Andrew W. Mackie	C. Ellis Staehlin	James C. Glass
William Esrac	Jane Mailander	Eolake Stobblehouse	**1991**
Christopher Ewart	Pete D. Manison	Tawn Stokes	Brian Burt
Larry Ferrill	Steve Martindale	Jay Sullivan	**1992**
Stephen C. Fisher	Marc Matz	M. C. Sumner	Karawynn Long
Marina Fitch	Lisa Maxwell	Mike E. Swope	**1993**
Lauren Fitzgerald	Paula May	Terri Trimble	To be announced
Eric Flint	A. J. Mayhew	Mary A. Turzillo	

> *"L. Ron Hubbard was a creator of the first order, blessed with an imagination beyond description. He saw and wrote the future, inspiring millions and awakening the genius of writing in thousands."*
>
> — HANS JANITSCHEK
> *President, Society of Writers at the United Nations*

P. Photographic Reference Section

L. Ron Hubbard translated a life of adventure and penetrating observation into a body of genuinely American literature that possesses both liberating perceptions and the unmistakable ring of authenticity.

This photographic reference collection provides a brief look at his life, works and creative legacy, as well as some of his fiction awards and the exhibitions about him. It is cross-referenced to other pertinent sections.

L. RON HUBBARD

L. Ron Hubbard
The Adventurer

Top: L. Ron Hubbard at the family homestead near Helena, Montana, circa 1915.

Bottom: L. Ron Hubbard in Guam, circa 1928.

Top: L. Ron Hubbard near Seattle, Washington, circa 1923.

Bottom: L. Ron Hubbard adventuring in the West Indies, 1932.

*Top left: L. Ron Hubbard
panning for gold in 1933.*

*Top right: L. Ron Hubbard
aboard his 32-foot ketch
Magician in Ketchikan, Alaska.*

*"Barnstorming" with powered aircraft in Washington, D.C., 1931.
L. Ron Hubbard is on the far left.*

L. Ron Hubbard became one of the most widely published and popular authors of the 1930s and 40s. He had already produced an extraordinary one million words of published fiction when this early promotional flier appeared around 1936.

L. RON HUBBARD
BESTSELLING AUTHOR

Celebrating his 50th Anniversary as a professional writer, L. Ron Hubbard wrote [Battlefield Earth—A Saga of The Year 3000], internationally acclaimed as the biggest science fiction bestseller ever written. It was released in the U.S. in 1982. This was followed by his magnum opus—the Mission Earth dekalogy, a science fiction satire of more than 1.2 million words released in 10 separate volumes. In response to public requests for copies of his earlier classics, republication of the plethora of L. Ron Hubbard masterpieces written during the 1930's and 1940's was begun. Between May 1982 and May 1994, more than 12 million of his fiction works have been sold in 17 languages, available in 72 countries around the world.

L. Ron Hubbard Awards & Recognitions

The international acclaim for his literary achievements and contributions to the field of the arts is evident in the countless recognitions and awards bestowed upon L. Ron Hubbard. Shown above is but a small sampling of the types of awards which continue to be received on L. Ron Hubbard's behalf by his literary representatives and publishers in the U.S. and abroad.

L. Ron Hubbard
Audio/Visual

Since 1987, L. Ron Hubbard's fiction works have been regularly produced on audio cassette, featuring top professional theatrical talent. (See Section E.)

*Original musical albums—marking a publishing milestone—written by L. Ron Hubbard to accompany his bestselling fiction books, **Battlefield Earth** and **Mission Earth**. (See Section EE.)*

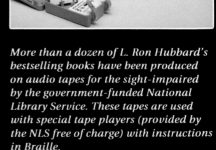

More than a dozen of L. Ron Hubbard's bestselling books have been produced on audio tapes for the sight-impaired by the government-funded National Library Service. These tapes are used with special tape players (provided by the NLS free of charge) with instructions in Braille.

*The complete and unabridged audio edition of **Battlefield Earth** — an astonishing 45 hour program.*

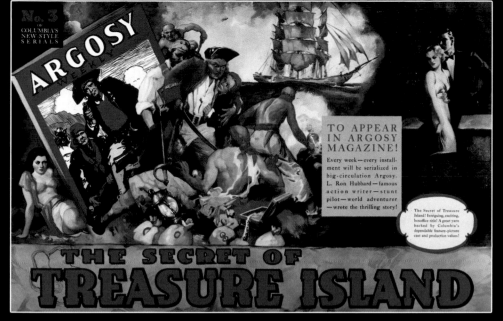

A movie poster from the 1937 Columbia Pictures hit serial **The Secret of Treasure Island,** *based on an original story by L. Ron Hubbard. (See Section F.)*

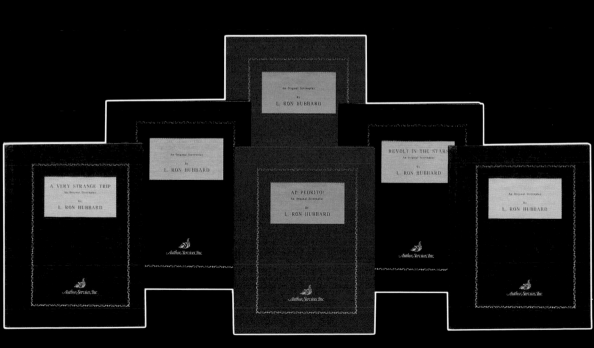

L. Ron Hubbard's original screenplays include **Ai! Pedrito!, A Very Strange Trip** *and* **Revolt in the Stars.** *Adaptations of several of his bestselling novels—including* **Fear, Battlefield Earth** *and* **Final Blackout***—have also been developed for the screen. (See Section F.)*

L. Ron Hubbard Gallery

Top left: Located in Hollywood, Author Services, Inc., is the international representative for the literary, theatrical and musical works of L. Ron Hubbard. (See Section M4.)

Top right: The L. Ron Hubbard Gallery at Author Services displays limited edition art prints which depict cover art, characters and scenes from L. Ron Hubbard's bestselling fiction works.

Right: Author Services' gala release events such as this one for **Mission Earth** *are attended by international celebrities.*

Below: Original covers of magazines featuring hundreds of novels, novelettes and short stories by L. Ron Hubbard line the walls of the boardroom at Author Services.

L. RON HUBBARD LIFE EXHIBITION

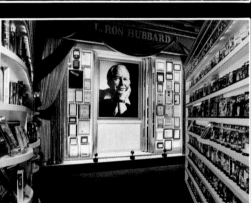

Top left: The opening of the L. Ron Hubbard Life Exhibition was a festive event with ribbon cutting, fire-works, celebrities and many thousands of spectators.

Exhibits depict the renaissance quality of L. Ron Hubbard's life— from his study of different cultures (top right) to his screenwriting in Hollywood and his prodigious literary output (middle right), and his humanitarian awards (middle left).

Bottom row: The L. Ron Hubbard Life Exhibition is a walk through his fascinating life and, with remarkable animation, through several of his most celebrated fiction works. (See Section M4.)

L. RON HUBBARD HALL

The School of Journalism of Moscow State University, incorporating the Departments of Russian and Foreign Literature, is the home of the new L. Ron Hubbard Hall where his works are available in a dozen languages. L. Ron Hubbard became the first foreign recipient of the Honorary Degree of Doctor of Literature of Moscow University. (See Section M4 and Section H.)

L. Ron Hubbard's Writers of The Future and Illustrators of The Future Contests

Grand Prize winners in the **Writers of The Future** *and* **Illustrators of The Future** *Contests receive the L. Ron Hubbard Gold Award Trophy to acknowledge their achievements, along with a generous cash award. (See Section O.)*

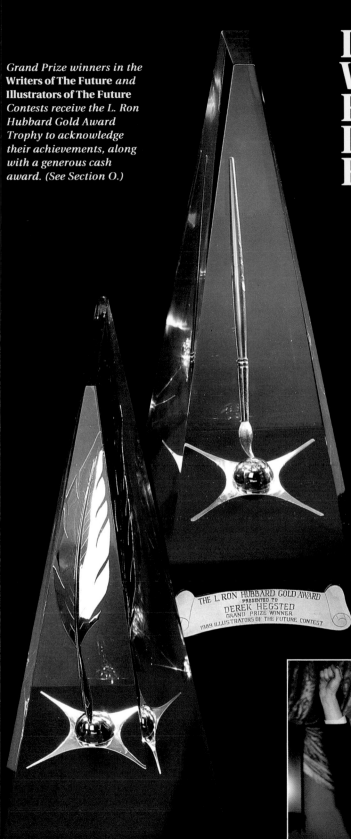

THE L. RON HUBBARD GOLD AWARD
PRESENTED TO
DEREK HEGSTED
GRAND PRIZE WINNER
1989 ILLUSTRATORS OF THE FUTURE CONTEST

THE L. RON HUBBARD GOLD AWARD
PRESENTED ANNUALLY TO THE
WINNER OF THE WRITERS OF THE FUTURE
STORY OF THE YEAR

A symposium on writing, held at the United Nations as part of the 1989 **Writers of The Future** *awards event.*

1990 **Illustrators of The Future** *winner, Sergey Poyarkov of the Ukraine. Winners of both contests have come from around the world. (Section O.)*

WRITERS OF THE FUTURE

Q. Series Index

This section lists the works of L. Ron Hubbard that comprise or form a series of stories. It provides a series synopsis and is cross-referenced to the individual entries in Sections A and B.

1. The Conquest of Space

2. Hazardous Professions (Hell-Job Series)

3. Kilkenny Cats

4. Ole Doc Methuselah

5. The Secret of Treasure Island

6. Mission Earth

Q. SERIES INDEX

Q1. **The Conquest of Space.** Approx. 52,000 words.

Nine stories related by theme, settings and characterization which were published between July 1948 and November 1950 in *Startling Stories*.

The stories are based on information obtained from archives in the future—after man has conquered space—that deal with the human barriers that man must overcome to reach the stars.

Published as an Italian hardcover anthology, *L'impero dei mille soli* (The Empire of the Thousand Suns), by Libra Editrice, 1981.

The series will also be published in two volumes (English) by Author Services, Inc., in 1999 as part of the *L. Ron Hubbard Classic Fiction Series*. (See AA63 and AA64.)

STORIES

1. "When Shadows Fall" (B177)
2. "Forbidden Voyage" (B181)
3. "The Magnificent Failure" (B183)
4. "The Incredible Destination" (B188)
5. "The Unwilling Hero" (B191)
6. "Beyond the Black Nebula" (B194)
7. "The Emperor of the Universe" (B199)
8. "The Last Admiral" (B206)
9. "Tough Old Man" (B216)

Q2. **Hazardous Professions (The Hell-Job Series).** 150,000 words.

A series of 17 thematically related stories based on hazardous occupations experienced, or researched, by L. Ron Hubbard. The stories appeared in *Argosy* between July 1936 and December 1937.

The stories were republished in the United States in hardcover under the title, *Lives You Wished To Lead— But Never Dared.* (See A19.)

The series will also be published in seven volumes by Author Services, Inc., in 1996 as part of the *L. Ron Hubbard Classic Fiction Series*. (See AA23 to AA30.)

STORIES

1. "Sleepy McGee" (B66)
2. "Don't Rush Me" (B67)
3. "Mr. Luck" (B77)
4. "Test Pilot" (B78)
5. "Deep-Sea Diver" (B79)
6. "The Big Cats" (B80)
7. "River Driver" (B84)
8. "The Ethnologist" (B85)
9. "Mine Inspector" (B87)
10. "The Shooter" (B88)
11. "Steeplejack" (B90)
12. "Flying Trapeze" (B91)
13. "Mountaineer" (B92)
14. "A Lesson in Lightning" (B96)
15. "Nine Lives" (B100)
16. "Cargo of Coffins" (B105)
17. "Orders Is Orders" (B107)

Q3. **Kilkenny Cats.** 36,000 words.

A series of five stories related by setting and characterization which were written under the pen name "Kurt von Rachen." They appeared in *Astounding Science Fiction* between July 1940 and February 1942.

In the year 2893, after a number of revolutions have taken place, the government attempts to rid itself of future threats by sending rival forces to colonize a planet—knowing that they will destroy each other.

Among them, however, are two rebels who devise means to prevent the rival groups of scientists and longshoremen from killing each other, and whose goal is to return to Earth and topple the dictatorial regime.

The series appeared in Italy in the Libra Editrice hard-cover collection, *I ribelli dell'universo* (The Rebels of the Universe). (See A25.)

Author Services, Inc., also published the series in 1992 as part of the *L. Ron Hubbard Classic Fiction Series.*

STORIES

1. "The Idealist" (B148)

2. "The Kilkenny Cats" (B150)

3. "The Traitor" (B154)

4. "The Mutineers" (B156)

5. "The Rebels" (B162)

Q4.   Ole Doc Methuselah. 70,000 words.

A collection of seven short stories related by character-ization and theme, written under the pen name "Rene Lafayette" for *Astounding Science Fiction.*

The stories appeared in *Astounding Science Fiction* be-tween October 1947 and January 1950.

A seven-hundred-year-old Soldier of Light, "Ole Doc Methuselah," travels throughout the galaxy performing medical miracles, and gets involved in planetary politics—violating the rules of his profession.

First hardcover anthology in the United States pub-lished in 1970 by Theta Press (A16). DAW Books published the same stories in paperback in 1970.

Bridge Publications, Inc., published them again in hard-back in 1992, with an introduction by Robert Silverberg and also released the book in audio with narration by Roddy McDowall.

Author Services, Inc., will be releasing the Ole Doc series in 1997 as part of the *L. Ron Hubbard Classic Fiction Series.*

STORIES

1. "Ole Doc Methuselah" (B172)

2. "The Expensive Slaves" (B173)

3. "Her Majesty's Aberration" (B174)

4. "The Great Air Monopoly" (B178)

5. "Plague" (B185)

6. "A Sound Investment" (B190)

7. "Ole Mother Methuselah" (B203, also D91)

Q5.   **The Secret of Treasure Island.** 70,000 words.

Written as a single story (*Murder at Pirate Castle*) for magazine serialization. Produced as a fifteen-part full-length screenplay series by Columbia Pictures in 1937. See F2 for series names and additional annotation.

Q6.   **Mission Earth.** 1,200,000 words.

Technically written as an unprecedented 1.2 million-word science fiction satire in ten volumes—the longest science fiction novel in the history of the genre, and generally considered to be Hubbard's "magnum opus" for its imaginative scope and bold complexities of character, plot and situation, its brilliantly innovative use of the narrative viewpoint, and as a tour de force of broad satire and antic farce.

Mission Earth has received wide critical acclaim, academic interest and all 10 volumes have been *New York Times* bestsellers. It has been published in numerous languages in countries around the world where it has received the same interest and acclaim. See A29-38 for complete notes and the already extensive publishing history.

VOLUME TITLES

1. The Invaders Plan

2. Black Genesis

3. The Enemy Within

4. An Alien Affair

5. Fortune of Fear

6. Death Quest

7. Voyage of Vengeance

8. Disaster

9. Villainy Victorious

10. The Doomed Planet

R.   INDEX OF QUOTES AND CRITICAL APPRECIATIONS

This section is an alphabetical index of critical quotes and appreciations regarding L. Ron Hubbard and his fiction works that are referenced in this volume.

S. TITLE INDEX

This section contains a title index, in alphabetical order, of the published and unpublished works of L. Ron Hubbard that are referenced in this volume.

NOTES